Golfing with Lewis and Clark:
My Rediscovery of America

Path Finder Books—Gettysburg, PA
ISBN: 979-8-9870744-0-4
eBook: 979-8-9870744-1-1
Library of Congress Control Number: 2022919174
Title: *Golfing with Lewis and Clark: My Rediscovery of America*
Author: Lex McMillan
Digital distribution | 2022
Paperback | 2022

All photographs by the author

Golfing with Lewis and Clark:
My Rediscovery of America

Lex McMillan

Dedication

In grateful memory of Stephen E. Ambrose (1936-2002),
whose *Undaunted Courage* inspired my journey.

Contents

Preface

"For the men who entered the unknown and returned, and for those who knew the land and watched from the heart of wilderness, nothing would be the same ever again. It was the most difficult of journeys, marked by extraordinary triumph and defeat. It was in the truest sense a vision quest, and the visions gathered were of profound consequence. All that we are, good and bad, was in it."

N. Scott Momaday, "The Voices of Encounter"[1]

As my long-anticipated retirement approached in May 2017, the thought of driving across the country emerged from a pleasant daydream to serious planning. From that angle, it looked like an adventurous way to make a clean break with my career and declare a new chapter in my life, a redeployment of my forces. It would also be an opportunity for me to test my belief that despite all the troubling features of American life, there was good reason to hope that we would emerge stronger and better, that we could continue to be a beacon of hope for all those seeking freedom and greater economic opportunity.

The restless impulse to head west appears to be hard-wired in Americans' DNA. I like to think that I inherited some vestige of the pioneering spirit from my Scotch-Irish forebears who arrived on our shores in colonial times. They were fleeing the oppressive hand of the British crown and greedy landlords who raised their land rents to unbearable levels in the nine counties of Ulster or Northern Ireland from whence they came. These rugged and restless people played a large role in the American Revolution and the subsequent exploration and settlement of our nation. Their story is told well in *The Scotch-Irish: A Social History*[2] by my beloved mentor and friend the late James Graham Leyburn (1902-1993), who was a distinguished scholar, teacher, and advisor to generations of students at Washington and Lee University. Like many others who had the benefit of his guidance and friendship, I count him as my best teacher and the embodiment of excellence in scholarship, character, intellect, and faith.

Three dimensions shaped my planning. First, I recalled with admiration the late Stephen Ambrose's account of the Lewis and Clark "Voyage of Discovery" in 1803-06 across the just-acquired Louisiana Territory. Aptly entitled *Undaunted Courage,*[3] Ambrose's account is a fine biography of Meriwether Lewis, the young Virginian and protégé of Thomas Jefferson who led the expedition with his friend and co-captain, William Clark. It is also a gripping account of the adventure that the small band, initially 44 men including Clark's slave, York, undertook in making their way up the Missouri River from St. Louis to its source in the Rockies, across the Continental Divide, and ultimately down the mighty Columbia River to the Pacific at what is today Astoria, Oregon. One cannot read this account without being moved by the adventure of stepping off into the unknown. It is, simply, a great American story. I decided that re-tracing the Lewis and Clark Trail would be the core of my route west.

The second dimension that shaped my plans was my love of golf. Although not a very good golfer, I share with some 25 million other Americans a passion for its endless challenges, frustrations, and occasional rewards. In the summer before my 50th birthday, I picked up the game and got badly hooked. Although some may shudder at the "wasted" hours and money one can spend on golf, nothing recreational compares with the pleasure the game has given me. One of my enduring treasures was learning to play when my youngest son, Patrick, was just 11. He said he wanted to learn the game, so I bought him a set of starter clubs, and off we went to various public courses always looking out for "twilight rates" and other bargains where we could roll our hand carts across the hills of Adams County, Pennsylvania, chasing the unpredictable flight of the little white ball that is the sometimes-maddening focal point of the game. Patrick quickly showed the advantages of starting young and became a good golfer playing on his high school teams. Our early golfing days created a special bond.

The compulsive attraction of the game is a perfect illustration of the "variable reinforcement ratio" in classical conditioning. Many will recall from an introductory psychology course, the work of the Russian physiologist Anton Pavlov, who was studying salivation in dogs. Pavlov discovered by accident that dogs could be made to salivate even when no food was present, simply by associating food with some other stimulus, in this case a bell that rang each time the dog was fed. Of course, if no food showed up, at some point the dog ceased to salivate. Pavlov discovered that the salivation could be sustained for the longest amount of time if the food arrived on an unpredictable schedule: "the variable reinforcement ratio."

As most of my golfing buddies know, I have tested this idea on many golfers. Some seem to get the idea immediately; some seem unsure; others wonder if I've insulted them by comparing them to salivating dogs. Since I readily include myself in the image, I certainly mean no offense. As every golfer knows, even the great ones rarely hit the ball perfectly. On those occasions when the ball springs off the club and heads straight along the intended line toward the target, the feeling is hard to beat. It is, as they say, the shot that brings you back, especially after a frustrating round where one seriously wonders why the heck he or she ever took up this often-frustrating game.

One of the occupations that captures all golfers' attention is comparing, ranking, and rating golf courses. It is a source of endless dispute and generally good-natured argument. We are helped along in this pastime by various publications that attempt to identify the best public and private courses. *Golf Digest* is one of the more venerable sources of such lists, annually publishing the top 100 courses in the U.S., both public and private. I wondered how many such courses might be within reach of my route.

The third dimension of my voyage of discovery emerged from the increasingly toxic and divisive political atmosphere of the 2016 presidential race and the surprising election of Donald Trump. I wondered what was becoming of our beloved country. Was there more that held us together than divided us? Were our common values and bonds stronger than the charged antagonisms so evident in the daily news cycle? Three questions emerged from these thoughts:

1. What is most valuable, most worthy of appreciation about America?
2. What is most troubling or worrisome about America today?
3. If one had a magic wand, what are one or two things in the American past or present that one would change to make our country a better place?

Would the people who I met on my journey be willing to answer these questions, and if so, would their responses be reassuring?

As the lovely Pennsylvania spring bloomed, I grew increasingly excited about a drive across the country, retracing the path of Lewis and Clark, playing golf at some of the best courses that were within striking distance of the historic trail, learning a great deal more about that epic journey, and finally meeting a lot of folks on golf courses and elsewhere who would be willing to share with me their perspectives on our nation today. I had many moments of doubt about the sanity of my project and realized soon after my departure that I could have spent many more weeks in research and preparation. Nevertheless, I roughed out an itinerary, bought a very fine guidebook entitled *Traveling the Lewis and Clark Trail* by Julie Fanselow,[4] selected about 20 possible courses, packed my bags, and set out from my home in Gettysburg, on the morning of June 20, 2017. My day one goal was Clarksville, Indiana, overlooking the Falls of the Ohio where Lewis and Clark met up to proceed down the Ohio River to the Mississippi near St. Louis, which is just south of the Missouri River's terminus.

I would be on the road for 40 days, travel 9714 miles, play 16 rounds of golf, set foot in 18 states beyond Pennsylvania and enjoy a pleasant detour with my wife, who joined me in Portland after I completed the outbound leg of my trip. Together we explored the Pacific Northwest for about eight days before she flew home and I began the long drive back.

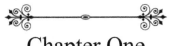

Chapter One
Westward Ho!
From Gettysburg to Clarksville, Indiana

June 19, 1803: Meriwether Lewis writes William Clark inviting him to share command of the Corps of Discovery. Clark is living with his famous older brother, George Rogers Clark, in a cabin overlooking the Falls of Ohio in Indiana Territory overlooking Louisville, Kentucky. Historian Donald Jackson described Lewis's letter as "one of the most famous invitations to greatness the nation's archives can provide."[1]

Eager to get on the trail, I planned one of my longer drives for day one, June 20, 2017, some 583 miles in all. It was a perfect day for travel. Bright, clear blue sky. Low humidity and 70 degrees as I pulled away from our home in Gettysburg that morning around 8:30. No deadlines, no clock to punch, just a reservation at a Best Western in Clarksville. An auspicious beginning. I headed west from Gettysburg, across Western Maryland on I-68, then on to West Virginia where I discovered that June 20 was the 154th birthday of the Mountaineer State. A nice piece of serendipity. I had selected June 20 with the summer solstice in mind but arriving in West Virginia on its birthday felt like a good omen.

Born of Virginia's secession from the Union in 1860, forty western counties refused to go along and seceded from Virginia, a nice poke in the eye to their Eastern brethren. West Virginia was accepted into the Union in 1863. Festivities were apparent at the state's well-appointed rest stops, including an opportunity to have my picture taken with Smokey the Bear. Tempting, but I let that one pass. Many children were clearly thrilled with the chance as they danced around the familiar big brown costumed figure in their brightly colored summer outfits.

After some 35 years of work-related travel, I couldn't help but ponder whether I was sane to undertake such a journey on my own. Truth to tell, I was excited. I like travel, the sense of anticipation around every curve and over every hill, the visual delight of varied landscapes, discovery, the unknown, the motion itself. In a certain sense, life is simple on the road. You get up every morning with a plan and you proceed. If you're lucky, the travel doesn't go perfectly to script, opportunities and diversions arise, unplanned detours are inevitable. Being alert to such opportunities is part of the adventure.

If every journey is a spiritual quest, then Jackson Brown's words in his memorable "Your Bright Baby Blues" are worth recalling: "no matter how fast I run, I can't run away from me." I also recalled C. S. Lewis's trenchant reminder that "mere movement in space will never bring you any nearer to Him [God] or any farther from Him than you are at this very moment."[2]

Not sure I was running away from anything, but I did hope that during my travels I would learn a lot—about Lewis and Clark, of course, but also about our country and whether golfing might bring me closer to its heart.

Being alone on the road for more than a month may have had spiritual benefits. Hours of time for reflection helped me to see myself a little more clearly, not all of it encouraging. Some would think I have led a charmed life, and there's some evidence to support that impression. From any perspective, my blessings or good fortune, if you prefer, outweigh the hardships. But deep within is a darkness and a hunger that nothing in this world completely removes or satisfies. If my journey west was a spiritual quest, I was not quite clear on the end I was seeking. Although I met a lot of interesting and pleasant people, I spent many hours alone, simply a reminder of our human predicament. No matter how hard we work to fill our lives with family and friends, no matter how many diversions we create to pass the time and entertain ourselves, all of us are securely locked in a cell called the self. None of us can escape it. Some appear to be better at avoiding that reality than others, but all must confront it eventually, even if it's not until we face our death.

Nevertheless, I felt that I was in good historical company, like Huck Finn resisting Mrs. Watson's offer to "civilize him," I was "lighting out for the territories," at least to those parts of the U.S. that were territories not so long ago. It has been a perennial American impulse from our earliest days. The farther west I traveled, I was repeatedly reminded that we are a very young country. Are we still in our adolescence? If we are, perhaps there is reassurance to be taken from that possibility. We are still growing up, still finding our way in the wilderness—some of which we continue to create—still imperfectly resolving the darker parts of our history, which are inescapable in following the Lewis and Clark Trail, particularly our repeated betrayal of the American Indian tribes who were scattered across our vast continent when the first Europeans arrived.

When Columbus arrived in the "new world," between six and sixty million people who spoke more than 500 languages already inhabited the area now comprising the United States, Canada, and Latin America, from the Arctic to Argentina. The conflict between these original immigrants from Asia and the newcomers from Europe was probably inevitable—a clash of cultures that would be hard to exaggerate. There is no reason to doubt the sincerity of Jefferson's benevolent intentions in charging the Lewis and Clark Expedition. The familiar history that followed, however, make the words of the U. S. Congress in 1789 now appear cruelly ironic:

The utmost good faith shall always be observed towards the Indians; their lands and property shall never be taken from them without their consent; and, in their property, rights and liberty, they shall never be invaded or disturbed, unless in just and lawful wars authorized by Congress (1789).[3]

"By 1900, survivors of the Indian Wars had been confined to reservations totaling only four percent of all the lands within the borders of the United States. [By 1972], Indian reservations comprise[d] only 2 percent of the contiguous 48 states; in Canada, reserves occupy only a fourth of one percent of all the provinces." [4]

Neither Jefferson, nor Lewis and Clark could possibly have foreseen the astonishingly rapid invasion of pioneers across the expanding frontiers of what would become the "lower 48" states only 106 years after the Corps of Discovery returned to St. Louis. Clark, himself, however, played a key role in that expansion and its inevitable adverse impact on the indigenous people.

After returning from their historic journey, William Clark settled in St. Louis where he served as "Indian agent" for the Louisiana Territory, later Missouri, and later yet as territorial governor till Missouri was admitted as the twenty-fourth state in 1821. In that capacity, he was the federal agent for negotiations with the Indian tribes west of the Mississippi and those from the East who were relocated there by the federal government. Although necessarily an instrument of unjust treatment of the Indians, he was sympathetic to them, befriended many, including Sacagawea's two children, whom he adopted, and was known as an enlightened and generous public servant. At Clark's monumental gravesite at the Bellefontaine Cemetery in St. Louis is a granite marker with the following inscription: "'It is to be lamented that the deplorable situation of the Indians do [sic] not receive more of the human feelings of the nation.' William Clark writing to his old friend Thomas Jefferson, Dec. 15, 1825."

The "deplorable situation" that Clark described is repeatedly evident across the Lewis and Clark Trail, but on this fine morning I was charmed by the rural beauties of West Virginia. Although a somewhat antiseptic way to experience the state, my interstate highway route from Williamsport, Maryland, to Morgantown and Charlestown then on to Kentucky afforded me repeated grand mountain vistas. It's a superficial way to experience West Virginia, but having previously visited many points in the state, camped in its parks, hiked its trails, and fished its streams, I was eager to move on to my destination, the beginning of the Lewis and Clark Trail.

I reached Kentucky around 3:30 p.m. Although I know this state much less well than others east of the Mississippi, for several years in the late 1970s I passed through it traveling from Atlanta, where I grew up, to South Bend, Indiana, for my doctoral studies at Notre Dame. I recall being impressed with the route from Nashville to Louisville on I-65. The impression offered to travelers from West Virginia on I-64 is strikingly different.

The Tug Fork, a meandering tributary of the Big Sandy River that originates deep in the Appalachian Mountains to the southeast, forms a large part of the border between Kentucky and West Virginia and runs northwest into the Ohio River a few miles north of the bridge that connects the two states on I-64. Immediately across the river in Kentucky is some sort of industrial processing plant complete with belching smokestacks, gravel drives, and chain link fencing. Apparently, Kentucky doesn't care much about the first impression of travelers crossing into the state from West Virginia.

From the state line across The Tug Fork, it's still some 175 miles to Lexington and the landscape improves, but I'm not sure I saw the

4

famed bluegrass; perhaps it's elsewhere in the state. About ninety miles south of that bridge over The Tug Fork lies Pike County, famed for the bloody feud between the Hatfields and McCoys, which raged from 1863 till 1891. This was one of many tempting detours, but the day was already long enough.

I bypassed Louisville, founded in 1778 by Revolutionary War hero George Rogers Clark, elder brother to William Clark, crossed the Falls of the Ohio, as it's called, and rolled into Clarksville, Indiana, around 5:30 p.m. After ten hours and 583 miles, I was ready to call it a day. The Best Western where I had made reservations is in an utterly charmless development of big box stores and cheap apartments bounded and defined by acres of concrete and asphalt. Although I hated to get back in my car, the local eateries were not in convenient walking distance. A clerk at the hotel suggested "Bubba's," a casual burger and pizza place nearby, so I settled for modern American tacky and a high-fat dinner surrounded by happy families with small children in tow. I was probably a little biased toward the place because of another "Bubba's," an outstanding barbeque place just off I-77 north of Charlotte.

Chapter Two
Where Did the Journey Begin?

October 15, 1803: Lewis and Clark meet near Clarksville, Indiana, overlooking the rushing waters of the Ohio River. Stephen Ambrose writes: "When they shook hands, the Lewis and Clark Expedition began." [1]

"When They Shook Hands" at Falls of Ohio State Park, Clarksville, Indiana

Clarksville, Indiana. Soon after arriving at the impressive Falls of Ohio State Park and Interpretive Center, I discovered a bone of contention among aficionados of the Corps of Discovery. When I described my ambitious travel plan to the attendant working at the center, he asked me where I thought the Lewis and Clark journey began. Up to that point, I had thought that Clarksville had a good claim to primacy because this was the point where Lewis and Clark met to continue preparing for their great adventure. When Lewis wrote to Clark in 1803 inviting him to join him as a co-captain of the expedition, the latter was living with his aging brother in a modest cabin on a magnificent bluff overlooking the Falls of the Ohio from the Indiana side. A replica stands there today with helpful historical markers. It faces south overlooking the great river and the sprawling city of Louisville across the Ohio's rushing turbulence.

Outside the Visitors Center, overlooking the river just to the east of the Clark cabin, is a larger-than-life sculpture of Lewis and Clark striding toward one another and grasping hands in glad reunion. The sculpture was dedicated on October 26, 2003, to commemorate the 200th anniversary of the Corps of Discovery departing the area on their way west. Inscribed on a brass plaque set in the ground in front of the monument is the following: "'When they shook hands, the Lewis and Clark Expedition began.' *Undaunted Courage*, Stephen E. Ambrose." The statue is dedicated to the memory of Ambrose and is mounted on a 16.5-ton native slab of Jeffersonville limestone dated to the Devonian Period (350-400 million years ago), reflecting the rich geological and fossil resources of the area, which are well presented and interpreted in the Visitors Center.

Here is the description of the Center from its web page:

> In all the world, there is no other place like it. The Falls of the Ohio State Park and its Interpretive Center are the crossroads of ancient lives and future hopes. The park features the largest exposed Devonian fossil bed in the world and is part of a 1,404-acre National Wildlife Conservation Area. Perched on a small bluff overlooking a wide sweep of the expansive Ohio River, a newly revitalized state of the art, immersive and interactive Interpretive Center brings to life giant fossil beds telling a story 390 million years in the making. The Falls of the Ohio connects the environment of the ancient past with the natural and cultural history of yesterday and today.[2]

The sculpture was made by the late Carol (C.A.) Grende from Montana, who designed a series of Lewis and Clark sculptures at different points along the trail. Of her passion for such projects, she wrote: "To walk in the footsteps on the original trails of these explorers fills my heart with honor and humbles me. I feel so fortunate to have lived in the West where the traces of the past are etched into the earth."[3]

One would think that the matter was settled with the authoritative words of the late Stephen Ambrose, who became a tireless advocate for the Lewis and Clark story for the remainder of his life after publishing *Undaunted Courage* in 1996. But one would be wrong! This is America after all, and nothing is quite as attractive as the desire for what a historian friend of mine once called "sterile claims of primacy."

My next significant visit to a historical site on the trail was the Lewis & Clark State Historic Site in Southern Illinois at the confluence of the Mississippi and Missouri Rivers and a smaller stream called Dubois or Wood River. The captains selected the site on December 12, 1803, and called it Camp Dubois. Because of various delays, it would prove to be their first winter camp, a particularly bitter, cold, and snowy winter where the Corps took formal shape and underwent sustained military training and discipline primarily under Captain Clark's direction.

One compelling reason for selecting this site is that it was on American soil, east of the Mississippi River. Until the transfer of the Louisiana Territory was complete, the Spanish officials in St. Louis would not permit an American military camp on the west side of the river. Lewis was an official witness in St. Louis to the formal transfer of Upper Louisiana, first from Spain to France on March 9 and then from France to the United States on March 10.[4]

At this site one quickly finds a prominent rendering of Lewis's words in his journal: "The mouth of the River Dubois is to be considered as the point of departure" (ca. May 14, 1804). Another claim to primacy. It is worth noting that the official National Park Service brochure "Lewis and Clark Trail," which is an excellent overview of the entire journey, states "The journey began on May 14, 1804, as the Corps of Discovery left Camp Dubois in the keelboat and two pirogues, crossed the Mississippi River and headed up the Missouri."

Leaving the issue of primacy aside, this site, which describes itself as "The Point of Departure" is well worth visiting. Although a little off the beaten path north of I-270 and just south of the tiny hamlet of

Hartford, Illinois, the 14,000 square foot interpretive center and a full-scale replica of the camp itself, according to Clark's own drawings, gives one a clear sense of the primitive conditions under which the Corps lived through that bitter winter.

It is also worth noting that in 1978 the U.S. Congress established the Lewis and Clark National Historic Trail as part of the National Trails System. Some 3700 miles in length, the trail begins in Hartford, Illinois, and ends at Fort Clatsop (near present-day Astoria, Oregon), on the southern bluffs overlooking the mouth of the Columbia River. The Lewis and Clark Historic Site in Oregon was the location for the first National Signature Event on May 14, 2004, the bicentennial of the Corps' departure from Camp Dubois. The Corps spent a miserable, wet winter of 1805-06 at Fort Clatsop before starting their return journey.

Inside the impressive interpretive center at Camp Dubois is a full-scale model of the 55-foot keelboat split in a cross section from stem to stern to better show the details of this craft. Lewis had commissioned the keelboat in Pittsburgh before traveling down the Ohio to meet Clark. Could one make a legitimate claim for Pittsburgh to be the point of origin? Perhaps someone has. But the best answer to the question came from the same attendant at the Falls of the Ohio Center: "it began in Jefferson's head." I found this to be a useful response at several points along the trail although only St. Charles, Missouri, made a competing claim to be the point of departure.

During their brutal winter in Camp Dubois, spring looked as if it would never arrive. It was mid-May before the rivers were passable and they could "proceed on," as they habitually described their journey in their voluminous journals. After further provisioning in St. Louis, they departed up the Missouri River amid much fanfare from the local citizens of tiny St. Charles, just north of St. Louis, on May 21, 1804. One could argue that St. Charles has the most compelling claim to the start of the expedition since it was the Missouri River and the newly acquired Louisiana Territory that Jefferson charged the Corps to explore. St. Charles was founded in 1769 as a fur-trading post by Louis Blanchette, a French-Canadian hunter. It was the first permanent white settlement on the Missouri River and served as Missouri's first state capital from 1821 to 1826.

9

Chapter Three
Golf in Southern Indiana

October 16-25, 1803: Lewis and Clark interview and evaluate scores of young men eager to join the expedition. "How many applied is not known, but one of those eventually selected, Private Alexander Willard, boasted in his old age that 'his fine physique enable[d] him to pass the inspection' that more than one hundred others failed." [1]

Eighteenth hole at Sultan's Run, Jasper, Indiana

S nugly nestled in the graceful, rolling hills of Southern Indiana, are the little tourist towns of French Lick and nearby West Baden Springs. Among other attractions, are the historic French Lick Springs Hotel and Casino as well as the elegant, grand old West Baden Springs Hotel and Conference Center with its vast dome across an equally vast atrium. Gambling at the resort was legalized in 2006 after a major renovation of the property, but illegal gambling dates back into the early 20th century. The colorful history includes visits by prominent political figures and entertainers as well as shadier characters. Although its history has had periods of decline and revival, it appears now to be thriving.

Only about 75 miles northwest of Clarksville, the resort is also home to two *Golf Digest* top 100 public golf courses, the Pete Dye Course, ranked #17 in 2016, and the Donald Ross Course, ranked #83. After falling to #19 in 2017, the Pete Dye Course returned to #17 in 2020. The Donald Ross Course fell to #99 in 2020. I hope it wasn't anything I said.

I called the Pro Shop at the famed Pete Dye course to see about a tee time and a preferred rate for a traveling writer on a budget. The response was not encouraging. It was the first such call that I had made, and perhaps my pitch got better as I went along. The young man who answered the phone listened to my story and my plan to write about my adventures on select golf courses and elsewhere along the trail. I expressed my hope to get on and perhaps join a twosome or threesome for a round and asked if he could give me a "preferred rate." There was a longish pause and then he rather curtly informed me that "we don't do discounts." The published rate is $350, a bit outside my budget.

Now I don't want to quibble with the fine folks at this justly celebrated course, but I have never yet known a course that didn't have a variable pricing policy that gives the pro a good deal of discretion. Either my pitch had failed or the young fellow who answered the phone lacked the authority, so I asked if he could suggest another good course nearby that might be a bit less stress on my budget. He didn't hesitate to suggest Sultan's Run just outside nearby Jasper. I thanked him kindly and gave Sultan's Run a ring. I later learned that both Sultan's Run and the Pete Dye course are owned by French Lick Resorts.

The response at Sultan's Run could not have been more gracious. I spoke with the pro, Jeff Howerton, who showed genuine interest in my project and welcomed me out for an afternoon round at a very agreeable fee. We booked a 1:30 tee time. He said he'd try to get me a game with some locals but didn't promise, given the time on a Thursday afternoon.

My visit to Sultan's Run was another instance of serendipity or just dumb luck. Having never heard of the course, I had no great expectations, just curious and eager to get out on a local course after my long travel day from home to Clarksville. The course is a pure delight from the impressive entrance off North Meridian Road just east of Jasper to the visually stunning (and challenging) 18th hole set below the stately clubhouse, framed by a rugged rock wall with water splashing down its face into a pond that runs along the back side of the green and off into the adjacent woods. (You don't want to be long on your approach shot to the green!)

The course rambles gracefully across some 224 acres of rolling woods, water, and wildlife. Designed by Pete Dye disciple Tim Liddy, it clearly bears the marks of the master—challenging, tempting, rewarding, and humbling—a fine test of golf and a visual delight.

In 2015, the Indiana Golf Course Owners Association named Sultan's Run as the Indiana Public Golf Course of the Year for displaying "the highest quality of ownership and facilities" as well as exhibiting "a thoughtful contribution to the game of golf."[2] *Golf Digest,* in its "Places to Play Guide," gushes: "A killer scenic layout . . . . The waterfall behind #18 takes your breath away . . . . Scenic, challenging, and worth the trip to Jasper . . . . The views are all breathtaking and the 18th is the one of the best finishing holes in Indiana . . . an absolutely beautiful course!"

Opened in 1992, the history of the course adds another element of charm. Formerly owned by the horse-breeding Ruxer family, the land now sculpted into a majestic golf course was home to the renowned American Saddlebred show horse Supreme Sultan (March 12, 1966-Dec. 6, 1983), who sired many other champions in his time. That legacy is celebrated on engraved stone markers at each tee box of the course recalling the champions that Supreme Sultan sired. Sometimes called "the peacock of show horses," the American Saddlebred has a proud legacy dating back to the early days of the Republic. Known for their presence and style as well as a spirited but gentle temperament, they have devoted fans and a complex web of legend and story. I learned that this breed was a favorite among officers in the Civil War. Many of them have figured in film, including the "talking horse" known as "Mr. Ed" in the popular 1960s TV show of that title.

I ran across an amusing story about this famed show horse. Its owner sold it as a yearling in 1967 and then bought him back a year later after his sire had died unexpectedly. He paid twice what he had sold him for but never expressed anything but satisfaction, being quoted as saying "Anyone can have a million dollars, but only the Ruxers have the Sultan."[3] When Supreme Sultan died, he was buried at the Kentucky Horse Park in Lexington where a full-sized bronze sculpture stands over his grave.

The rhetoric around golf courses can sometimes run to hyperbole, but I don't think the effusions about Sultan's Run overshoot the mark. Here's a good sample:

> What an enjoyable surprise Sultan's Run was. We had no expectations going into this course and it ended up being a ton of fun. Sure, there are a couple of pedestrian holes on the course, but the property is really good for the most part and I think Tim Liddy did a heck of a job in getting some really fun holes out of the site. I hate to sound clichéd, but Sultan's run is a course that can be played and enjoyed by all skill levels. There are only a few really challenging tee shots for the high handicapper and single digits will have fun with the risk/reward holes and gauging distance on the uphill and downhill shots. Considering that the green fees [sic] is $60 (including cart . . . if you want one that is) for weekend play this is a great value and I'm really glad that it worked out for us to add it to our French Lick visit. [4]

When I arrived at Sultan's Run, it was clear that most local golfers and visitors had wisely gotten in their rounds in the cooler morning air. The Pro apologized that it looked like I'd be playing alone. Although disappointed, I headed out to the first tee box, debating whether I should test myself with the "Gold" tees at 6429 yards (71.5/138) or be sensible and play from the "Silver" tees at 5762 yards (68.8/129). Not for a moment did I consider "playing from the tips," as they are called. In this instance, these are the "Black" tees at 6859 yards (73.5/143). The rolling terrain makes all those distances play longer. The golfing advice, often given and probably just as often ignored, is to "play within your game," which is to say, know your limitations, accept them cheerfully and make the most of what you've got. Good advice for lots of situations beyond the golf course. And probably ignored just about as often in those other situations.

As I was about to tee off, I noticed a pair of golfers in a cart hanging around the putting green in front of the clubhouse. Hoping to get a game after all, I waited. Courteously, so did they. Realizing they were not going to pull up to the first tee till I was off, I turned my cart around and went back to introduce myself and ask if they'd mind my joining them. After assuring them that I was more interested in their company than the quality of their play, we set off. My first tee jitters resulted in a triple bogey and convinced me that I'd be wise to play the silver tees with my somewhat older companions.

Jim and Tom were local retired businessmen, proud of their town and community. Although I had never heard of Jasper, by the end of our round, I felt that I should be proud of it as well. Tom, who proudly reminded me several times that he was 79, referred to Jim as a mere boy. I would guess that Jim was in his early 70s. They clearly shared a lot of history, just a couple of overgrown boys out for another round.

I learned that Jasper is a small town of about 15,000 residents, the county seat of Dubois County, and was founded in 1830 by German immigrants—a recurring theme on my travels. The story goes that it was named by the wife of one of the founders who found her inspiration in the following verse from the Book of Revelation: "And the foundations of the wall of the city were adorned with all manner of precious stones. The first foundation was jasper" (Rev. 21:19).

I told them about my envisioned project, and they expressed interest and encouragement, but neither ventured comments on my questions about the state of the country today. They did, however, proudly tell me about Jasper, its economic vitality, healthy community, and great work ethic. Both men were surely members of the Chamber of Commerce, and they did a great job of convincing me that Jasper is a special place. It is, in fact, a rather remarkable small town with an enviable economic vitality. It appears to reflect the very qualities that are extolled on the town's website: "a rich German heritage" that is credited with the stability, permanence, hard work ethic, good management, and excellent craftsmanship to be found there. It is remarkable that more than a dozen regional, national, and international firms have a headquarters or significant presence in Jasper. This economic vitality draws people from across the region resulting in a work force that is larger than the town's population.

We finished our enjoyable round on a very warm June afternoon, wished one another well, and parted ways. I did not think to ask for any personal contact information, so I figured that I'd likely never hear from either of them. The chances of getting back to Jasper were slim.

In September, to my surprise, I received an email from Jim expressing his hope that I could one day return for another round at Sultan's Run. He listed three things he appreciates about our country: 1. Freedom of speech and the right bear arms, 2. Three branches of the U.S. Government, and 3. Religion of choice. He worried that we don't lose the three items above, that ISIS "doesn't make inroads in our Country," possible nuclear war with radical nations, our national drug epidemic, and bullying in our school system. I found his last concern touching in its contrast to the larger, global focus of the others and had to wonder if it reflected personal experience of his own or of younger family members. As anyone with children knows, it is a very real problem and devilishly difficult to address.

He described two magic wand wishes. First was his desire that English would be the "official language of the U.S." and that "anyone entering our country must be able to speak our language." I infer that he meant all immigrants who wish to become permanent residents or citizens. He elaborated on this wish with the conviction that the government could provide assistance in language learning to all such individuals. He then added that all U.S. residents should be encouraged to learn other foreign languages and that "Spanish would be at the top of that list." His second wish was that we "secure the borders" to help combat our drug problems and keep criminals from trying to enter our country.

In December 2017, I was delighted to receive an email from Jeff Howerton, the Pro at Sultan's Run who had greeted me so warmly the previous June. Jeff wrote:

1. Being an American citizen is a blessing. I can think, dream and act as I please as long as it is law abiding.

15

2. America is a great nation but our sovereignty has been under attack the last eight years and I hope we can stay a great nation another 250 years!
3. My magic wand would put people back in civility mode. People would use manners, take pride and be humble.

Well, I guess as I get older my sentiments are stereotypical . . .
I hope you will travel back to southern Indiana sometime in the future and play Sultan's Run again.

Thanks for making contact with me and you may use my name!

Merry Christmas and Happy New Year Lex!

Sincerely
Jeff Howerton, PGA
Sultan's Run Golf Club

The Donald Ross Course

The next morning, I played The Donald Ross Course at French Lick. Upon arriving, I discovered that it was the centennial year for this fine, old links-style course, which is shrouded throughout by stretches of knee-high grass that should not be in play, but woe to the golfer who pulls or pushes his ball into these sinewy hazards. The course is rated #2 in Indiana (after the Pete Dye course just down the road) and has been consistently among the top 100 for *Golf Digest*. It is a fine test of golf, a par 70 laid out on rolling hills across 7000 yards for those who want that much challenge (74.7/135). I am pretty sure I played the black tees at 5950 yards (69.5/131). Given the terrain, it played longer.

After a $5 million restoration, the course is in excellent condition: some 80 of "Ross's trademark bunkers with flat bottoms and deep, gnarly faces were once again in place along with expanded, square or rectangular shaped greens that severely undulate." The course's web page adds that 35 of the bunkers "are original to the course that Ross constructed in 1917." They are scattered with such devilish care that only the most precise shot makers can hope to escape without some sand in their shoes.[5]

The head pro, Robert Koontz, gave me a generous discount, and I teed off on a fine sunny morning at 9 a.m. In honor of the centennial, I bought a colorful golf shirt; to my surprise, this shirt proved to be the only one I added to my already overstocked inventory during my journey.

By chance I joined up with a local player from nearby Jasper who had been born in Boiling Springs, just up the road from Gettysburg along the shores of the famed Yellow Breeches trout stream. It is a lovely stretch of water that I have spent many often-frustrating hours lashing with a line and delicate lure. Few trout deigned to rise to my efforts. Even if the fish are a challenge, just standing in the cool waters of the Yellow Breeches among the heavily wooded banks on a warm spring day is a complete pleasure.

The adjacent village of Mt. Holly Springs claims former Atlanta Braves first-baseman Sid Bream as its most famous son. Bream played major league ball for about 11 years; the peak of his career was in the early 90s with the red-hot Atlanta Braves who went on to win five league championships but only once captured the World Series trophy in 1995. It was the third for the Braves but their only one since they moved from Milwaukee to Atlanta in 1966 until their unexpected championship in 2021.

My golfing companion was a decade my elder, bearded and casually rumpled but in fine condition and a solid golfer, patient with my errant shots on this challenging course, made more so by shifting winds, the rolling terrain, narrow approach shots, and subtle breaks on the fast, smooth greens that caused me too many three putts. Although he was a more consistent player than I, we were matched evenly enough to make our game interesting. He did, however, beat me by 3 to 1 in match play. In strokes I was ten behind him but mostly because I struggled on the front nine. I was down only one stroke on the back nine.

As we played, I told him about my trip, and we talked about the state of our country. He expressed concern about the increasing polarization in our politics, the apparent dominance of the extremes, and shared his conviction that the extremes fail to reflect the will of the majority. Although he does not have an email account and thus presumably doesn't spend much time on our increasingly toxic social media, his intuition of a large, pragmatic, mostly silent and politically disengaged "moderate middle" is consistent with my experience and my reading. There is substantial evidence that the noisy extremes dominating our political discourse give us an exaggerated sense of a nation divided. Social media and 24-7 cable "news" amplify this impression. My travels confirmed this intuition, if only anecdotally.

If he had a magic wand, he'd have us return to a healthy fear of God and reminded me of the Proverb (9:10) that such fear is the "beginning of wisdom." Having been superintendent of two different Christian schools, he quietly but firmly shared his deep faith. I felt blessed to have spent the morning with this thoughtful, articulate, and warm-hearted citizen.

After a light lunch, I drove out to the Pete Dye course. Although I had decided against playing it (a decision I now regret), I thought I should at least give it a look. As I drove up through dense, silent woods to the second-highest point in Indiana (about 900 feet), I couldn't help but feel that I was entering sacred ground.

At the top of the winding drive stands an imposing, red-brick Georgian clubhouse known as The Mansion. Built in 1928 by Thomas Taggart, the former mayor of Indianapolis, for his son Thomas D. Taggart, it reaches out to visitors with its chevron-shaped footprint and grand white columns like an elegant lady of a more gracious era. The Taggarts owned the French Lick Springs Hotel from 1901 to 1946.[6]

By contrast, I couldn't miss the welcoming committee of one at the head of the drive: a life-sized bronze sculpture of Indiana native son Pete Dye himself, standing with hands on hips on a modest platform with a plaque on a rough stone at his side. It reads, "The ardent golfer would play Mount Everest if somebody would put a flagstick on top . . . golf is not a fair game so why build a fair golf course." Dye's signature is engraved below, lest there be any doubt.

It being a lovely summer afternoon, I was surprised that the course was so lightly used. The handsome practice facility at the bottom of the hill was empty, and I spotted only a couple of groups out on the sweeping vistas afforded by the prominence of The Mansion. Opened in 2009, the majestic course was honored in the January 2010 issues of both *Golf Digest* and *GOLF Magazine* as the best new course in the U.S. Canadian journalist and photographer Anita Draycott has a fine review of the course in which she offers this succinct description: "Imagine an impeccably manicured anorexic green snake of a fairway that slithers along a roller coaster terrain atop a ridge."[7]

The course measures more than 8000 yards from the tips, characteristically including many Dye trademark bunkers, including distinctively nasty "volcano bunkers" designed to capture and not easily release errant balls. The forward tees measure 5151 yards. But most memorable are the majestic vistas said to be as much as 40 miles across the undeveloped woods of the surrounding Hoosier National Forest. Even from The Mansion, the vistas are breathtaking, feeling much higher than the reported 900 feet.

Dye is reported to have sketched out the original concept for the course on the back of a napkin at the nearby resort, initially doubting that the site would accommodate a great course. After winning the 2015 Senior PGA Championship there, Colin Montgomerie dubbed it an "iconic" American course that golfers all over the world would want to play.[8]

The resort offers packages that include an overnight in either the French Lick or West Baden Springs Hotel and both the Dye and Ross courses. I recommend the "Triple Play": it requires a two-night stay that includes a third round at the lovely Sultan's Run course. In fact, the best order of play would be Sultan's Run, then Donald Ross, and finishing with Pete Dye.

I spent the afternoon planning the next segment of my trip, securing tee times in St. Louis, Kansas City, and Omaha. I had a very good dinner of pork chops and asparagus at 33 Brick Street in the charming little commercial district of French Lick then headed over to the grand old West Baden Springs Hotel and even spent a couple of hours losing $40 at blackjack at the nearby casino. I can see how it's a popular tourist attraction.

Chapter Four
Rest for the Weary: I-64 to the Mississippi

October 26, 1803: The Corps of Discovery departs Clarksville in the 55-foot keelboat, whose detailed design and construction Lewis had overseen in Pittsburgh, and two pirogues proceeding west down the Ohio River to find winter quarters on the east shore of the Mississippi River across from St. Louis.

Reconstruction of Camp Dubois, Lewis & Clark State Historic Site, Hartford, Illinois

On the morning of Friday, June 23, rain was falling as I left the Best Western Plus in French Lick, where I had spent two comfortable nights. Located a little south of the main tourist attractions, this relatively new hotel feels a bit isolated, but the price was one of its attractive features.

Unlike Steinbeck, who voiced disdain for the Interstates in *Travels with Charley* (1962), and William Least Heat-Moon, who avoided them as much as possible in his circumnavigation of the nation, which he memorably recorded in *Blue Highways* (1982), I had made no pledge to renounce these modern roads that annihilate time and space. I used them selectively to cover as much territory as possible in my self-imposed time limit.

Although the interstate highways are convenient and far safer than any other roads, I readily acknowledge that they cut you off from serendipity, discovery, immersion in local attractions, and the texture of the communities that they both connect and bypass. They also almost always prevent you from getting stuck behind an International Harvester lumbering down the highway at 17 mph scattering dust and grain across your windshield. Like so much of life, they are a mixed blessing. On balance, I'm grateful for them, especially as I reflect on what travel was like before the system was begun in the 1950s under President Eisenhower's visionary leadership.

When Eisenhower was a young Army officer, he was bitterly disappointed to be posted to a tank-training camp in Gettysburg, for the duration of WWI. Like all ambitious career soldiers, he longed to be where the action was. Ironically, Ike regarded his career as likely to be undistinguished as the war wound down and he went about the task of demobilizing his command.

In the spring of 1919, under pressure from advocates for the emerging new technology of the automobile, the War Department launched a transcontinental motorized convoy of some 300 men to travel from Washington, D.C., to San Francisco. Always excited by new technology—and the automobile in particular—Lt. Colonel Eisenhower was delighted when his application to join the convoy as an observer was accepted. The convoy set off from the nation's capital on July 7, 1919. Many expressed doubts that they would succeed, and their progress was tediously slow—61 days, or an average of 46.2 miles per day. The 2800-mile trip would take an estimated 39 hours of drive time today.

It is difficult to imagine the conditions that the convoy confronted. As Michael Korda observed in his fine biography *Ike: An American Hero,* "Some notion of what the roads were like can be gleaned from the fact that on the first day out of Washington, D.C., the convoy 'traveled forty-six miles in seven and a quarter hours,' with three breakdowns of vehicles."[1] Indeed, although their path was roughly what is now called The Lincoln Highway, or U.S. Route 30, in many places there were no paved roads at all. The convoy reached San Francisco on September 6 to raucous celebration and fanfare, medals, speeches, dinner, and a dance.[2]

This experience, along with being deeply impressed by Hitler's autobahn as Ike led the victorious allies in WWII, convinced him that the U.S. must have a modern system of highways for economic development as well as national security. With his passionate advocacy, Congress passed the Federal Aid Highway Act of 1956, envisioning a nationwide network of some 41,000 miles connecting every town or city of at least 50,000 population and thousands of smaller ones in its complex web. At the time, the American Association of State Highway Officials estimated that once completed the interstate system "comprising little more than 1% of the Nation's total road and street mileage, will carry 20% of all the motor vehicle traffic."

Eisenhower regarded the interstate system as one of the most significant domestic accomplishments of his administration. The impact of the interstate highway system on American life cannot be exaggerated. Indeed, there are few items in our homes today that were not at one point in a box and traveling along one or more Interstates in a truck. In October 1990, President George H. W. Bush signed a law designating the nation's Interstate System as the Dwight D. Eisenhower National System of Interstate and Defense Highways.[3]

On this rainy morning, I-64 was a welcome means of getting over to southwestern Illinois with some dispatch, have time to tour the Lewis and Clark Historic Site at Camp Dubois, just south of the tiny village of Hartford, Illinois (2020 pop. 1769), and still get to St. Louis in time for dinner. It was an easy drive of only some 280 miles.

After meandering across the rolling pastoral countryside of Southern Indiana, I reached Interstate 64, near the Illinois line. This 953.7-mile interstate runs from Chesapeake, Virginia, in the Hampton Roads area, to Wentzville, Missouri, about 40 miles west of St. Louis. Begun in 1961, I-64 is the second longest east-west route in the system, exceeded only by I-94 further north. It has a familiar ring from my years living in Virginia and frequently traveling from the Richmond area out to the Shenandoah Valley beyond the majestic Blue Ridge Mountains that define the western spine of the Old Dominion. There are few more beautiful spots in the world.

Not long after getting on I-64, I was pleased to see signs for a Rest Area just across the state line in Illinois. When I got to the exit, however, I was disappointed to see that it was closed. I "proceeded on" and was soon pleased to see that another Rest Area was only about 40 miles further west near the town of Mt. Vernon. Sadly, it too proved to be closed without explanation. I wondered whether the well-publicized fiscal challenges facing Illinois along with a governor recently jailed had something to do with it.

Soon after Congress approved in 1956 what is today our complex interstate highway system, The American Association of State Highway Officials called for the rest areas that we now take for granted:

> Rest areas are to be provided on Interstate highways as a safety measure. Safety rest areas are off-road spaces with provisions for emergency stopping and resting by motorists for short periods. They have freeway type entrances and exit connections, parking areas, benches and tables and may have toilets and water supply where proper maintenance and supervision are assured. They may be designed for short-time picnic use in addition to parking of vehicles for short periods.
> ~ *A Policy on Safety Rest Areas for the National System of Interstate and Defense Highways, 1958*

I later learned that Illinois has some 30 highway rest areas scattered across the state. There are only three on the 135-mile stretch of I-64 from Indiana to the Mississippi River. Like many other states, Illinois has been considering the future of these aging facilities. Many need substantial renovation, and the costs, borne entirely by the states where they are located, can be considerable. Indeed, the maintenance of the facilities is a significant item in the states' budgets, running to hundreds of thousands of dollars per year.

It's not surprising that many states are closing their rest areas. According to an April 2017 article in *USA Today*, "Ohio had 294 rest areas . . . in 1961—today it has 89." In addition to the cost, the principal reason given for closing these convenient facilities is the explosion of commercial development alongside the interstates. When first constructed, our interstates were, by design, sited away from the towns and cities they connected, so that drivers would find long stretches of road with no amenities, particularly in rural areas. All that has changed with the explosion of fast-food options, sprawling truck stops, and chains of convenience stores like Sheetz and Wawa in my area. It's not hard to foresee a day when the rest areas will vanish from the American scene, but I hope it's not in my lifetime.

Not surprisingly, the rest areas have passionate defenders and even an impressive website devoted to their history: "'Shutting them down would be the end of an era,' said Joanna Dowling, a historian who researches rest areas and runs the website RestAreaHistory.org. 'Rest areas take you away from the road and the hecticness of travel and immerse you in the natural landscape.'" [4]

According to RestAreaHistory.org, Safety Rest Areas, as they were officially named, were originally envisioned to provide minimal amenities for the traveling public:

> early in their developmental history, . . . safety rest area sites emerged as unique and colorful expressions of regional flavor and modern architectural design. Safety rest areas functioned to create a context of place within the Interstate System; achieved through the implementation of unique and whimsical design elements and the use of regionally signifying characteristics.

In my travels across the country, these regional expressions of place and local culture ranged from the woodsy log-cabin textures of West Virginia to Spartan, low-profile "burrows" on the Dakota plains. All, however, in various ways attempted to tell the story of place and thus mitigate the deracinating experience of sustained Interstate highway travel. They also, frankly, were the most time-efficient and safest way to take a break so long as food was not the objective. Rest areas on the Pennsylvania Turnpike now frequently are full-service plazas with commercial food and beverage options from the omnipresent Starbucks to Burger King.

At any rate, on this day, I-64 got me to the Lewis and Clark State Historic Site in the early afternoon despite "losing" an hour crossing into the Central Time Zone. By the time I arrived, the sky had cleared and ushered in another bright, warm June day with dappled clouds across a clear blue sky.

After touring the impressive historic site, I drove just north to what was called River Dubois where Lewis and Clark stood on its shore as it flows into the Mississippi. I did the same, took a selfie with the Mississippi at my back and felt a sense of accomplishment in having reached this point. Nearby is a large stone on the otherwise rough, unadorned, flood-tumbled point with a polished marble plaque commemorating the spot's historic link to Lewis and Clark and nearby Camp Dubois.

The stream once known as River Dubois is now known as Cahokia Creek in honor of the nearby Indian Mounds built by a pre-Columbian tribe of Native Americans that are now known as Mississippians. The little stream is much more of a creek than a river, only about 40 feet across where it flows into the Mississippi. Perhaps it was larger when Lewis and Clark stood on its banks and determined that the area just south of it would be good for their first winter camp.

The Cahokia Mounds State Historic Site directly across the Mississippi River about 10 miles east of St. Louis preserves and interprets a pre-Columbian city that flourished between 1050 and 1350 AD. There is evidence there, however, of Native American culture dating back another 500 to 700 years. Archeologists estimate the peak population in the 13th century to have been as large as 40,000, which would make it the largest urban area in North America till Philadelphia reached that number in the 1780s. London, England, had a similar population in the 13th century, about a century before Geoffrey Chaucer lived.

Although the name of the pre-Columbian tribe is unknown, the name "Cahokia" was linked to later inhabitants who were there when French explorers first arrived in the 17th century. Cahokia Mounds is regarded as the largest and most complex archaeological site north of the great pre-Columbian cities of the Aztecs in Mexico. It is a National Historic Landmark and one of only 23 World Heritage Sites in the US. This 2200-acre, historic archaeological site preserves 80 mounds— estimated to be about two-thirds of the original total at the city's peak. It's easily reached just off Interstate 64 near its intersection with I-55.[5]

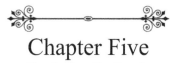

Chapter Five
Exploring St. Louis

May 14, 1804: After a long, bitterly cold winter, the 41-man crew, including William Clark's slave, York, depart Camp Dubois to cross the Mississippi into the newly acquired Louisiana Territory.

Gateway Arch, St. Louis, Missouri, June 24, 2017

A fter leaving Camp Dubois, I headed west on surface streets across the rural countryside of southern Illinois and crossed the Mississippi on a rusty old bridge which had been named for Martin Luther King Jr. soon after his assassination in 1968. Although it's been renovated a couple of times since it was built in 1951, the bridge was showing its age. I was not surprised to learn later that it was closed in the fall of 2018 for a $24 million overhaul. The bridge connects East St. Louis, Illinois, to downtown St. Louis just north of the Gateway Arch National Park at Laclede's Landing. This entrance to the city is named for Pierre Laclede, one of the two Frenchmen who established a trading post here in 1764. It claims to be the city's oldest district and only riverfront entertainment and dining destination. Once a busy manufacturing, warehousing, and shipping hub of St. Louis, it now boasts more than 20 restaurants, clubs, shops, and other historic attractions.[1] Exploring Laclede's Landing was tempting, but I was eager to find my hotel and get settled.

In the November 7, 2018, issue of *Forbes*, the award-winning food critic and reviewer John Mariani offers a succinct appreciation of St. Louis that shows how much there is to see and enjoy in this historic city. From the towering Gateway Arch to its museums, parks, gardens, and restaurants, St. Louis has much to offer visitors and long-term residents. Mariani acknowledged its share of urban challenges, including a dramatic decline in population following World War II, but it has rebounded with a focus on historic heritage. One of the more impressive reflections of that rebound is the restoration of the old Union Station, built in 1894 and once the busiest in the world. With the decline of passenger rail travel, the grand old building fell into decay, but it is now an upscale Hilton Hotel after a $150 million renovation. Mariana also mentions the city's world-class medical institutions, led by Washington University's medical school, among the top ten in the nation.[2]

Although I was only there for two days, my little taste of the city whetted my appetite for a more leisurely and extended visit. It's good to have a standing invitation from an old friend from grad school to do just that. As Mariani notes, the city of some 320,000 feels much larger, and it should be noted that the greater metro area is home to more than 2.8 million, making it the largest in Missouri and 22nd in the U.S. It also shows the wear and tear of so many American cities that have suffered from suburban exoduses:

> There is much decay surrounding the downtown area, gray stretches of un-patched roads and trash-strewn vacant lots; in fact, today its population is 100,000 people less than it was in 1950, when a flight to the suburbs began. Only Detroit and Youngstown, Ohio, have seen such precipitous declines. The city has had to battle its image as having the highest murder rate per capita in the U.S.[3]

The decay that Mariani describes was quite evident in my drive across the northern part of the city on my way to the clumsily named Home2Suites by Hilton near the city's graceful Forest Park, which hosted the World's Fair in 1904 and the Summer Olympics that same year. A variety of smaller parks add charm and warmth to many of the city's 79 neighborhoods.

The Hilton where I stayed for three nights is a comfortable, contemporary design and convenient to many of the city's attractions, including the Gateway Arch National Park, which is only four miles to the east, the Fox Theatre, Missouri Botanical Gardens, City Museum, and the Cathedral Basilica of Saint Louis. Many dining and shopping options are nearby. Forest Park, one of the city's most treasured assets, is only two miles away, near the Shriner's Hospital, Washington University School of Medicine, and multiple other medical facilities.

On Friday evening, I had the good fortune to dine at Bar Italia, which is located on Maryland Plaza in an upscale shopping and restaurant venue in the city's Central West End. I came upon it by chance, looking for a nicer place for a good meal. I was not disappointed. My server in this elegant bistro was a 30-something military veteran who guided me through the many appealing menu options. The wine list is impressive. Ambiance was warm and comfortable. I would return. It would be more fun with a companion. I was surprised that I was able to walk in and be seated without a reservation; although there were others enjoying this fine ristorante, it was not very crowded, especially for a Friday night.

28

Described as one of the city's most treasured resources, Forest Park, known as "the heart of the city," is one of 110 city parks under the jurisdiction of the Department of Parks, Recreation and Forestry. Opened to the public in 1876, it is one of the largest urban parks in the U.S. At around 1,300 acres it is far larger than New York's Central Park at 843 acres.[4]

Attracting more than 12 million visitors a year, Forest Park includes monuments, historic buildings, wildlife, waterways, and landscapes to form a unique cultural institution that is vitally important to the entire St. Louis region. The park is home to the region's major cultural institutions – the Zoo, Art Museum, Missouri History Museum, Science Center, Muny Opera, Boathouse, Steinberg Skating Rink, Dwight Davis Tennis Center, as well as the Probstein and Highlands golf courses. It also serves as a sports center for golf, tennis, baseball, cycling, fishing, soccer, rugby, running, walking and more.[5]

Sadly, I did not visit this major asset. When researching top-rated golf courses in the area, the park's 27-hole Norman K. Probstein Course, which was designed by Robert Foulis, an assistant to Tom Morris at St. Andrews' Old Course, did not make the lists that I consulted. Built between 1912 and 1915, the course was completely redesigned by Hale Irwin's firm in 2001. It sounds like a must play if I find my way back to St. Louis.

Neither of the two courses that I selected were in the city proper. Tapawingo National Golf Club, designed by Gary Player, is a 27-hole track located in Sunset Hills, about 13 miles southwest of my hotel, just outside I-270. The other course I played was The Missouri Bluffs Golf Club near St. Charles, about 25 miles west of Forest Park. Designed by Tom Fazio and opened in 1995, it is a spectacular natural beauty on the bluffs of the Missouri River. Superior in design and natural beauty, it is a fine test of golf. Teeoff.com lists Aberdeen and Spencer T. Olin among the top four in the area. There are many public and private courses in and around St. Louis.

Tapawingo Golf Course

I left my hotel early on Saturday morning, June 24, for Tapawingo Golf Course and had the good fortune to join two local golfers who had a tee time of 8:36, just before mine. We hit some balls on the spacious practice range at the foot of the hill below the handsome club

29

house. The recent rains had left the course a bit soggy but quite playable on a fine early summer's day of sunshine and scattered high clouds. The nearby Meramec River, which flows into the Mississippi south of the city, had caused some damage on a few of the holes, and the golf carts were well beyond their expiration date with Velcro and duct tape holding them together, bald tires, and poor brakes, especially noticeable on some of the more elevated holes. The clubhouse was nicely appointed with a well-stocked pro shop. Service and hospitality were quite good.

Dave and Dan were regulars on the course, so they provided helpful suggestions throughout, all of which helped my play when I was able to follow their guidance. Indeed, I had a great start, only one over after the first five holes, but my play went down to my average afterwards, and I posted a 92 only because I took no more than a 7 on three holes. We played the Woodlands/Prairie course from the white tees (5910 yards, 68.9/126). From the tips, the black tees, the yardage is 7040 with a rating and slope of 73.8/140. The gold and blue tees between provide nice options for golfers seeking more or less challenge. The forward, red tees measure 5484, 70.7/125. The Meramec was the wettest of the three nines.

I would rate Tapawingo as a three-star course, good but not great. The greens were a bit bumpy, perhaps not typical given the recent rains.

My playing partners were both former executives with locally based Anheuser-Busch, one of the nine *Fortune* 500 companies based in St. Louis. Dave was an executive with Eveready Corp., also based in St. Louis. I did not record Dan's current job. Both expressed enthusiasm for my project with Dave promising to send me responses to my questions via email. Surprisingly, it was Dan who sent me a thoughtful email a few days later.

As a first-generation college graduate, Dan expressed his gratitude for the opportunities he had been given and the "high work ethic" that his parents had instilled in him and his siblings. He shared his belief that "if you worked hard at something, good things would happen." He wondered if most Americans appreciate how our powerful economy provides opportunities that would not otherwise be available.

His worries focused on the adverse social and political impact of extreme voices at both ends of the political spectrum, amplified by social media and drowning out the "moderate people in the middle." He expressed his hope that the "current extremism" would wake up the "moderate middle of both parties" and sway our politics toward the middle.

With a magic wand, he'd "get people involved so the true voices of the country are being heard, not just the loudest." Although acknowledging progress, he said, "The divide between the economic success of different races is too wide and we need to continue to improve in this area."

Dan's comments touched recurring themes of my journey. The sense of gratitude for tangible and intangible blessings of being Americans did not surprise me, as was the recognition that we are a young country where so many are only a generation or two removed from hopeful immigrants who came here seeking freedom and economic opportunities. Dan's recognition that being a first-generation college graduate had opened many doors not available to his parents was also a recurring theme and struck a familiar note in my own experience working in higher education. At Albright, in particular, the number of students who were the first in their family to attend college was large, and the evidence of the advantages it gave them was clear and encouraging even if many graduated with substantial debt. Although some had much more, the average debt of Albright graduates when I retired in 2017 was less than $30,000.

Dan's comments about the impact of social media also struck a familiar theme, as did his conviction that extreme voices are dominating our political discourse and obscuring more moderate ones. Our ugly historical burden of racism is also widely recognized. It is, perhaps, our deepest scar, but a good case can be made that our treatment of Native Americans is an equal cause for shame. As he observed, we have surely made progress, but we have miles to go. The horrific Charlottesville debacle on August 12, 2017, shortly after I returned from my trip, was a grim reminder of the darker angels that are part of the American story, never very far from the surface. Subsequent events have driven this home repeatedly as our former president seems to have emboldened these darker angels to speak and act with increased and explicit frequency. The backlash against this toxicity as evidenced by the extraordinary diversity of successful candidates in the Congressional midterm election of 2018 was cause for hope as was Trump's resounding defeat in 2020. But I have no illusions that the toxic fever has been defeated. We are clearly in for a difficult time as a nation.

Gateway Arch National Park

That afternoon, I drove into the city to visit the Old Courthouse and the Gateway Arch National Park or, more formally, the Jefferson National Expansion Memorial. Although, the Arch was a "must-see" on my trip, I was more moved and impressed by this marvel of engineering than I had expected. Unfortunately, the Museum of Westward Expansion beneath the Arch was closed for renovation; a considerably condensed selection of its exhibits was temporarily located in several rooms of the Old Courthouse across the street--the site of the famous Dred Scott trial, where one of the saddest chapters in U.S. history was written (1846).

Scott and his wife, Harriet, were slaves who sued for their freedom in this courthouse after having spent some time with their owner, a military surgeon, at posts in Illinois and the Wisconsin Territory, where slavery was prohibited by the Missouri Compromise (1820). The Scotts' case ultimately made its way to the U. S. Supreme Court, where the infamous decision of Chief Justice Roger B. Taney denied them citizenship and freedom (1857). Most historians view the case as having increased sectional tensions that ultimately led to the election of Lincoln and the Civil War. Ironically, Scott was freed by his then owner a few months after the Supreme Court decision ruling against him. He died of tuberculosis 18 months later.

"On June 8th, 2012, the Dred Scott Heritage Foundation, the National Parks Service, and master sculptor Harry Weber were incredibly proud to unveil a statue of Dred and Harriet Scott on the south lawn of the Old Courthouse in downtown St. Louis. The Scotts are depicted standing close, holding their heads high, their eyes directed not only Arch-ward and across the Mississippi River, but toward a horizon of freedom in which they believed enough to one day finally see."[6]

Constructed between 1963 and 1965, the elegant Gateway Arch was designed by Eero Saarinen (1910-1961), the son of a famed Finnish architect who immigrated to the U.S. in 1923. He grew up in Bloomfield Hills, Michigan, where his father taught and served as dean of the Cranbrook Academy of Art. Saarinen also designed the Washington Dulles International Airport Terminal and the TWA Flight Center at JFK International in New York City. Saarinen's design was selected from 172 entries in an international competition held in 1947-48.

The Arch is described as "a sandwich made of stainless steel on the outside, carbon steel on the inside, and concrete in the middle."[7] Visible from miles away in Illinois and Missouri, its impact grows as one moves closer until one can stand along either leg of the soaring monument that reaches 630 feet, the exact same distance between each leg of the structure.

Although the Memorial invites contemplation of America's westward expansion, its graceful grounds can lead one's thoughts in multiple directions like the curving walks that wind through open vistas, two curvilinear ponds, allays of plane trees, and plantings of native flora. Under construction during my visit, the entire site was surrounded by plastic webbed and chain-linked fencing, so the grace and beauty that is its hallmark was somewhat impaired. (Yet another reason to return to St. Louis!)

The extensive re-landscaping was designed by Michael Van Valkenburg Associates of Brooklyn, NY, which gave me a frisson of delight. I was familiar with the renowned landscape design firm because one of its principals, Matthew Urbanski, is an alumnus of Albright College, who several years ago led a small team of his colleagues in a dramatic remaking of the central pedestrian pathway through campus and the creation of an inviting commons at its center. Although a very small project by the firm's typical standards, the impact is stunning. It is also a nice coincidence that the oldest son of one of my regular golfing buddies in Gettysburg went to work for MVVA after graduating from Penn State and has moved up to Senior Associate with the firm.

On that warm June afternoon, with a bright, azure sky overhead and gentle breezes wandering through the trees, the significance of the place in our history and in my personal voyage of rediscovery opened before me. In one respect it seemed fitting that this grand memorial to the visionary aspirations of Thomas Jefferson and so many who came after him was under construction. Not only does the remaking of the park reflect the restlessness that is a dominant trait of the American spirit, but the always unfinished work of seeking a more perfect union is reflected here as well. Guided by lofty, inspiring ideals, we have become a great power. We are very likely the wealthiest nation in the history of humanity. We have been a force for great good and have been a principal force for peace and stability in the world since World War II.

And yet, and yet, I can hear my critical friends already. What about the cruel horrors of slavery, standing as an ever-present reminder in the bronze statue of Dred and Harriet Scott just across the street from the Arch? What about Vietnam, Iraq, Manifest Destiny, and the crimes committed in its name, the genocide perpetrated against the indigenous peoples who occupied this land thousands of years before Columbus, before the Pilgrims landed at Plymouth Rock, before Jamestown? All part of our story too. But all those evils are not the only theme of our story. There is much more. Plenty of mistakes; plenty of well-meaning projects that failed; plenty of malevolence, just plain meanness that comes from the darkest corners of the human heart. But through it all, one theme remains, although sometimes very softly, quietly sounding in the darkest moments; it is hope. It is hope that drove us forward; hope of explorers and adventurers and, yes, fortune seekers. Hope that drove our ancestors to these shores seeking a better life, whether they were disinherited sons of English gentry, starving Irish, or terrorized Vietnamese "boat people" fleeing almost certain death. All were driven by hope for something better for themselves, for their families, for their descendants. It is this idea that Lady Liberty holds high in New York harbor. This idea still lives. Its sound is the heartbeat of America.

I recently read an admirable definition of patriotism:

"There are three kinds of patriots, two bad, one good. The bad ones are the uncritical lovers and the loveless critics. Good patriots carry on a lover's quarrel with their country, a reflection of God's lover's quarrel with the world." [8]

Lovers without hope cannot hope to have love.

After several hours of my reflective rambling through the Gateway Park, I headed for my car parked nearby. The temporary access walk led me out along Walnut Street just south and east of the Old Courthouse and alongside the Old Cathedral, built by the St. Louis Catholic community in 1834. I noticed that the old church had a Saturday vigil mass at 5:30, just minutes away. I went in, admired the historic church, and gave thanks for a beautiful day and much more.

Dinner at Pappy's Smokehouse
I can't recall now how it got on my radar, but that evening I was in the mood for BBQ and found my way to Pappy's Smokehouse at 3106 Olive Street in Midtown, just a couple of miles from my hotel. Pappy's bills itself as serving the "best Memphis-style BBQ in St. Louis." It's a casual atmosphere with concrete floors and wooden picnic tables in a large dining room. Customers order at a window in a fast-moving environment that reminded me of the famed Varsity drive-in across from Georgia Tech in Atlanta. The house specialties include dry-rubbed and slow-cooked meats smoked over apple and cherry wood. The smells were intoxicating. I enjoyed a hearty meal of pulled pork with a side of slaw and baked beans and left fully satisfied. Pappy's ships free anywhere in the U.S.: https://www.pappyssmokehouse.com.

Saint Charles and Golf at Missouri Bluffs Golf Course: The following morning, a Sunday, dawned bright and beautiful. (I was very lucky with the weather throughout most of my trip.) I left the hotel for Missouri Bluffs Golf Course around 7:45 a.m. My tee time was not till 10:30, so I also planned to spend some time touring the nearby historic city of Saint Charles where some would say the Voyage of Discovery started in earnest on May 21, 1804. Thinking I had ample time, I went first to the golf course, which proved to be a bit further up the river from St. Charles than I had expected. I looped back some 14 miles to visit this charming historic site that amply celebrates the Lewis and Clark legacy.

The historic district along Main Street faces the broad sweep of the Missouri River just a few miles upstream from its terminus in the Mississippi. It boasts scores of lovingly preserved buildings, some dating to the early 1800s. The city of some 70,000, now the county seat, traces its beginning to a French trading post established in 1769. Among its earliest American settlers was famed frontiersman Daniel Boone, a native of Berks County, Pennsylvania, near present-day Reading, who moved to Saint Charles in 1799 to join his son Nathan, who had built a home nearby.[9]

In 1821-26, it served as the new state's first capital. Missouri became the 24th state in August 1821, admitted under the terms of the Compromise of 1820 that permitted slavery in Missouri but nowhere else north of 36 degrees, 30 minutes, west of the Mississippi. To maintain the balance between slave and free state, Maine—a free state—was admitted at the same time, resulting in 12 free and 12 slave states.

The Missouri Compromise of 1820 is a reminder that the issue of slavery was a festering wound from the earliest days of the nation's history. Indeed, the acrimonious debates over the divisive issue during the writing of the U.S. Constitution in 1787 foreshadowed the conflict that would not be resolved until Lee surrendered his troops at Appomattox Court House in April 1865. Although slavery is long-gone in U. S. law, its bitter legacy of racial conflict that has defined and defaced our history continues to the present day.

Across from Main Street's multiple shops and restaurants, the city maintains a shady Riverfront Park with trails, multiple plantings, and many appealing sites for a leisurely picnic or siesta. The central attraction is a grand sculpture of Lewis and Clark accompanied by Lewis's great Newfoundland, Seaman, which he had acquired in Pittsburgh while impatiently waiting for the 55-foot keelboat to be completed by a builder who was in no hurry and was further slowed by his devotion to liquor. This fine, larger-than-life sculpture, by artist Pat Kennedy of Colorado was dedicated on May 18, 2003, like so many others along the trail, in celebration of the bicentennial of the Lewis and Clark expedition. Surrounded by a stunning variety of flowers and plants in full bloom on this warm summer day, the 15-foot high, bronze sculpture appears even higher on its ample stone base with Lewis standing to Clark's left, his right hand on his comrade's shoulder, both staring off to the west. It is clearly a point of pride for the citizens of St. Charles. [10]

Lewis & Clark Sculpture, St. Charles, Missouri

Also located at Riverfront Park is the Lewis and Clark Boathouse and Nature Center, a well-regarded small museum focused primarily on the Corps of Discovery. It includes scale models of the Corps' keelboat and pirogues, which are often taken out on the river for demonstrations.[11] Much more about visiting this charming historic city can be found easily on the internet.[12] Like so many other places along the trail, Saint Charles would reward more time than I had allotted for my visit.

After my ramble through the area, I headed back to Missouri Bluffs Golf Club. Everything about this round of golf was a pleasure— except another mediocre score of 95. At least I had only one triple bogey, but only two pars.

Although not among the top 100 on *Golf Digest's* annual list of public courses, the magazine did rate it as third best of new public courses opened in 1995. Designed by Tom Fazio, it is located in a pristine forest of rolling hills and wildlife adjacent to the famed Katy Trail a 240-mile rail-to-trail biking and hiking path that crosses the state alongside the Missouri River from Machens, just northeast of Saint Charles to Clinton, about 80 miles southeast of Kansas City. It claims to be the longest such trail in the U.S. (Yet another tempting excursion!)

Missouri Bluffs is a visual feast from start to finish. It has a gracious old-South clubhouse of 12,000 square feet, embraced by a wide verandah with white wooden rockers for admiring the multiple wooded views it affords. The course has hosted qualifying tournaments for the PGA and USGA. Here's the description from its website:

> The course is gently carved from the best that nature has to offer. With tees perched high, pristine zoysia fairways are edged by huge hundred-year-old trees and lead to perfect bent grass greens. You'll see an occasional deer and to the delight of golfers, sometimes even a small herd. You'll often stumble across a fox or wild turkey that are as startled by you as you are by them. You'll sense the faint hint of honeysuckle in the air as hawks glide high overhead.[13]

Even accounting for the hyperbole of such writing, this is not far from the mark. From the tips, the course is more than 7,000 yards; given the rolling terrain and twisting turn of the fairways, this would be a very substantial test of golf for single-digit players. There are four additional sets of tees at 6,610, 6,205, 5,807, and 5,191 yards. I failed to mark my card, but I think we played the white tees at 5,807 yards. From these tees the slope and rating of 67.1/113 does not reflect the challenge for a mid-teen handicapper.

When I arrived, I was able to join a threesome of locals, a cardiologist from nearby St. Louis University Hospital, a medical implement sales rep., and a software salesman. All were good guys with easy manners and, like me, delighted to be out on a beautiful early summer's day. I shared with them my adventure and the questions I hoped they'd consider answering and got emails for each of them. Only one of my new friends did respond, just a couple of days later.

John's email of June 29, 2017, reflects the sunny optimism of an American salesman who has done well. He graciously expressed his pleasure in meeting me and delight in a great day for golf. As for what he most valued about being an American, he first cited the cornerstone of freedom to pursue "life, liberty, and happiness." He added capitalism and our form of government. He acknowledged "it seems that we are a bit dysfunctional lately," but expressed his confidence that "the checks and balances are still the best for a nation to extend its prominence for hundreds or thousands of years to come." Given the nation's experience over the intervening years since we met, many would be hard pressed to share his optimism.

He described his worry as a hope "that future generations never forget the values our founding fathers put forth as we established a nation and the continual sacrifices the generations who came before them made. These values are key to sustaining our nation."

His magic wand wish struck me as modest as he focused on the Federal Government being forced to operate on a balanced budget. Leaving aside the debate over whether such a practice would be beneficial to our economy, the chances of that happening are close to zero. So perhaps it's not such a modest wish after all.

The spectacular Missouri Bluffs Golf Course is owned and operated by the Whittaker Family, which was battling local opposition to develop a residential complex in the adjacent pristine forest surrounding the course. Having obtained an option to purchase from the University of Missouri, Whittaker set about developing an extensive housing plan for the area. The University of Missouri had received the land for $1 back in 1948 so long as it was preserved for natural wildlife research. Apparently, the terms of that agreement had recently expired, so the University found a buyer for what is undoubtedly a very valuable 8,000-acre property. Not surprisingly, the opposition from neighbors and environmental groups was loud. Their concerns were supported by the 8-1 vote of the St. Charles County Planning and Zoning Commission opposing the development plan.

After some modifications to the plan, the County Council approved it on June 25, 2018, 5-1 with one abstention. Although an environmental group filed suit to stop the development, that effort ultimately failed. The first phase of residential development—221 homes on 48 acres—began in 2020 and plans for a second phase on 87 additional acres are moving forward.[14]

Later that day, I had the pleasure of meeting an old friend from my graduate studies at Notre Dame who now lives and works in St. Louis. He's now a priest and a New Testament scholar. We visited for a while at his home and then headed out for a restaurant he had selected: Vin de Set Rooftop Bar and Bistro (https://vindeset.com.). Located atop a nondescript warehouse in an industrial strip near Lafayette Park, the restaurant describes itself as having an "approachable creative cuisine using straightforward ingredients much of which is grown in [its] hydroponic greenhouse." Owned by Paul and Wendy Hamilton, their inspiration for opening Vin de Set (2017 is the street address on Chouteau Avenue) in 2006 was a trip to Provence. They aim to bring the warmth of Southern France to St. Louis, a city with deep roots in French history and culture. It was a delightful environment for a delicious meal and good conversation with an old friend who I had not seen in many years. A memorable way to conclude my visit to St. Louis.

Chapter Six
Bellefontaine Cemetery

May 2, 1804: France and the U. S. sign the treaty completing the transfer of the 828,000 square mile Louisiana Territory to the U.S. for $15 million or about $18 per square mile. Although now almost universally regarded as one of Jefferson's greatest accomplishments, it was hotly contested at the time and cleared the Senate by just two votes.

William Clark Memorial, Bellefontaine Cemetery, St. Louis

W hile checking out of my hotel in St. Louis on Monday morning, I shared with the pleasant clerk something about my journey. She asked if I had visited Bellefontaine Cemetery and reminded me that William Clark's grave and memorial site is located there; it was erected in 1904, the year that St. Louis hosted the World's Fair. Deferring my departure, I drove five miles northeast to see this early example of what is called "rural cemeteries." Not surprisingly, the Clark memorial is the most visited in the 314-acre park and arboretum, which was opened in 1849, the same year that a devastating cholera outbreak decimated the rapidly growing city.

Of course, today with the sprawl of the city, Bellefontaine is far from rural. It's located in a densely developed neighborhood just east of the International Airport on the bluffs overlooking the Mississippi. But when the visionary and ambitious city leaders planned this gracious park as a dignified pastoral resting place for the dead, it was well beyond the bounds of the rapidly growing city.

The rural cemetery movement is traced to the opening in 1804 of the Pere Lachaise Cemetery outside Paris. It became the model for Mount Auburn Cemetery (1831) in Cambridge, Massachusetts. New York and Philadelphia were not far behind. "The rural cemetery movement sought to establish 'cities of the dead' in park-like settings outside of urban centers, so that those who had died could truly rest in peace. The rural setting also allowed visitors to reflect and remember in dignified, natural surroundings, far from the distractions of the city." The leaders of St. Louis wanted to stake their own claim as an American city worthy of comparison with their older siblings on the East Coast.[1]

According to experts in this field—yes, it's a serious subject of academic study and a popular topic for amateurs as well—the rural cemetery movement reflected the early 19th-century romantic view of nature and art as well civic pride and practical considerations of increasingly crowded cities, rising real estate prices, and concern about disease. A quick glimpse at offerings on Amazon reveals at least 18 such books "frequently bought" with *Cemeteries* (2010) by Keith Eggener, a distinguished professor of architectural history at the University of Oregon, who Rebecca Greenfield (I assume that's not a pseudonym borrowed for the occasion!) interviewed for an article in *The Atlantic* entitled "Our First Public Parks: The Forgotten History of Cemeteries" (March 6, 2011).

Cemeteries, which includes 650 black & white photographs, is described as a "bountifully illustrated exploration of the cemetery in American landscape and narrative." Other suggested titles include the following: *Rest in Peace: A History of American Cemeteries* (2008) by Meg Greene; *Stories in Stone: A Field Guide to Cemetery Symbolism and Iconography* (2004) and *Going Out in Style: The*

Architecture of Eternity (2017) both by Douglas Keister; and *199 Cemeteries to See Before You Die* (2017) by Loren Rhoads, who hosts a popular Cemetery Travel blog! Along with Bellefontaine, Rhoads's list includes cemeteries on every continent.

As Eggener observed, before 1831, America had no cemeteries. It's not that Americans didn't bury their dead—just that large, modern graveyards did not exist. With the construction of Mount Auburn, the movement spread rapidly across American cities before and after the Civil War. He reminds us that in the early days of the Republic, there were no public parks, art museums, or botanical gardens in American cities. "People flocked to the cemeteries for picnics, for hunting and shooting, and carriage racing."[2]

Bellefontaine is a beautiful example of the species and lovingly maintained. Entering its imposing stone pillared gate on West Florissant Avenue, I was reminded of Westview Cemetery in southwest Atlanta where the Dillard family plot holds the remains of my mother, father, sister, maternal grandparents, and great-grandparents among others. Westview, like Bellefontaine, was built as an expression of civic pride and contains the remains of many notables in that city's history. Opened in 1884, its 600 acres is the final resting place to more than 100,000 among its "towering trees and winding roadways." Westview claims to be the largest of its kind in the Southeast.[3]

Bellefontaine conveniently provides visitors a helpful guide and map with a key to some 50 significant graves and memorials— significant for those buried there as well as for the impressive variety of architectural styles including Classical, Romanesque, Gothic, Egyptian and modern. Indeed, one might use the site as an open-air classroom for the study of architectural styles. Still an active cemetery, Bellefontaine is the final resting for more than 87,000 remains.

"In spite of many changes, the cemetery continues to reflect the original design of Almerin Hotchkiss. While the cemetery's original 138 acres have grown to 314, Bellefontaine's fourteen miles of curved roadways still afford beautiful views of the landscape, including thousands of shrubs and trees and hundreds of works of art. Bellefontaine has become an outdoor museum, containing fine sculptures and memorial art reflecting the changing tastes of our culture."[4] It is also recognized as a Level II Accredited Arboretum, listed in the Morton Register of Arboreta. The magnificent variety of trees is worth the trip.

Among the notable graves and tombs is that of Williams S. Burroughs, the author of *Naked Lunch,* along with his grandfather of the same name who invented the adding machine. One will also find the grave of Thomas Hart Benton, the first U.S. Senator from Missouri, who as a hot-headed youth fought a duel with Andrew Jackson. The future President carried Benton's bullet in his body for the remainder of his life. As a Democrat, Benton later became a stalwart supporter and great friend of his former dueling antagonist.[5]

Not surprisingly, the monumental tombs of the Busch and Anheuser families reflect the fortunes they amassed in brewing America's favorite alcoholic beverage. The Busch Mausoleum is a perfect gem of Gothic Revival style in unpolished Missouri granite. Inscribed over the bronze doors is Julius Caesar's famous proclamation, "Veni, vidi, vici!" I don't suppose Mr. Busch intended irony in directing this inscription over his final resting place, but one cannot avoid the thought.

Among the most visually striking and celebrated monuments is the Wainwright Tomb, which was commissioned in 1891 by the local multi-millionaire brewer Ellis Wainwright as a memorial to his wife, who died suddenly of peritonitis. Designed by architect Lewis Sullivan, the tomb "is a domed cube with simple carved decorations in Sullivan's signature stylized plant patterns. The mausoleum's double doors are bronze grills framed by delicate stone carvings. Sullivan's draftsman for the project was the famed American architect Frank Lloyd Wright. The unique tomb was added to the National Register of Historic Places in 1970.[6]

Wainwright Tomb, Bellefontaine Cemetery, St. Louis

At the time of his wife's untimely death, Wainwright had recently completed the 10-story office building bearing his name that is an early example of the modern "skyscraper." The handsome terra cotta structure located at 709 Chestnut Street was saved from demolition by the National Trust for Historic Preservation and is now a National and city landmark owned by the state and housing state offices.[7] It is an encouraging example of the impulse to preserve our limited history in the face of the competing itch that is often called "progress."

As I meandered through the cemetery, I came upon a McMillan tomb and wondered which of my restless forebears of Scotch-Irish descent had found their way to St. Louis. As noted earlier, the story of these early frontier settlers was told by my beloved mentor from my undergraduate studies, James Graham Leyburn (1902-1993), in his seminal *The Scotch-Irish: A Social History* (UNC, 1962). Daniel Boone is likely the best known of these colonial immigrants who descended from the Scottish Highland Clan MacMillan but found their way to American shores by way of Northern Ireland and a scheme envisioned by Elizabeth I but effected by her successor, King James I, to lure Lowland Scottish farmers to the nine counties on land the English essentially stole from the indigenous Irish. Thus was planted the seeds of what has come to be known as "The Troubles" in Ulster.

After returning home, I visited the Bellefontaine website and used its helpful search function to discover that there are 32 burial sites for McMillans dating back to Eliza on October 8, 1852, to John S. McMillan Jr. on October 9, 2018. Seeking further information, I had a good conversation and several emails with Dan Fuller, Bellefontaine's helpful archivist and volunteer coordinator. I learned that the McMillan mausoleum was built around 1901, by William P. McMillan who died that year. He or his descendants had the remains of his parents, Percy and Mary, moved into the mausoleum soon after it was completed. His wife, Eliza, was buried there in 1915.

On the campus of Washington University in St. Louis is a McMillan Hall, the first dormitory for women at the University, named for William P. McMillan and given to the University by his widow, Eliza, who was known for many acts of charity among the poor in the city.

According to the Washington University website, William P. McMillan was born in Canada in 1841 and established a wholesale hardware store that bore his name. He moved to St. Louis in 1870 and established the Missouri Car and Foundry Company, which built railroad cars, and later merged with William K. Bixby's American Car & Foundry Company. McMillan became Chairman of the Board of that company. At one point the McMillans gave $100,000 to Mary Institute, a college preparatory school that had been operated by Washington University, which enabled the Institute to move from dilapidated quarters into a new building. At her death, Eliza McMillan left many bequests to friends and family, including her household staff, to whom she gave "lifetime" salaries.[8]

After a few days of exploring the McMillans of St. Louis, it became clear that this could become a major digression—perhaps already is—so I thanked my helpful guide at Bellefontaine and decided to move on.

Before doing so, however, I must mention several African Americans who share my surname. Beyond St. Louis, these include Terry, the esteemed novelist, but in St. Louis I discovered several who had achieved some distinction. Among them are Ernie, the 1960s NFL star tackle for the St. Louis Cardinals; and his son Erik, an outstanding defensive player for the N.Y. Jets in the 1980s. Although I cannot know exactly how the McMillan surname came to these and many other African Americans, it is clearly part of our sad legacy of slavery.

In my research after returning home, I discovered a profile of Michael McMillan, who at age 41 had been appointed in 2013 the CEO of the Urban League of St. Louis. Although one might not know it from his photograph, McMillan is, indeed, a proud member of the city's African-American community. A life-long resident of St. Louis, McMillan acknowledged in the interview that people continue to be surprised that he is an African American because of his very light complexion. Nevertheless, he notes that his family has roots in the South and still has some of the slave papers of his ancestors. Reflecting on that grim legacy, which has been trenchantly called America's "birth defect," McMillan somberly affirmed the difficulties for "a race of people in 150 years to go from being a piece of property to being fully equalized in terms of all aspects of life in society." He added that "we have obviously made tremendous strides, and the Urban League is trying to help finish the job."[9]

The William Clark grave and memorial monument is an impressive array of sculpture and engraved steles celebrating the life and legacy of this courageous soldier, explorer, and St. Louis civic leader. Located on a small hill at the northernmost point of the cemetery, the focal point is a 35-foot granite obelisk that shone brightly in the sun in the cloudless morning sky on the day of my visit.

After returning from the expedition in 1806, Clark remained in St. Louis for the rest of his life. President Jefferson granted him 1600 acres, gave him the rank of Brigadier General overseeing the Louisiana Territory Militia, and made him superintendent of Indian affairs, a post he held for the remainder of his life. From 1813 to 1821, Clark served as Governor of the Missouri Territory.

When Clark died in 1838 at the age of 68, he was buried with full military and Masonic honors on a farm owned by a nephew, Col. John O'Fallon. The grave was later incorporated into Bellefontaine Cemetery. When Clark's youngest son, Jefferson Kearney Clark, died in 1902, he left a bequest to build the monument, and Clark's widow supervised the construction. It was unveiled in 1904 in conjunction with the Louisiana Purchase Exposition World's Fair and the centennial celebration of the Lewis and Clark Expedition. This history is memorialized on a granite plinth erected adjacent to the monument in conjunction with the bicentennial celebration of the expedition in 2004.[10]

At the base of the obelisk is a handsome bust of Clark with the following inscription: "William Clark—Born in Virginia August 1, 1770—Entered Into Life Eternal September 1, 1838—Soldier, Explorer, Statesman, and Patriot—His Life is Written in the History of His Country."[11]

Clark's compassion for Native Americans is memorialized on what appears to be a more recently installed granite slab at his monument with the following inscription:

IT IS TO BE LAMENTED THAT
THE DEPLORABLE SITUATION OF
THE INDIANS DO NOT RECEIVE
MORE OF THE HUMAN FEELINGS
OF THE NATION.
WILLIAM CLARK
WRITING TO HIS OLD FRIEND
THOMAS JEFFERSON, DEC. 15, 1825

My serendipitous visit to Bellefontaine was a highlight of my time in St. Louis. An impressive example of the rural cemetery movement, it is also a compact expression of civic pride and creativity. Even as one admires the diverse architecture of monuments and tombs as well as it's carefully nurtured and cultivated natural beauty, Bellefontaine is a solemn reminder of all our journeys' final destination.

Chapter Seven
Crossing Missouri: An Immigrant Story

May 21, 1804: At long last and after many vexing delays, the Corps of Discovery departs the tiny riverside city of St. Charles, Missouri, cheered on by its enthusiastic citizens. Traveling upstream against often-unfavorable winds and currents, the Corps made just over three miles to its first camp.

The Missouri River, in the state whose name it bears, flows east
from Kansas City in a series of lazy curves and arcs north of I-
70 along the northern outskirts of Harry Truman's hometown
of Independence, where the Presidential Library is worth the visit. Just
east of tiny DeWitt (population 78 in 2020) the river cuts a wide
horseshoe arc and dips sharply south of I-70 to the charming state
capital of Jefferson City, then proceeds on through the southern hills
of the state to its conjunction with the Mississippi north of St. Louis.

If you're in a hurry, I-70 will get you from St. Louis to Kansas City
in fewer than four hours. But a much more interesting route is to find
State Road 94 near the beautiful Missouri Bluffs Golf Course west of
Saint Charles and follow it westward upstream along the wide and
lazy flow of the river through a series of small towns founded by
hopeful nineteenth-century immigrants, mostly German, seeking the
promises of what has always been America's enduring attraction—
economic opportunity, freedom from oppression, more room,
independence.

Following the Lewis and Clark expedition, St. Louis and the
Missouri Territory attracted settlers from the east and thousands of
immigrants, many from Germany who were drawn to the new frontier
by promotion of what was called the "Missouri Rhineland."

The legacy of these adventurous pilgrims is evident in St. Louis and
all along the river that was quickly settled and developed along its
shores, the principal mode of transportation and commerce until
superseded by the railroad beginning in the 1850s. The exploding
population of St. Louis reflects this booming migration. With fewer
than 5000 residents in 1830, St. Louis ranked as America's 57th largest
city. In just a decade, the city's population had more than tripled, and
by 1850, St. Louis was the eighth largest city in the U.S. with more
than 77,000 residents, a classic boom town that soon became known
as the "gateway to the west." Although none of the towns that grew
up along the Missouri River to the west compared in size to St. Louis,
the growth is still evident today.[1]

I left Bellefontaine Cemetery around 11:30 and headed west toward
lunch in nearby Washington, just 54 miles from St. Louis, along the
river's meandering path among rolling hills and neatly tended
farmland. Washington is located on the south bank of the river on State
Routes 47 and 100. With a population of just under 14,000, it proudly
claims to be the largest city between St. Louis and Jefferson City, the

state capital, some 77 miles to the west. Although my visit was brief, the lively charm of this thriving riverfront community is evident in its many stores, restaurants, museums, and parks. Its civic pride is well represented in its impressive website: http://www.washmo.org.

Known as the "corncob pipe capital of the world," Washington is home to the famed Missouri Meerschaum factory. Founded in 1869, the factory is among the prominent red-brick buildings along Front Street facing the river and the railroad line for a passenger train now known as the Missouri Runner. The train connects St. Louis and Kansas City on its 283-mile route that includes daily Amtrak passenger service. During my brief visit, a long freight train sped through town carrying many cars of coal. The clapboard-sided passenger station is neatly maintained and houses the city's visitor center.

Among the area's attractions are more than 40 wineries within an hour's drive, celebrated by a Fine Arts Fair and Winefest each May. Other events in this bustling town are an annual BBQ and Blues Fest in April, the Town and Country Fair in August, a lively Farmer's Market each Saturday from April to October, and Music at the Market on the second Thursday of May through October. The range and scope of its special events calendar is particularly impressive for such a small town.

By luck, I selected one the city's best BBQ restaurants along Front Street, Sugarfire Smokehouse, and feasted on a delicious beef brisket, one of the featured dishes among its "award-winning" selection of barbecued meats. Truth to tell, the flavors were succulent, but I was surprised by the amount of fat in my cut. I still prefer the lean, pulled pork of Eastern North Carolina with a shot of the traditional vinegar-based sauce to moisten it and bring out the wonderful, smokey flavor. After a stroll along the river, I reluctantly pulled myself away from Washington and headed west on State Route 100, along the southern shore of the wide Missouri.

New Haven & Mountain Man John Colter

My next brief stop was the tiny city of New Haven (pop. 2000), just 13 miles west of Washington. Originally known as Miller's Landing, it was a busy port in the first half of the 19th century when steamboats carried settlers, restless adventurers, and supplies into the territory. My principal interest there was the legacy of John Colter (c.1770–

1775 – May 7, 1812, or November 22, 1813), a famed member of the Corps of Discovery and the prototype of the "mountain men" who still stir the American imagination.

Following his service with the Corps of Discovery, Colter returned to the west to trap beaver and trade with the Indians. Over the following four years, he had harrowing adventures, "discovered" what we now know as Yellowstone Park and the Grand Tetons, and finally settled down in New Haven, where he died in 1812 or 1813 at the age of 37 or 42.

The grandson of an Irish immigrant, Colter was born in Stuarts Draft, VA, in Augusta County near present-day Staunton. Although Colter is justly remembered and celebrated in New Haven, the site of his grave is unknown. The exact dates of his birth and death are disputed. But in his short life, he had more adventures than many who lived much longer, and his story has inspired many since.

Colter's family moved to Maysville, Kentucky, around 1780. Located in northeast Kentucky along the banks of the Ohio River, the small city became an important crossroads in the development of that region and famously an important stop on the Underground Railroad. Harriet Beecher Stowe is reputed to have witnessed a slave auction in Maysville that she incorporated in *Uncle Tom's Cabin*.

Maysville is about 65 miles northeast of Lexington. Frontiersmen Simon Kenton and Daniel Boone were among the city's founders. It's interesting to note that the first steamboat to travel from Pittsburgh to New Orleans passed Maysville in 1811, just five years after the Corps of Discovery returned to St. Louis. Steamboat traffic on the river contributed to the growth and prosperity of Maysville in the early 19th century as it did for so many other towns along the waterways of the rapidly growing country. It must have been an exciting time to be alive with a sense of adventure and opportunity at every turn.[2]

Although Maysville is some 300 miles to the southwest of Pittsburgh, Colter appears to have found his way there to apply for membership in the Corps. Ambrose records that both Lewis and Clark received many such applications and could, therefore, be selective. As they were undertaking preparations separately while Lewis made his way from Pittsburgh to the Falls of the Ohio, each of the captains agreed that the other would have a veto over any recruit selected by the other.[3]

Colter was among the first men recruited by Lewis in the fall of 1803 while he waited impatiently for the completion of the keelboat in Pittsburgh. Lewis offered him the rank of private with pay of $5 per month. In August 1806, when the expedition returned to the Mandan villages near present-day Bismarck, North Dakota, on its return to St. Louis, Colter petitioned the captains to be discharged early so that he might join with two others and return west to hunt, trap beaver, and explore.

On April 2, 2006, a handsome granite memorial to Colter was dedicated in New Haven by the Missouri State Society of the Daughters of the American Revolution. The memorial inscription records William Clark's journal entry regarding Colter's request for the early discharge: ". . . we were disposed to be of service to anyone of our party who had performed their duty as well as Colter had done, we agreed to allow him the privilage [sic]." Also recorded on this stone is the following, "Military records show that Private John Colter died May 7, 1812, while serving in the United States Mounted Rangers commanded by Captain Nathan Boone, son of Daniel Boone." Other sources say that Colter died late the following year of jaundice. Given the uncertainty of his birth year, we can only know that Colton was no more than 43 when he died and possibly as young as 37.

Nearby the DAR memorial overlooking the river is a small museum and visitor center as well as a tidy, log shelter honoring Colton. Dedicated in 2003 to commemorate the expedition's bicentennial, the shelter contains framed prints retelling Colter's many contributions to the Lewis and Clark Expedition, his skill in hunting and trapping, his effectiveness in negotiating with the Indians, and most famously his grueling near-death experience and escape from hostile Blackfoot Indians while trapping beaver in Montana.

The Memorial adjoins a pleasant river walk along the levee with additional information about the Lewis and Clark Expedition as well as local history. It's an impressive accomplishment for such a tiny town, which like so many others along my travels, gave ample evidence of civic pride, a sense of history, and a commitment to hospitality.[4]

The famed episode known as "Colter's Run" has been told and retold in story and film. It is not known whether Colter could write; other than a signature, he left no written records, so all we know about his adventures trapping and exploring the Rockies is based on his memories shared with others. There is no reason to question the essential shape of his desperate escape from the hostile natives who made his capture a sort of contest among young braves; the details of his harrowing experience attest to his toughness and perhaps succumbing to a degree of exaggeration that is common to many of the tall tales of the frontier. It is certain from what we do know of the Expedition that the men—and the Indian woman Sacagawea—endured hardships that tested the extreme limits of human endurance. Surely, there has never been a more hardened group of courageous explorers. Their grueling adventures, particularly in crossing the Bitterroot Mountains from Montana into Idaho, attest to the human capacity for enduring physical and mental adversity.

In 1809 while traveling by canoe on the Jefferson River, Colter and his companion John Potts suddenly encountered several hundred Blackfoot warriors who demanded that they come ashore. Although the Blackfoot, also known as Blackfeet, had already proven their hostility to the invading whites, Colter had previous experience negotiating and trading with them and other tribes. Accordingly, as the story goes, Colter complied and came ashore where he was promptly disarmed and stripped naked. Potts refused and fired on the Indians killing one of them; he was promptly filled with arrows and lead, fell dead in the water, was dragged ashore and hacked to pieces as Colter watched.

To his surprise, his captors told Colter to run for it. He did not wait for them to change their minds and took off realizing soon that he was the prize in a game of capture the man. Pursued by a pack of young braves, Colter ran naked for several miles across brutal terrain. Having outrun all but one of his attackers, exhausted and bloody, he turned on the surprised brave who, equally exhausted, made a feeble throw of his spear, which Colter retrieved and "pinned him to the earth" with his own weapon. Continuing his flight with only a blanket he had taken from the dead Indian, Colter reached the Madison River and hid himself in a beaver lodge—or according to another account, among some floating logs—where he waited till nightfall. He then walked for eleven days to a traders' fort on the Little Big Horn, arriving more nearly dead than alive, but survived to contribute one of the more exciting tales to our common legacy of the West.

After other adventures, more trapping, and more close calls with the Blackfoot, Colter finally departed for St. Louis late in 1810. He had been in the wilderness for almost six years.

Among the popular productions based on Colter's adventures is a 1912 silent film entitled *John Colter's Escape*; *The Naked Prey*, a grisly 1965 film set in Africa starring Cornel Wilde; *Run of the Arrow*, a 1957 western starring Rod Steiger; and *The Mountain Men*, a 1980 film starring Charlton Heston. One would think that we're about due for a re-make!

The 1994 novel *Wilderness* by Roger Zelazny and Gerald Hausman is loosely based on Colter's adventures and another harrowing survival tale of a mountain man named Hugh Glass, whose ordeal was more recently portrayed in the 2015 film *Revenant* starring Leonardo DiCaprio. T. Coraghessan Boyle's *The Harder They Come* is a 2015 novel in which Colter's legendary life figures prominently.[5]

Although my visit to New Haven was brief, it was a stirring reminder of the adventures and hardships that our forebears endured as they fanned out across the vast, uncharted land that Jefferson had purchased for roughly three cents an acre in 1804.

Just 18 miles upstream is Hermann, population 2500. Also known as "Little Germany," it was founded by the German Settlement Society of Philadelphia in 1836 as "a colony where German customs and language could be preserved amid the benefits of America," according to a local historical marker. Hermann prospered as a shipping port for commerce on the river and became known for its extensive vineyards, which flourished until destroyed by Prohibition. The region along the river from Jefferson City to the western frontier of St. Louis is known as the Missouri Rhineland both for the strong immigration from Germany and for topography and soil similar to that found along the Rhine River. The wine business rebounded and has been booming since a revival that began in the 1960s. Before Prohibition, Missouri was the second-largest wine producer in the country. Today, the countryside around Hermann and all along the river is thick with vineyards. They have become a major tourist attraction for the region.

The Corps of Discovery camped near the future site of Hermann on May 26, 1804, and organized into two detachments and three so-called "messes" under three sergeants, each of whom commanded one of the three vessels: the keelboat, a red pirogue, and a white pirogue. The smallness of this force against the challenge of their mission is a continuing source of wonder.

The history of Hermann is one of many vignettes that illustrate the central role of immigration in the growth and vitality of the United States. Clearly, the promoters of this area saw it as an attractive way to preserve their German culture in the new world. The idea of assimilation would have been utterly foreign, even repugnant. They kept a German-language newspaper well into the 20th century. I am reminded that one of the treasures in the archives at Gettysburg College is an original of the broadside sheets of the Declaration of Independence published in German. Apparently, the Founders were not too concerned about English being the only acceptable language for Americans and understood quite well that if they hoped to have the support of German-speaking Americans, they darn well better make their bold Declaration available in German. Although the distinctive German heritage of Hermann is still evident in even a brief visit, one can hardly doubt that it is, in this very distinctiveness, another thoroughly American town.

I can't help but note that when I began work on this chronicle in 2017, I could not have imagined how what then appeared a disturbing level of toxicity in our civic and political discourse could have gotten worse. As I write these words on Saturday, August 3, 2019, the campaign for the next presidential election is in full swing, and it has become evident that our president is positioning himself to run for re-election by a campaign rooted in hatred, fear, division, xenophobia, and racism. I suppose that the recurring nativism that Mr. Trump has cultivated is as American as the multitude of diverse immigration stories like the ones found along the Missouri River in the Missouri Rhineland. One can only hope that the "better angels" in which Lincoln expressed hope and confidence will once again prevail.

After departing Hermann, I crossed the river on the nearby Christopher S. Bond Bridge, which opened in July 2007, replacing the old Hermann Bridge that dated back to 1930. Bond is a popular former Republican two-term governor of Missouri and four-term U. S. Senator. It is a curiosity that there is another Christopher S. Bond Bridge across the Missouri in Kansas City. It was opened in 2010.

It was after three p.m. and Kansas City, where I had plans to meet friends for dinner, was still 250 miles away. I picked up the pace of my leisurely ramble, but still had to squeeze in a short visit to Jefferson

City, the state capital. I arrived in Jefferson about 4:10 as the sky became increasingly gray and overcast, the temperature became cooler, and it began to drizzle. Although not ideal conditions for even a cursory visit, I did manage to admire the handsome classical capitol and the impressive sculpture of Lewis and Clark that sits just below the capitol, fittingly overlooking the river below the bluff on which it stands. The sculpture features Lewis, Clark, York, the guide George Druillard, and Lewis's Newfoundland dog, Seaman. Overlooking the Jefferson Landing Historic Site and the Missouri River, the large sculpture was dedicated on June 4, 2008, to commemorate the date that the Corps of Discovery encamped in the area on its outbound journey in 1804. The beautifully landscaped monument is the work of the Missouri native sculptor Sabra Tull Meyer.[6]

The Lewis and Clark monument in Jefferson City is at the Katy Trailhead Plaza, which is part of the Katy Trail State Park. The country's longest recreational rail trail, stretching 240-miles, it was built on the right of way of the former Missouri-Kansas-Texas Railroad. Made of firmly crushed and packed limestone, the almost level Katy Trail affords hikers and bikers a smooth path through the historic Missouri heartland with a variety of amenities and attractions along the way. Autumn is a highly recommended time to visit.[7]

After my too-brief visit to Jefferson City, hardly more than a wave of the hand, I made my way north to I-70 and hustled to cover the 160 remaining miles to meet my Kansas City friends for dinner.

Chapter Eight
Two Kansas Cities

June 26, 1804: The Corps of Discovery arrives at the mouth of the Kansas River, site of present-day Kansas City, Missouri, and Kansas City, Kansas.

As most everyone knows, there are two Kansas Cities, one in Missouri, the other just west in Kansas. I had hoped that my visit would help me understand better how the two adjacent cities came to have the same name and what the relationship between the two was like. The easiest shorthand for the two cities is KCM and KCK, which I hope requires no further explanation.

After my ramble across Missouri, I arrived in KCM around 7 p.m. on June 26 for dinner with friends at one of the area's famed BBQ places: Jack Stack in the Country Club Plaza, a busy, upscale shopping and restaurant mecca, which claims to be the first planned shopping center in the U.S.[1] With five locations in the metro area (four in KCM; one in KCK), Jack Stack is worth the wait that appears inevitable even on a Monday night. No reservations accepted. Kansas City is justly proud of its BBQ. One could explore the city for a week eating only BBQ. Leaving aside the doubtful health benefits of such an adventure, it would surely be a pleasure for those who like this quintessentially American dish. Worth mentioning here is Joe's Kansas City BBQ in a renovated gas station on W. 47th at Mission Road. Located on the Kansas side of the metro area, many claim that Joe's BBQ is the best in the metro area.

By chance, my arrival in Kansas City was the same date that the Lewis and Clark Corps of Discovery arrived in the area in 1804 and made camp near the confluence of the Kansas and Missouri Rivers. A somewhat neglected, interpretive park is now located at Kaw Point near where the Corps camped for three days, undertook repairs, and built a modest defensive "redoubt" in the event of attack. Although they saw buffalo for the first time, they did not kill one. They also did not encounter any of the indigenous tribes in the area, most notably the Kanza or Kansa, from which "Kansas" is derived. Now known as the Kaw Nation, they operate out of Kaw City, Oklahoma, where like so many others they were relocated in a series of treaties and maneuvers orchestrated by the U.S. Government in the long tragic war of attrition against the native inhabitants of our country. The Kansas River is also known as the Kaw in recognition of those native peoples.

Although worth visiting, Kaw Point Park is not easy to reach. Even my Google Maps, usually so reliable, was flummoxed by the challenge of navigating through a heavily industrialized complex that surrounds the park on the Kansas side of the rivers.

The greater Kansas City metro area is comprised of 15 counties straddling the river in both Missouri and Kansas with a population of more than 2.3 million. Taken together, the area is one of our often-overlooked urban gems with a thriving and diverse economy, many artistic and cultural attractions, museums, monuments, and more than 200 "registered" fountains across KCM, which is known as the City of Fountains. There are also major league sports including the Royals and Chiefs in KCM, Sporting Kansas City (the professional soccer team) and the Kansas Speedway in KCK. The Speedway hosts two major NASCAR events each year.

The population growth of the region has been steady since 2010, at about 15,000 per year. In 2016, however, the population growth spiked at 20,000, reflecting the healthy economy of the region and a dramatic, ten-fold jump in domestic migration.[2]

The earliest origins of Kansas City are traced to John McCoy, who established West Port in 1833 along the Santa Fe Trail to serve the growing numbers of pioneers making their way west. The following year, McCoy established Westport Landing along a bend of the Missouri to serve as a landing point for his trade. Soon thereafter a group of investors known as the Kansas Town Company began to settle the area. The Town of Kansas, Westport, and nearby Independence were important points along the Santa Fe, California, and Oregon Trails that ran through the area that is now Jackson County, in which the bulk of KCM is located.

I was surprised to discover that the KC metro area has more than double the population of St. Louis. Indeed, KCM, is the most populous city in the state. According to a recent story in the *Kansas City Star,* the population of metro St. Louis recently dipped below one million for the first time since 2011, largely because of net domestic outmigration. Folks were leaving St. Louis looking for better economic opportunity while Kansas City was enjoying just the opposite.[3]

A newcomer might expect the river to be the natural border between Missouri and Kansas, but it is not, at least, not entirely. After all, the river flows roughly from west to east, and the two states share a border that runs north/south. Although the river forms the Missouri/Kansas border north of the two Kansas Cities, most of the border between the two states is defined by the helpfully named State Line Road, which runs due south from the downtowns of the two cities near Kaw Point. For the visitor exploring the greater Kansas City metro area, south of the two downtowns, one can easily slip into Kansas and back into Missouri without knowing it. If one wished to follow State Line Road to its terminus, one would arrive in extreme northeast Oklahoma not far from Joplin, Missouri, and about 100 miles from Tulsa. Such an excursion, although tempting like so many others along my journey, would have taken me too far afield. Plus, I hadn't identified any alluring golf courses down that way although I have no doubt that they are there.

I had reserved a room at a Hilton Garden Inn for my two-night stay in Kansas City. After a very long day driving across the state and a most enjoyable dinner with my friends, I wearily made my way to my hotel, which is just across the river in Kansas. It was late and dark, so I noted little of my surroundings and was glad to find a clean and comfortable room awaiting me. It was my first time in Kansas, the Sunflower State, and home to the beloved Dorothy from "The Wizard of Oz." It's also known as "The Free State," reflecting the tumultuous conflict over whether Kansas would be admitted to the Union as a free state or slave state. Abolitionists from New England and elsewhere won that battle, which earned the state another nickname, "Bloody Kansas," and the state entered the Union in January 1861. The geographic center of the contiguous "lower 48 states" is located a few miles north of Lebanon, Kansas, about 250 miles west of KCK. East to west, the state measures 410 miles from Missouri to the Colorado line.

Like every American city, KCM shows wear and tear of neglected infrastructure and the effects of many leaving the inner city for more attractive business and residential options in the suburbs. More subtle, but just as important, is the heavy hand of racial segregation, white flight in the face of court-ordered school desegregation and restrictive covenants designed to keep "undesirables" out. But Kansas City shares this sad legacy with most U.S. cities. Despite this, however, KCM shows multiple signs of downtown growth and renewal, with several attractive hotels, including the grand old Hilton President in the "Power and Light District" near its impressive convention center, The Sprint Center, Union Station, the World War I Monument and Museum, J.C. Nichols Fountain, Kaufmann Stadium, and Arrowhead Stadium.

It was not till the next afternoon that I discovered the surprising contrast between the two downtowns called Kansas City. The two are linked by the Lewis and Clark Viaduct, a series of nine bridges across the Kansas River near its confluence with the Missouri. But the first impression of crossing into Kansas City, Kansas, suggests the harsh reality of two Americas. The contrasts can be found in any metro area in the U.S., but it was particularly dramatic to have these two cities bearing the same name showing such contrast on either side of the great river that divides and unites them.

After a delightful morning round of golf at Shoal Creek Golf Club (see Chapter 9) with a group of international educators, I went searching for the Lewis and Clark Memorial at Kaw Point, which proved to be challenging, as noted above. Despite the challenges of finding the park, it was well worth the visit. It has good historical plaques (although damaged by vandalism), hiking and biking trails, a small, rustic amphitheater overlooking the river, and a fine view of the KCM, skyline. That said, when I arrived, I was the only visitor. Given the location tucked behind warehouses in an industrial zone, I felt a bit as if I had wandered into a not-entirely safe place. I imagined it would provide an excellent, after-dark rendezvous for illicit transactions. The entire site was coated with a light, gray grit. I did not realize it at the time, but the park is a foretaste of many other contrasts between the two Kansas Cities.

Following my visit to Kaw Point, I crossed back into Missouri and found my way to the graceful Richard L. Berkley Riverfront Park, an elegantly designed 17-acre urban oasis that runs along the southeast bank of the Missouri just north of the KCM downtown. Once a landfill for construction debris and the site of a sand and gravel company, the park now features some 300 trees, a nearly mile-long esplanade with period lighting, grassy lawns, and six sand volleyball courts. A reflection of good urban planning, it is a fitting tribute to the popular, visionary mayor (1979-1991) for whom it is named.[4] On that sunny afternoon, the park was far from crowded, but there were joggers, bicyclists, a father and son playing Frisbee, people walking dogs. It felt pristine and lovingly cared for, a striking contrast to the gritty and ghostly Kaw Point site I had just left.

As the hot, humid afternoon began to take its toll, I headed back over into KCK thinking I'd find a bistro or café for an early dinner and call it a day. Then the adventure began, food desert! To be fair, I should have checked Google Maps for places to eat; as I later discovered, there were several ethnic options nearby, Mexican or Asian, as well as a couple of BBQ joints, but I trusted to luck and headed west on Minnesota Ave., where the Hilton is located. After driving several miles through a dreary succession of run-down strip malls, grimy auto repair shops, thrift stores, and empty properties, I turned left on 18th Street, heading south.

About a mile down the road, just before reaching I-70, I saw a Sun Fresh market and decided to check it out. I was only about three miles from my hotel, but it seemed further. The store was clean and well stocked with a nice variety of fresh produce, a bakery, and good meats. It was the first grocery store I had seen in KCK. I picked up a couple of items and went looking for a bottle of wine. Proving that one is never too old to learn, it was here that I received a succinct tutorial in the liquor laws of Kansas. They are among the strictest in the U.S. "in sharp contrast to its neighboring state of Missouri," as archly noted in Wikipedia:

> Kansas had statewide prohibition from 1881 to 1948, longer than any other state, and continued to prohibit general on-premises liquor sales until 1987. The state's tightly regulated approach to alcohol shows that the vestiges of prohibition are alive and well. As of December 2012, Kansas had 13 "dry" counties, where on-premises liquor sales are prohibited, but the sale of 3.2% beer is permitted.[5]

Kansas is yet to ratify the 21st Amendment, which ended Prohibition in 1933.

Given the Byzantine liquor laws of Pennsylvania, I am not about to sneer at another state's. It is also worth noting that both Pennsylvania and Kansas have modestly liberalized their liquor laws in recent years. Without further research, I am reluctant to insist that the availability of liquor has a beneficial effect on economic development, but I'm pretty sure there is good evidence to support that thesis. Intuitively, it seems highly likely. Having grown up in Georgia, which is still a "local option" state, my home county of DeKalb was then "dry" while Fulton County and Atlanta just to the west had long since shaken off the burden of "temperance" and offered liquor in stores as well as by the drink in restaurants. The result was a booming restaurant business in Fulton County and a much leaner range of options in DeKalb. All that has since changed, and 105 of Georgia's 159 counties, including DeKalb, now allow liquor sales. Up until 2011, however, no alcohol could be sold on Sundays; even now, Sunday sales, where permitted by local option, cannot commence till after 12:30 p.m. What a wonderful country!

The helpful clerk at Sun Fresh suggested a liquor store just up the road. It was not difficult to find but did not look promising. The store appeared to be a converted gas station, narrow in front and extending back toward what must have once been the garage bays for auto repairs. The windows were covered with iron bars. Perhaps I imagined smelling gasoline fumes as I entered the modest shop. They did, indeed, have a wine selection, quite limited and dwarfed by the much larger stock of hard liquor. After peering at the few shelves for a bit and calculating a graceful exit, a personable young man asked if he might assist me. I gamely asked for a pinot noir. He looked a bit uncertain, asked his colleague and apologized that this was not an option they stocked. "How about a pinot grigio," he helpfully suggested. I purchased a simple bottle of red table wine from California, thanked them, and departed.

I later learned that many parts of Wyandotte County, which is home to KCK, are "food deserts." Indeed, Wyandotte County is the poorest and least healthy county in the state of Kansas. The U. S. Department of Agriculture defines a food desert as an urban area where at least 500 people and/or 33 percent of the census tract's population live more than a mile from a supermarket or large grocery store. Not surprisingly the correlation between food deserts and poverty is high. Many of the folks who live in such areas do not own cars and must rely on public transportation, a bicycle, or their own two feet to get to stores. What one does find in such areas are local convenience stores offering processed, sugary and fat-laden products that are known contributors to our national obesity epidemic.[6]

Sarah Biles, a spokesperson for Harvester, a regional food bank serving 26 counties in and around the Kansas City metro area, offers further details: "In Wyandotte County, nearly 18 percent or 28,000 people—12,000 of them children—are considered 'food insecure' [which] means they may have a meal today, but they don't necessarily know where their next meal is coming from."[7]

Key demographic data confirm my impressions of the striking contrasts between the two Kansas Cities:

	KCM	KCK
Population:	475,361	148,155
Median Household Income:	$50,259	$38,749
Poverty Rate:	17.9%	24.9%
Race/ethnicity:	55%	39.5% white
	29.6%	25.1% black
	9.7%	28.7% Hispanic

My brief visit stuck with me as I proceeded up the river into Nebraska. When I got home, I reached out to my friend in Kansas City for insight into the striking contrast between the two cities. Although the "what" is easy enough to see, the "why," as with most things involving humans, is more complicated. To be safe, one might say that the relationship between the two cities is complex with deep historical roots that go back to the creation of the Kansas Territory (1854), the hotly contested issue of slavery, and bloody intrastate conflicts during the Civil War. When Kansas entered the Union in 1861 as a "free state," slavery still existed in Missouri.

One of the famed episodes that my friend mentioned was the Quantrill Raiders' assault on Lawrence, Kansas, in 1863 in which the town was destroyed and more than 200 people were killed. For his actions, William Quantrill, although a partisan of the Confederacy, was roundly denounced by both his supposed allies and the Missouri authorities. The scars of that infamous event and the often-bloody contests between "free stater" abolitionists and pro-slavery forces from Missouri and other slave states before Kansas entered the Union have not completely healed. At one point, KCK attempted to incorporate KCM, into Kansas, but the Missourians defeated the effort.

The Mid-America Regional Council (MARC) representing 119 municipal governments in the nine core counties of the Kansas City area encourages cooperation and collaboration on matters of shared interest. These include transportation, childcare, aging, emergency services, environmental issues, and others that extend beyond the jurisdiction of a single city, county, or state. The Council is governed by a Board of Directors comprised of local elected officials and is funded by federal, state, and private grants, local contributions and earned income.

The existence of MARC suggests a substantial commitment to regional collaboration, and there is good evidence of its success. To help me understand better the perplexing issue of the two Kansas Cities, my friend Michael put me in touch with Pete Levi, the celebrated and longest-serving president of the Greater Kansas City Chamber of Commerce, who retired in 2009 after 19 years of distinguished service. Earlier in his career, Levi was executive director of MARC. Described as a "consummate consensus builder," he now lives most of the year in Florida, where I reached him by phone.

Having grown up in Kansas City, Levi earned his bachelor's degree from Northwestern and both the J.D. and a Master of Laws degree at the University of Missouri, Kansas City. He knows his hometown well.

When I described the startling contrast between the two downtowns, Pete's first question was whether I had gotten down into Johnson County, Kansas, south of the Kansas River. I admitted that I had not. He pointed out that Johnson County has a larger population than KCM, estimated to exceed 580,000 in 2015. Its largest city is Overland Park. The entire area is affluent. Median household income was $82,892 in 2015, and the median property value was $230,900. Poverty rate was 5.29%. It is more than 80% white. It is the most populous county in Kansas and undoubtedly among the wealthiest.

If I had continued down 18th Street from the Sun Fresh grocery story, I would have been in the heart of Johnson County in minutes with spacious, well-maintained homes, multiple golf and country clubs, restaurants, shops, and all the elements one expects in an affluent suburb. Mission Hills rang a bell very likely because of the elegant private golf and country club located there, not to mention the one in Rancho Mirage, California, with its Arnold Palmer Signature Course. The golf course at the Kansas Mission Hills was designed by the prolific Scotsman Tom Bendelow (1868-1936), sometimes known as the "Johnny Appleseed of American golf," who is credited with designing more than 500 American golf courses including Medinah and East Lake.

Pete then pointed out that if I wanted to see poverty in KCM, I would not need to search far. Traveling east from Johnson County, one reaches Troost Avenue in just a few miles. It is named for Dr. Benoit Troost (1786-1859), an immigrant from Holland and reputedly the first resident physician in the area, who was a founding father of KCM. At one time, Troost Avenue was known as "millionaire's row," but in the 20th century it became a racial dividing line that for a time was explicitly enforced under Jim Crow laws. Today, Pete pointed out, Kansas City remains a deeply segregated city. East of Troost is almost entirely black and poor. West of Troost, one finds little racial diversity and much more affluence, like that surrounding the Country Club Plaza where I ate delicious BBQ with my friends on my first night in KCM.

Levi described the relationship between the two cities as a mix of cooperation and competition. When Google was looking for a site, both cities competed for it; KCK won. They also beat KCM, in competing for the NASCAR track and the professional soccer team that located in KCK, "Sporting KC." Those competitions reflect the demographics of the two cities with KCM being justly proud of its World Series winning Royals (1985 & 2015) and Super Bowl Champion Chiefs (1970 & 2020). The large Hispanic population in KCK likely was a factor in that city securing a professional soccer team, and NASCAR has a decidedly more blue-collar fan base than football and baseball.

The sheer size of KCM contributes significantly to its economic health, but so does the form of government, Levi suggested. KCK has a "strong mayor" form of government; KCM has a longer history of professional city management. KCM also has had some dynamic and visionary leaders. He mentioned J. C. Nichols (1880-1950), a builder and developer who conceived the Country Club Plaza and was a founder of the Mission Hills Country Club. Nichols was also an architect of the residential racial and ethnic segregation that still characterizes both Kansas Cities.[8]

Although the two Kansas Cities have a unique history born of demographics and geography, they are a microcosm of America today facing many of the same challenges that can be found across the country. From the outside, it appears that KCM has had greater success than its sister city. The key to their future clearly lies in continued regional collaboration as called for in a 2014 Brookings Institute study that was commissioned by the Mid-America Regional Council: "It's time to coalesce economic development around regional goals and build on the area's strongest collection of industries," the study concluded.[9]

Chapter Nine
Golf at Shoal Creek

June 30, 1804: Heading upriver toward the future state of Nebraska, William Clark recorded with wonder the abundance of deer and other wildlife "as plenty as Hogs about a farm.*"*[1]

Although not a golfer, my Kansas City friend steered me well in recommending that I play Shoal Creek Golf Course, located about 15 miles northeast of the city's center. It is a moderately priced, beautifully maintained public course that is comparable in quality to many suburban privates. Built in 2001 and designed by architect Steve Wolford, it plays about 7000 yards from the tips with a rating and slope of 74.0/135. The white tees, which I played, are a bit more manageable at 5571 yards, rated 66.6/119, but the elevations, tight turns, and numerous sand bunkers make that rating seem low for a bogey golfer. The greens are fast and smooth bent grass; the fairways and tee boxes are Zoysia grass. Among the remarkable features of this lovely, forested course is that it's owned by Kansas City Parks and Recreation, one of five in the area including Swope Memorial designed by A. W. Tillinghast in 1934 and completely restored in 1989. In sum, it's one of the best maintained municipal courses that I've ever played. I shot a typical 95, with just a few holes—as usual—that kept me from getting into the 80s.

Among its accolades is a four-star rating by *Golf Digest*, ranked #2 public course in Missouri by *Golf Week's* America's Best You Can Play, ranked #1 course in Missouri by *Golfadvisor.com* in 2017 and 2018, and ranked #1 public course in Missouri by the Golf Card Traveler. Its many amenities include golf carts equipped with GPS, always a helpful tool even if one brings one's own rangefinder.

The handsome 11,000 square-foot clubhouse offers a gracious first impression of casual elegance in cream stucco with stacked stone accents. Designed for special events and entertaining, it features a well-stocked Pro Shop (which boasts three PGA professionals), the

Fireplace Lounge, Players Grill, and a large ballroom with a capacity to serve 250. An outdoor covered patio overlooking the 12,000 square foot, 34-station driving range and practice area will seat another 60 guests.

In short, Shoal Creek has earned its accolades through a lovingly maintained facility, a spectacular location, and a course that embraces and highlights the distinctive features of the terrain. It is a must-play for golfers visiting Kansas City.[2]

My delightful day at Shoal Creek began auspiciously with a bright, sunny sky and morning temperatures in the low 70s, a perfect, early summer day. I arrived a little before 9 a.m., early enough to get in some practice before my 9:30 tee time. As it turned out, in making the tee time, there was confusion over the different time zone, so my actual time was 10:30. Given the attractive practice area, I was not in the least dismayed, and it turned out quite delightfully because it enabled me to join a threesome of international educators who provided me with some of the most pleasant company of my trip.

All three were in their forties and clearly had some history together. This was something of a reunion as one of the three had traveled from Salt Lake City and another from Venezuela. The third was their local anchor. I was delighted to receive thoughtful emails from two of my companions offering their perspectives on the state of our country. Despite their depth of friendship and shared memories, they very gracefully made me feel included. This was not the only time that I experienced such a friendly embrace as I traveled.

Like many others I met on my journey, they were keenly interested in my project and expressed some envy. I discovered that my wanderlust is shared by many a restless man curious about what's just over the next ridge or around the river's bend.

My new buddy who lived in Venezuela was a Canadian who was married to a woman from Mexico. To complete the global profile, he happily chomped on a Cuban cigar and later noted that among them they had taught in international schools in 15 different countries.

His admiration for America was deep and thoughtful. Several months after our round of golf, he wrote me his responses to my questions. "America," he wrote, "leads, builds and educates. Opportunity is abundant and for those who are creative and willing to do the work, America pays dividends. Also, I believe that the US Constitution is the finest document ever created by man." I felt certain that he had read our Constitution, indeed, perhaps studied, and taught it to his students. I don't think any other individual along my trail commented on our Constitution. I was moved and impressed that a neighbor from the north would do so.

What worried him about America today was less unique, but certainly thoughtful in his nuanced description of what he called a "PC culture" that "has emboldened many and quieted even more." He said the result is a "major rift between the left and the right that is becoming comparable to the Catholics and Protestants in Northern Ireland." The result is a missed opportunity for "interesting conversation and polite debate" and an emerging culture of reparations that is "contributing to increased economic and racial tensions that will prevent the US from solving the major problems it faces." He also faulted the news media for making the problem worse by "highlighting the negative and contributing inflammatory, and often dishonest, accounts of the supposed facts to support the right or left leaning opinions of their stakeholders."

Writing in late December 2017, his observations were not exactly prophetic but certainly an astute assessment of circumstances that have only grown more evident since then. I am writing as the House of Representatives debates the articles of impeachment for Donald Trump, December 2019. Who could have guessed that he would be impeached again in the last days of his term for inciting an insurrection? It feels like we are in a nosedive of unparalleled political polarization. Whether we can pull out before it's too late remains to be seen.

Jonathan's use of his "magic wand" was also distinctive and surprisingly ahead of its time. He wished for a way to provide "free, high-quality education at every level for all who are interested and qualify (at the higher learning level), eliminating the heavy, and sometimes crippling, debt" that some college graduates bear as they enter the work force. He added his hope to see "less indoctrination at the university level in the name of diversity, equality, or fairness. America was built on merit, and merit-based accomplishments; merit has no color or race." He closed his thoughtful note, "Relentlessly positive."[3]

His buddy, Wendell, an administrator and science teacher at a private preK-12 school in Salt Lake City, also offered thoughtful comments reflecting his education as well as his global experience teaching for 22 years in four different countries (Colombia, Venezuela, Qatar, and Belgium). I was not surprised that he chiefly valued the diversity of America, especially in comparison to other countries where he had lived and worked. He wrote, "it was always striking to me to come home and see ALL those kinds of folks."

Like others I met along the way, Wendell worried about the increasingly divisive tone of our public discourse and "the marginalization of facts by political leaders, 'news' organizations, and too many U.S. citizens." He also expressed his concern over a decreasing appreciation for diversity of "thought, culture, race, etc." He closed with the plaintive fragment, "So much divisive rhetoric and intolerance of others . . ."

If he had a magic wand, he would eliminate "the tribalistic survival instinct" that might have once been crucial to our primitive ancestors but is now, he thinks, "the root cause for much of the racism, classism, and prejudice we still struggle with today." He also lamented the lack of integrity and "absolute partisanship" displayed by "our politicians" in recent days. "Finally," he said he would like to "wave that wand over everyone's social media feed so that the first source of news that everyone sees is a non-partisan one."[4] One must give him credit for thinking big!

I parted from this congenial group of friends with gratitude for their company and good cheer as well as for making me feel at home, so far from home. They wished me well on my adventure, and we all agreed that we'd been most fortunate to play Shoal Creek on such a spectacular day.

Chapter Ten
On to Omaha and Golf at Tiburon

July 21, 1804: The Corps reached the mouth of the Platte River just south of present-day Omaha, Nebraska. They had traveled 600 miles from Wood River in Illinois, a milestone which Stephen Ambrose described as the "equivalent of crossing the equator"[1]

"Corps of Discovery," by Eugene Daub, Kansas City, Missouri

On the morning of Wednesday, June 28, 2017, I departed Kansas City with a sense of having only scratched the surface of this complex and diverse area, rich in history and natural beauty. Before leaving town, I visited an impressive monument to Lewis and Clark that sits at 8th and Jefferson in downtown Kansas City, Missouri, on a bluff overlooking the river and Kansas to the west. Known as Lewis and Clark Point, the site is a graciously landscaped oasis in a dense urban setting. I was there early enough to beat the morning traffic and to see the homeless people beginning to stir from their ragged makeshift beds where they had spent the night. It is an all-too-familiar sight in American cities large and small and a daily reminder of our chronic failure to provide adequately for our neediest citizens.

Designed by American sculptor and Pennsylvania native Eugene Daub, the monument is a grand expression of Lewis and Clark's heroic achievement. Standing some 18-feet high, it is the largest of the many sculptures that celebrate the Corps of Discovery.[2] It was unveiled in 2000 and features finely detailed figures of Lewis, Clark, York, Sacagawea (with her baby on her back), and Lewis's great Newfoundland, Seaman. On the base of the sculpture is engraved Jefferson's oft-quoted tribute to Clark: "Of courage undaunted . . . and a fidelity to truth . . . I could have no hesitation in confiding the enterprize [sic] to him." It was a fine way to begin the ninth day of my journey, having already logged more than 1500 miles.

Heading north and west up the river, I reflected on Fr. Richard Rohr's meditation for that day: "All great spirituality teaches about letting go of what you don't need and who you are not." Could this journey help me grow spiritually, help me let go of unneeded burdens? I knew already that I was learning a great deal and certainly enjoying the adventure, but those are not the same as the letting go that Rohr and many other spiritual advisors recommend. Since reading Philip Roth's novel *Letting Go* when I was an undergraduate, that phrase has haunted me.

I headed for Tiburon Golf Club in Omaha, where I had a midmorning tee time and unknown prospects for company. Tiburon is not nationally ranked, but it's an excellent local course, which claims to have been "voted" the best in the area, but the website doesn't say who did the voting. Its 27-holes are laid out across gently rolling terrain with lots of water to keep one alert. The website boasts of 12 acres of natural woodlands and ponds. A few of the holes are a bit too clever for my taste, but that may reflect an effort to work within the constraints of the existing terrain. Some narrow fairways and approaches bounded by reedy ponds and woods make some of the holes especially challenging. Aside from a few soggy spots from recent rain, the course was in excellent condition when I visited.

Built in 1989 as an 18-hole course with a small clubhouse, a third nine was added a few years later. The property was acquired in 2005

73

by a local couple who already owned another well-regarded course in the area, and they made major improvements, notably a 13,000 square foot clubhouse with ample space for large, upscale events. It has become a popular site for the same.

Of course, this Tiburon, Spanish for "shark," bears the same name as the more famous Tiburon in Naples, Florida, designed by "the Shark," himself, Greg Norman. I have played both of its two 18-hole courses on previous Florida excursions. They are magnificent public-private courses owned by Host Hotels and Resorts and operated by Troon. They are adjacent to the elegant Ritz-Carlton Golf Resort. I could not discover why the considerably less elegant course in Omaha chose the same name. They honor the spirit of "The Shark" by naming the three nines Mako, Great White, and Hammerhead, somewhat amusingly given the distance to the nearest ocean.

I was fortunate to arrive in time to join a father and son from San Diego who were visiting the area for the Division I NCAA baseball championships. They had already played nine, so I played nine with them and the second nine solo. I played better with the company than without, carding a 44 on Mako and a 49 on Hammerhead. Not my best; not my worst. It was a fine day for golf, and I finished up around 2:45 p.m.

From Tiburon, I made my way to the Lewis and Clark Monument Park just north of Council Bluffs, Iowa, overlooking the city of Omaha. This imposing site affords a magnificent vista to the west with the river winding around at the foot of the lofty bluffs. The Colonial Dames of America constructed this monument park in 1935, and the view alone is worth the drive up through the little town of Council Bluffs.

It was around 3:30, a hot, still, and sunny afternoon, when I arrived. I noted a temperature of 90 degrees in my daily log. Not another soul was on the site that commemorates the first meeting (August 3, 1804) between the Corps of Discovery and the native people, the Oto and Missouri tribes. The actual site of this historic meeting is not certain, partly because of the ever-changing flow of the river and the inexact record left by Lewis and Clark.

It is certain, however, that the meeting did not occur at the lofty site of the Monument Park in the present-day state of Iowa. The park merely celebrates and commemorates that meeting with handsome stone pillars, benches, interpretive plaques, and a spectacular view of

74

the rolling prairie to the west. Clark left a good record of the dramatic change in topography that he and Lewis observed from a similar bluff—if not this very one—overlooking the river:

> This prairie is covered with grass of 10 or 12 inches in height, soil of good quality and at the distance of about a mile still farther back the country rises about 80 or 90 feet higher, and is one continued plain as far as can be seen . . . . From the bluff on the second rise immediately above our camp, the most beautiful prospect of the river up and down and country opposed presented itself which I ever beheld.[3]

My impulse as a former English teacher is to clean up Clark's tortuous syntax, but of course I wouldn't dare. Still, that dangling "which I ever beheld" is jarring. Fanselow acknowledges regularizing the highly irregular spelling in the journals.

As I drove from Kansas City up along the river into Nebraska, I had at last left the familiar leafy greens of the East and entered another section of the country, the beginning of the western frontier and the Great Plains.

Despite the explorers' ignorance and some disappointment among the Indians that the gifts the Corps offered were not more substantial, the meetings went well enough, ended peacefully, and with promises that some of the tribal leaders would travel with Lewis and Clark to Washington upon their return.

Looking back at this first meeting with the advantage of more than 200 years of tragic history, one cannot but feel the irony of these first encounters. Naïve though he may have been, Jefferson had firmly instructed Lewis to make it clear that while the native people now had a new "Father" in Washington, his intentions were honorable and primarily commercial. They came seeking peace, friendship, and opportunities for mutually beneficial commerce. I have no reason to doubt Jefferson's intentions; he had no way to foresee the disaster that he was unleashing on the native people of the Plains and beyond.

Here are Jefferson's written instructions to Captain Lewis:

> In all your intercourse with the natives treat them in the most friendly and conciliatory manner which their own conduct will admit. Allay all jealousies as to the object of your journey, satisfy them of its innocence, make them acquainted with the

75

position, extent, character, peaceable and commercial dispositions of the U.S., of our wish to be neighborly, friendly and useful to them, and of our dispositions to a commercial intercourse with them.[4]

With Jefferson's hopeful words ringing in my ears, I made my way down from the heights of Council Bluffs to Omaha's Aksarben Village area to the Hampton Inn where I would spend the night. Once the site of a coliseum and horse track, since the early 2000s, Aksarben Village has been growing as an upscale, mixed-use development that is adjacent to the south campus of the University of Nebraska, Omaha. Blue Cross Blue Shield of Nebraska built and occupies a ten-story building that is its headquarters there. I had to be told that "Aksarben" is Nebraska spelled backwards. I hope I'm not the only one to whom this was not obvious.

With a helpful suggestion at my hotel, I made my way to a nearby Italian restaurant called Spezia.[5] I did not record my dinner that evening, but my logbook simply says "Excellent"! After the long, hot day, I recall being pleased with the comfortable ambiance as well as the good service, and departing feeling well fed.

Chapter Eleven
A Taste of Nature's Fury in South Dakota

August 20, 1804: Sergeant Charles Floyd, the youngest man on the expedition, died near today's Sioux City, Iowa, the only member of the Corps to die during its journey. The apparent cause was a burst appendix.

"Labor" by Matthew Placzek, Omaha, Nebraska

Yankton, South Dakota, is only about 160 miles up the Missouri from Omaha, so on Thursday, June 29, I planned to set a leisurely pace, see some sites of interest, admire the landscape of Eastern Nebraska, and reach Yankton before dark. I had not planned on my first exposure to the sudden, fierce weather changes that can blow through this region with little or no warning.

Alongside the river in downtown Omaha is the National Park Service Regional Office, which houses the Lewis and Clark Trail Headquarters and Visitor Center. The modern building is located on a knoll overlooking a grassy park that features a large sculpture entitled "Labor" by Matthew Placzek, dedicated in 2004. Described as a "salute to the dedication and hard work of all those who built the grand city of Omaha," it features five heroic figures, each roughly eight feet tall, laboring with hammers, tongs, and chains to manage a 35-foot-tall series of ladles, each weighing three tons, salvaged from the former Asarco refinery that had been located nearby. Closed in 1997, the refinery and smelting facility contributed to a major lead-pollution problem that is still being cleaned up in Omaha and other cities across the country where Asarco had plants. Nearby along the riverside is "Union Walk" which features a series of plaques commemorating significant moments in the history of organized labor in Omaha.

At the sculpture is a plaque describing the horrific flood of 2011, which lasted for 101 days and crested at more than 36 feet. The sculpture has a bronze plaque marking the flood's crest on the raised arm of the blacksmith, who stands at the front of the massive artwork. The sculpture's estimated total weight is 271 tons. Doubtful that any flood will wash it away, but nature's fury should never be underestimated. It is a lesson I would learn again later that same day.

Just a few miles north of Omaha is the Lewis and Clark State Park, near Onawa, IA. Easily accessible from I-29, my route to Sioux City, I pulled off to check it out. It proved to be a delightful, unplanned stop. Lovingly maintained by volunteers, the state park is located on a 200-acre "ox-bow" lake, flanked by camping sites, and crowned by a sun-bathed visitor center and museum that provides excellent exhibits as well as some hands-on opportunities for all ages. I recall a rig with a thick rope like the one used by the members of the Corps to pull the keelboat upstream when the winds were not favorable—which was most of the time on the outbound journey upstream and into prevailing westerly winds. That little experiment in elementary physics gave me a deeper appreciation for the raw muscle required of every man on the arduous journey.

The Park is particularly proud of its full-size replica of the Corps' keelboat as well as the smaller pirogues and canoes. It also has a replica of the experimental, collapsible iron boat that Lewis had constructed, but which quickly sank when they tried to use it near present-day Great Falls.

The life-sized replica of the keelboat was docked on the lake, where volunteers regularly take visitors on pleasure rides. I met there a man named John, one of the many volunteers, who insisted that everyone calls him "Lizard." He did not explain why. He was a friendly, knowledgeable guide who proudly gave me a private tour of the center.

My next stop was the Lewis and Clark Interpretive Center in Sioux City, where I was immediately impressed with the handsomely landscaped grounds alongside the river. Several large sculptures immediately capture one's attention. They include a life-sized grizzly bear, a bison, an elk, and a pair of gamboling foxes. The grounds are planted with native grasses and other indigenous plants that Lewis and Clark documented in their journals.

"Spirit of Discovery" by Pat Kennedy, Sioux City, Iowa

Near the entrance to the grounds is a 14-foot bronze sculpture of Lewis and Clark along with the dog Seaman entitled "Spirit of Discovery" by Pat Kennedy of Loveland, Colorado. The captains are in full military dress and as usual, gazing west. Lewis wears a Napoleonic "chapeau" with a fancy plume, but Clark is bareheaded, leaning casually forward with his arms resting across his right knee which is elevated by his foot atop a pile of rocks. Lewis rests his right hand on Clark's shoulder and Seaman stands patiently between them. The sculptor captured a delicate combination of their relative youth, their deep friendship, and the weight of the task to which they were committed.

A pleasant docent offered a warm welcome to the Interpretive Center and expressed interest in my project. The Interpretive Center is housed in a handsome stone and wood building opened in 2002 and focuses on a day in the life of the Corps of Discovery. It offers multiple hands-on opportunities to deepen one's understanding of the expedition. Adjacent is an "Encounter Center" opened in 2007, which offers a broader focus on the history of the area both before and after the Lewis and Clark visit. It's an impressive facility for families as well as those who seek a deeper understanding of the expedition. Best of all, there is no admission fee.

Docked nearby is a steamboat that was built in 1932 in Jefferson, Indiana, and served from 1933 to 1975 as a workhouse for the Missouri River Division of the Corps of Engineers. The old boat now serves as the Sgt. Floyd River Museum and Welcome Center. After serving for 18 months as a floating museum celebrating the bicentennial of the Corps of Engineers, she was moored for a time in St. Louis before being purchased by Sioux City in 1983 and moved to its present location where she is permanently dry docked. She offers visitors a history of the river's development through rare photographs and artifacts. She also boasts the country's largest collection of scale models of Missouri River steamboats and keelboats that navigated the river as the nation grew along its shores.[1]

From the Interpretive Center I set out to find the Sergeant Charles Floyd Monument under a sky that began to look threatening. One of the more surprising facts about the Corps' arduous adventure was that only one member died and that was apparently from a burst appendix. The journals record his increasing illness and his death on August 20 near present-day Sioux City. Captain Lewis presided over the funeral and burial with full military honors and erected a wooden pillar to mark the grave.

Over the ensuing years, Sergeant Floyd's grave became something of a tourist attraction. In 1900 a 100-foot concrete obelisk was erected over Floyd's remains on the bluff overlooking the river; dedicated the following year, it was the first site to be registered as a National Historic Landmark, as noted on a plaque nearby.[2]

One of the several plaques at the base of the Floyd Monument commemorates the Louisiana Purchase and "its successful exploration by the heroic members of the Lewis and Clark Expedition" as well as the "valor of the American soldier and . . . the enterprise courage and fortitude of the American pioneer to whom these great states west of the Mississippi River owe their secure foundation." On the plaque dedicated to Sgt. Floyd, is the following inscription: "Graves of such men are pilgrim shrines/shrines to no class or creed confined."

As dark clouds began to roll in from the west, I cut short my visit to Sioux City and headed for Spirit Mound, near Vermilion, South Dakota, 45 miles northwest. I had not traveled far before the threatening sky turned almost black, strong winds began whipping across the highway, and large hailstones began falling in furious waves. Like others along the highway, I sought shelter and was fortunate to pull under a highway overpass. Unfortunately, a fellow traveler immediately ahead of me captured a better berth leaving the back side of my car exposed to the fierce pounding of hail. It did not last long but left the rear half of my car covered with numerous dents that would require substantial body work after I returned home.

The fierce storm ended as suddenly as it had begun, the late afternoon sun emerged, and the sky was clear to the west. I proceeded to Spirit Mound arriving around 5 p.m. The local Native Americans regarded this prominent hill with superstitious dread, believing it to be occupied by fierce little spirits which Clark described in his journal of August 24, 1804:

They are in human form with remarkable large heads, and about 18 inches high, that they are very watchful and armed with sharp arrows with which they can kill at a great distance . . . . So much do the Omaha, Sioux, Otos and other neighboring nations believe this fable, that no consideration is sufficient to induce them to approach the hill.[3]

Lewis and Clark were determined to see this place for themselves and hiked to the top of the mound on August 25. Despite oppressive heat, which caused Lewis's dog, Seaman, to collapse, they made it to the top. Clark described it as "a most beautiful landscape; numerous herds of buffalo were seen feeding in various directions; the Plain to the north-northwest and northeast extends without interruption as far as can be seen."[4]

In addition to the promised impressive view across the Plains, Spirit Mound attracted me for its abundant flora and fauna. It is also one of the sites along the Lewis and Clark Trail where one can be sure to stand precisely where the explorers stood to admire the sweeping vista. I parked my car at the base of the well-kept hiking trail and set out on the three-quarter mile path up to the mound. A colorful variety of birds flitted among the waist-high native wildflowers and grasses. As I became absorbed in taking pictures of the birds and the variety of colorful plants, I did not notice the increasingly dark sky. Suddenly, large drops of rain began to fall as I was about 500 yards from my car. As I briefly toyed with the idea of continuing my hike, the rain grew more intense. With the fresh memory of the sudden, fierce hailstorm, I thought better of it and with regret jogged back to my car. By the time I got there, I was a bit soggy, but very glad of my decision, as the rain began to fall in torrents.

Around 5:30 p.m. I pulled out of the parking area at Spirit Mound, grateful for the well-maintained site complete with interpretive signs, recalling its place in the historic expedition. The rain was falling steadily as I headed west on SD Route 50 toward Yankton. What might have been an easy half-hour drive turned into another weather adventure, as the rain grew more intense, and another hailstorm arrived as I made my way through a stretch of single-lane highway construction.

By the time I arrived at the Holiday Inn Express in Yankton, the weather had cleared again, and I was just in time for the Manager's Reception where I met the Inn's personable manager. She asked about my journey and strongly recommended that I see the great sculpture at the Chamberlain exit on the way to Pierre the next day.

As I checked in, I discovered that Fox Run Golf Course was directly across from the Inn. I was ready to adjust my travel schedule but was disappointed to learn that an event was planned the following morning at the course, so I would be unable to get a tee time. Fox Run is an 18-hole municipal course built in 1993 and evidently a point of local pride.

After the reception, I drove around the small town, population just under 15,000. It is the county seat of Yankton County, which has an estimated population of 22,600. It was the first capital of the Dakota Territory and is named for the Yankton Sioux, who lived in the area when Lewis and Clark came through. Stephen Ambrose colorfully described the contentious encounter between the Corps of Discovery and the Sioux at a nearby site. Although the encounter almost resulted in a violent altercation, the Corps passed on without injury but with disappointment that they had failed to make the favorable impression that Jefferson had ordered.[5]

I drove across the river at the city's edge and into Nebraska as a rainbow appeared across the clear, blue western sky. I hoped it was an omen of better weather the next day. I also briefly visited the campus of Mount Marty College, a Benedictine liberal arts college with a well-maintained campus and an impressive church at its center. The enrollment is 1100 students from 25 states and 5 other countries. It was founded in 1936.

My late dinner at a place called "Back in Time," was a taco salad in an ambiance of the 1950s. Despite (or because?) of the clever décor, the dinner was not one of my more memorable ones. At the end of this eventful day, I had logged 219.3 miles.

Chapter Twelve
Pierre and Golf with Elton

September 25, 1804: The Corps has a tense encounter with members of the Teton Sioux (Lakota) tribe near present-day Pierre, S.D. Violence was averted by the calm of elder Chief Black Buffalo.[1]

"Dignity" by Dale Lamphere, Chamberlain, South Dakota

A fter breakfast at the hotel, I hit the road around 8:20 a.m. on Friday, June 30, departed Yankton and headed north on US 81 with Pierre, South Dakota, as my destination and hopes of a round of golf in the afternoon. I drove north through the rolling plains for a little more than an hour to reach I-90 and head west. I arrived at Chamberlain, South Dakota, around 11:20, having traveled about 155 miles.

An impressive rest area and information center at milepost 264 sits on the bluffs overlooking the wide Missouri just south of Chamberlain. This site features a magnificent vista west overlooking the river as well as an impressive interpretive center featuring a replica of the Corps' 55-foot keelboat that visitors can board and explore. Its most distinctive feature is that it is constructed partially inside the building and partially jutting out through its tall glass windows. The site also has a stylized tepee sculpture constructed of eight concrete beams that soar some 50 feet into the sky.

One of the newest attractions on the trail, the 50-foot sculpture entitled "Dignity" was constructed in 2016 in honor of the 125th year of South Dakota statehood. Also called "Dignity of Earth and Sky," the sculpture is a stainless-steel image of a Native American woman with arms outstretched to receive a star quilt. It was designed and crafted by Dale Lamphere, a South Dakota artist laureate. The figure in Plains-style dress honors the culture of Lakota and Dakota peoples who are indigenous to South Dakota.

This arresting sculpture, visible well before one reaches the exit for the interpretive center and rest area, was a gift from Norm and Eunabel McKie of Rapid City, South Dakota. Three Native American women from Rapid City served as models for the sculpture. Coincidentally, I later learned that the day after my visit, July 1, 2017, South Dakota enabled residents to purchase license plates with the image of "Dignity" on them.

"In a column published in the *Sioux Falls Argus Leader*, Susan Claussen Bunger, instructor of Native American social systems, wrote:

> As is evident through history, humans will ultimately disillusion and betray. As is such, I have a new role model who is solid and sturdy. She literally owns a spine of steel and reminds me of the injustice in the world, but also of strength, perseverance and survival. She signifies people who have

prevailed through the centuries. She represents all who resist and strive forward. She portrays a rallying cry for those who wish to be heard and valued. She stands strong and proud, meeting the morning sun and bracing against the nighttime cold. She contemplates the world through a poise of conviction and fearlessness. Her name is "Dignity."[2]

The massive sculpture reflects an aesthetic principle immortalized by Mae West's famed quip that "too much of a good thing is a good thing." There is no reason to doubt the good intentions of the generous donors, the artist, and his collaborators in constructing this tribute to the indigenous peoples, but one cannot but recall the long, succession of indignities visited on these people by the American government and the restless pioneers who overran their territories. It seems unlikely that the establishment of South Dakota statehood is a cause of universal celebration among the native peoples, so there is some irony in that event being honored by a sculpture of a proud and beautiful Native American woman cast in stainless steel. The irony and the ambiguity are rooted deep in the American story that unfolded in the footsteps of Lewis and Clark.

After visiting this site, I resumed my trek to the South Dakota state capital, where I arrived in the early afternoon. My overnight lodging was the Holiday Inn of Ft. Pierre, on the western bank of the river. Pierre is just across the river to the east. No one seems to know why Pierre is pronounced "peer," but so it is. The state capital and Ft. Pierre are named for the famed St. Louis trader Pierre Chouteau, Jr., who is credited with having built Ft. Pierre in 1817, the state's first continuous settlement.[3] Soon after my arrival, I discovered that Ft. Pierre is in the Mountain Time Zone while Pierre, just across the river is in the Central Time Zone. The opportunities for confusion are obvious, and I was not exempt.

Near present-day Pierre, the Corps of Discovery had an encounter in September 1804 with the Teton Sioux, who had a large village just north. The meeting was complicated by the Corps' lack of a translator and what Lewis and Clark regarded as the unreasonable demands of the chiefs whose expectations of tribute far exceeded what Lewis and Clark had anticipated. Although the encounter almost came to violence, with bows and arrows at ready, swords drawn, and rifles primed, it appears from Stephen Ambrose's account that a cooler-headed chief named Black Buffalo averted disaster.

Having discovered that Pierre has a municipal golf course aptly called Hillsview for the fine view of the hills that frame the otherwise relatively flat course along the eastern banks of the river, I secured a tee time and made my way to the course hoping for some company on this Friday afternoon. I was not disappointed. At the first tee, I met an older gentleman named Elton and his younger friend Ben. They were kind enough to invite me to join them, and we headed out on this deceptively challenging course.[4]

I soon learned that Elton had just retired as chief of the Pierre police force after many years of faithful service. He was clearly exulting in his newfound freedom on this warm, clear, blue-sky summer day. We had a fine round that started well with my 43 on the front nine. Unfortunately, young Ben had to leave us at the turn, so Elton and I finished the round as a twosome with lots of amiable conversation and devilishly difficult twists and turns that resulted in my shooting a disappointing 50 on the back nine and a couple of lost balls in tall grass.

On the Fourth of July, Elton promptly responded to my standing questions. So fitting and moving were his thoughts that they deserve quoting in full:

> On the 4th of July I am the most thankful knowing I am safe and free to [do] whatever I choose to do in this great country. I am my only obstacle to what choices I can make.
>
> I think of Charles Dickens in *A Tale of Two City's*. [sic] 'these are the best of times these are the worst of times.' I write that I think of 9-11-01. America was rocked by a ruthless person running a worthless cause--yet they hit the most powerful country and they hit us hard. The people of the U.S. came together as ONE!! We need that again. Our leaders need to realize whether they are Democrats or Republican they work for us. I spent my whole life working in the government either as an Airman or a city policeman. My job was to serve everyone, and I do mean EVERYONE!!! My personal agenda took the back seat to our team's mission. Our leaders need to

remember that and solve problems not come up with more problems.

What I would change? This is the tough question. I wish slavery did not happen. I wish December 7th, 1941. Did not happen. I wish our leaders did not let our troops down in Korea and Vietnam. It, and they did. I would hope that as Americans, hell as humans, we would learn and continue to learn to work as one to not let events like this occur anymore. I want us to be better not to let Rodney King, or the dumbness in Ferguson show up again. In summary we need to learn our history and be above our mistakes and we all need to enjoy our time God gives us on this earth because it ain't that long!!!! We need to focus on positives and rise above the negatives. Someday I am going to be standing in front of God. His judgment will and has always controlled my destination. We all need to remember that. Elton

In my last days as president of Albright, I had made some so-called "challenge coins" commemorating my term of service and celebrating the wisdom of Cicero that "gratitude is not only the greatest of virtues, but the parent of all others." (I subsequently learned that a more accurate translation is rendered "mother of all others," but this was after the die was cast.) The token, about the size of a silver dollar, I called a "gratitude coin." It was a gift I gave to golfers and others that I met on the trail. On one side, it bears the seal of Albright, with the inscription "Veritas et Justitia." On the other is the college logo bearing the founding date of 1856, my years of service, 2005-2017, and the phrase, "Presented by President Lex O. McMillan III, With Gratitude." It was warmly received as if it were a precious treasure by everyone to whom I gave it. I was surprised and delighted by every presentation.

Soon after I left Pierre, I got a note from Elton asking if I had received a similar challenge coin from him. He had left it at the hotel desk for me, but apparently the clerk failed to pass it on when I checked out the following day. Elton persisted and ultimately mailed it to me. Elton and I have continued to stay in touch, mostly through Facebook. If every public servant carried the values of Elton Blemaster, our world would be a better place.

Several weeks later I received an email from Elton's young friend, Ben, an officer with the South Dakota Housing Development Authority:

Good afternoon, Lex,

My apologies for the delay in responding to your questions. I hope your travels treated (or are treating) you well.

As for my responses to your questions below:

1. I first began drafting . . . my thoughts on this question on the night of July 4th, as the fireworks were echoing in the background while our country celebrated America. I appreciate nothing more than the security and safety this country provides to my children, my family, my friends, and all my loved ones. As the loud sounds in the night's sky reminds me that in too many places in this world, those sounds of bombshells send fear through millions of people.

2. What concerns me the most about our country today is our seeming inability to come together as an undivided union and focus on our core values, specifically taking care of each and every citizen of our nation. Taking care of those that cannot care for themselves should . . . be a fundamental goal always in our foresight in creating/revising policies. Our bipartisan divide and individual pride and selfishness prevents many of these commonsense values from finding long-term resolutions/improvements and sustainability so very much needed.

3. This magic wand question has me stumped a bit. There are so many significant events and policies in our country's history that would be fit to change/erase with the swipe of a wand. However, our mistakes have made this country what it is . . . and, what it will become. I cannot come up with one or two things I wish I could change. I hate to generalize, but I wish we simply had more unity to work together and care more for the general wellbeing of the whole. I believe with slight

change in how we should focus together in preserving the life, liberty and pursuit of happiness for all will help preserve the idea of the United States of America being the greatest country in the world.

The impressive depth and thoughtfulness of this young man's reflections gave me hope that he is not alone and that his generation, the Millennials, with their vision, hopefulness, and generosity, will give birth to a better future for our divided and suffering nation.

After golf, I toured the city of Pierre (population in 2020, 13,908), the second smallest state capital in the country, after Montpelier, Vermont. It was selected as state capital when South Dakota gained statehood in 1889; its location in the geographical center of the state was key in that decision. The handsome Capitol building, constructed between 1905 and 1910, is described as Colonial Revival, Classical Revival, and Renaissance; its dark iron dome stands on a rise overlooking the city.[5]

On Elton's recommendation, I had dinner that evening at the Cattleman's Ranch just east of Pierre, where he claimed I'd enjoy the best steak in South Dakota. I ate alone at the bar and enjoyed a very good steak in the rustic setting of a popular local tavern, perhaps not the best steak I've ever had, but certainly generous in size and well prepared. Having covered more than 300 miles and played a round of golf, I slept well that night. Since leaving Gettysburg ten days before, I had traveled 2259.4 miles.

Chapter Thirteen
Across the Deadwood Trail to Rapid City, South Dakota

October 8, 1804: The Corps reaches a three-mile-long island near the mouth of the Grand River, just north of present-day Mobridge, S.D., where they were warmly welcomed by the Arikara Tribe, which had been reduced in size by waves of smallpox dating back to the 1780s. Once thought to number some 30,000 members at the time of the Revolutionary War, the tribe then numbered about 2,000.[1]

Historic Trails (Deadwood, Indian, etc)

One of the famous trails is the Fort Pierre to Deadwood Trail which begins at the end of Hustan Ave in Fort Pierre near the southwest end of the present Colonel Waldron Missouri River Bridge.

Following the discovery of gold in Deadwood in 1875, hordes of prospectors, gamblers and storekeepers headed for the Black Hills which was in the heart of the Great Sioux Reservation. The fact that they were trespassing on Indian land didn't stop them and they kept coming from all directions. The shortest route to Deadwood was by steamboat from Yankton to Fort Pierre and then this famous trail taking them across prairie and creeks to Deadwood. The wooden sign above was one of 52 erected every two miles in 1975 by Roy & Edith Norman, hired hands, families and friends marking the Fort Pierre to Deadwood Trail from the Missouri River Bridge in Fort Pierre to the Pennington County line in South Dakota.[2]

W hile golfing with Elton on the preceding day, I told him of my plan to take a detour from the Lewis and Clark Trail to drive down to Rapid City and Mount Rushmore. Elton urged me to take the old, well-marked Deadwood Trail (U. S. 14) to the tiny town of Wall, just north of The Badlands National Park. It was good advice.

I left the Fort Pierre Holiday Inn Express at 7:50 a.m. (MDT) and enjoyed the rolling, grass-covered prairie through farms and the small towns of Hayes, Midland, Philip, Cottonwood, and Quinn, arriving at Wall around 10 a.m. In less than two hours, I had covered some 118 miles that had taken intrepid pioneers days on ox-pulled wagons and horseback in 1875. These fortune-seekers were, of course, trampling over sacred Indian land as they plodded across the South Dakota plains.

Wall is only two square miles with a population of 754 in 2020, but it boasts a famed drug store that seems to be its principal tourist attraction. I drove by but decided not to tarry to peruse the usual array of geegaws and bric-a-brac that some find irresistible. Although Wall appears to be a real town, it reminded me of South of the Border, South Carolina, where I have stopped many a time traveling along I-95 to points south. After a slow pass through the little village, I headed off to find the entrance to The Badlands National Park.

At one of the two visitor centers, I picked up a handsome pictorial guide entitled *Badlands: The Story Behind the Scenery* (2005) by Joseph W. Zarki, a career National Park Service employee, who also happens to be a graduate of Gettysburg College, where I had worked for eleven years (1993-2004). His well-written guide is an excellent keepsake of my too-brief visit to this grand geologic spectacle. It continues to be an active site for research by paleontologists, archaeologists, and others. Although I took some good photos, this wild preserve deserves more time than I could afford to give it.

In 1939, President Franklin D. Roosevelt declared the area the Badlands National Monument. Made a National Park in 1978, it is a stunning visual experience comprising some 244,000 acres of colorful canyons, buttes, pinnacles, and grassland that boasts one of the world's richest fossil beds. Its geologic story dates back some 70 million years to when the area was covered by a great inland sea. Once home to ancient mammals such as the rhino, the prehistoric horse, and saber-toothed tiger, today the Badlands afford visitors sightings of bison, bighorn sheep, prairie dogs, and black-footed ferrets roaming alongside the winding road that traverses the preserve. I did, happily, capture some charming shots of the prairie dogs that inhabit Roberts Prairie Dog Town north of the Sage Creek Rim Road. I also spotted several bison that roam the park.

Although I did not see a black-footed ferret, the story of this once-endangered species is one of the more hopeful legacies of the park. Previously thought to be extinct, scientists were delighted to discover in 1981 these rare ferrets alive and well in the wilds of Wyoming. The prognosis for their long-term survival, however, was not promising. They are dependent on the prairie for habitat and the prairie dog as their primary food source. Both were shrinking. By 1985 only 18 ferrets were known to be alive. In the face of some objections, the U. S. Fish and Wildlife Service in cooperation with Wyoming wildlife authorities, "captured the ferrets and launched a campaign to save them. Success came quickly. At seven breeding facilities, the ferrets flourished and multiplied. With high hopes and little fanfare, 36 black-footed ferrets were released in the park in the fall of 1994. In 1995, two litters of ferrets were born in the wild, an important milestone on their road to recovery." More of the captive-raised ferrets have been released in subsequent years, and it appears that these indigenous creatures have resumed their rightful place in the complex ecology of the region.[3]

In spring and summer, The Badlands are adorned with a wide variety of colorful indigenous wildflowers and other rugged plants. These include bright, yellow-crowned prickly pear cacti, royal magenta blooms of the spiderwort, red and pink thistles, the golden-petals of upright prairie cornflowers, the wispy red tentacles of the dotted gayfeather, and pure white blooms of snow-on-the-mountain scattered across the prairie grasses. One of the more striking images in Zarki's guide is two mating monarch butterflies gripping the stem of a woolly verbena blossom for balance during their delicate dance. I could not have hoped for a more beautiful day, with warm, caressing breezes under a clear blue sky that stretched to the horizon.[4]

Absorbed by one majestic vista after another, somewhere along the way I got off the main road and found myself wandering through the southwest side of the park. After a couple of turns, I realized I had left the park entirely. Reluctant to backtrack, with the help of my GPS, I charted a backroads way to Rapid City, where I arrived around lunch time and found my hotel, another Holiday Inn Express just south of the city on Caregiver Circle. With an overnight tariff of more than $250, the new inn proved to be one of my more expensive stays. Unlike many of my stops along the Lewis and Clark Trail, the Rapid City area is a major tourist attraction.

After lunch at a nearby Ruby Tuesday, I headed for Custer State Park, 30 miles to the south. I don't remember now how this attraction got on my itinerary, but I'm very glad I visited this majestic 71,000-acre state park that lies along the eastern edge of the much-larger Black Hills National Forest, a 1.2 million acre preserve of densely wooded hills and mountains that rises abruptly from the plains. The national forest is about 110 miles long and 70 miles wide. "Described as an 'Island in the Plains,' the forest has diverse wildlife and plants reaching from the eastern forests to the western plains."[5]

I spent a couple of hours slowly touring Custer State Park along with many other visitors attracted by the natural beauty and the abundant wildlife, including a carefully managed herd of bison, numbered at not more than 1450. The bison live on the native grasslands within the park, and careful assessment by wildlife experts has concluded that the number of bison must not exceed 1450. The story of the near eradication of these majestic beasts is well known. From once numbering in the millions before white settlers surged across the plains, displacing the Native Americans who depended on the bison for their way of life, by 1900 the bison had dwindled to an estimated 1,000.

Peter Norbeck (1879-1936), South Dakota's first Governor and three-term U. S. Senator was also a passionate conservationist. Often known as the "Father of Custer State Park," he took action to save the native bison. In 1914, the park, then known as Custer State Forest and Game Sanctuary, purchased 36 bison for breeding. By the 1940s the herd had grown to more than 2500, putting stress on the park's rangeland. From that time forward, the herd has been carefully managed so that the local habitat can sustain it. Each September, the park has a "roundup" in which all the bison are counted, branded, and inspected for health. Open to the public, the popular roundup is managed by cowboys and cowgirls on horseback, giving spectators a glimpse of another era in our history.

Norbeck's commitment to conserving this great natural treasure, reminded me of a paradox that has often puzzled me. Why are those who advocate conservation often opposed by those who call themselves conservatives? Why the hostility? There is clearly a fundamental difference between the members of groups like Ducks Unlimited and the Wilderness Society. The former would appear to emphasize responsible stewardship of natural resources but ultimately for the benefit and enjoyment of its members, in this case duck hunters. The latter sometimes betray an attitude that appears to value the same resources above the humans who too often have been responsible for spoiling them. What a powerful alliance it could be if one day conservationists and environmentalists consistently joined forces to protect and preserve our vast but threatened natural resources.

Other wildlife in the park include elk, pronghorns, mountain lions, coyotes, mule deer, bighorn sheep, mountain goats, and (of course) prairie dogs. I was fortunate to encounter a good-sized herd of bison, including their young, ambling casually across the road and up a grass-covered hill to our left. All traffic stopped to give these huge animals the right of way. One would not want to tangle with a bison; they can grow to more than six feet tall and weigh more than a ton. This small herd of not more than 50 gave me a sense of the wonder that Meriwether Lewis attempted to convey in his journal entry of September 17, 1804, near present-day Pierre:

> This senery already rich pleasing and beatiful was still further hightened by immence herds of buffaloe, deer, elk and antelopes which we saw in every direction feeding on the hills and plains. I do not think I exagerate when I estimate the number of buffaloe which could be compre[hend]ed at one view to amount to 3000.[6]

Lewis's idiosyncratic spelling is typical throughout the journals and was shared by Clark and the others who left written records of the epic journey. I am reminded of Andrew Jackson's reputed assertion, "damn a man who can spell a word only one way"! I have not been able to verify that source and have seen it attributed to Thomas Jefferson as well. Bear in mind that Noah Webster's *Compendious Dictionary of the English Language* was published in 1806. Up till that time, and surely for a long time thereafter, the idea of "correct" spelling was not universally recognized. Despite the best efforts of legions of demanding English teachers with their weekly spelling quizzes and spelling bees, it's clear that the battle has not yet ended.

Another common sight in the park is burros, which I also saw as we watched the passing bison herd. Although not native to the region, they are the descendants of a herd that once hauled visitors to the top of the park's Black Elk Peak. When the attraction was discontinued, the burros were simply released into the park, where they have thrived and become a tourist attraction. Whenever I see these sturdy, charming beasts, I am reminded of St. Francis's use of "Brother Ass" to refer to our own bodies, and C. S. Lewis's endorsement of the Franciscan perspective in *The Four Loves*:

> Ass is exquisitely right because no one in his senses can either revere or hate a donkey. It is a useful, sturdy, lazy, obstinate, patient, lovable and infuriating beast; deserving now a stick and now a carrot; both pathetically and absurdly beautiful. So the body.[7]

The park features many cabins and campsites, four lakes, trout streams, hiking trails, and more. One of its prominent structures is known as the State Game Lodge, which was built in 1921 but burned to the ground a few months later. It was rebuilt the following year, and in 1927 earned the title of "Summer White House" as President Calvin Coolidge tarried there for thirteen weeks.[8]

As the summer sun of this long day began easing down toward the pines on the slopes of the deeply forested Black Hills, I left Custer State Park to make my way to Mount Rushmore just beyond the north entrance. The long shadows that began to fall across these grand hills made me think of the dark shadow that had fallen across the nation in the wake of the most unexpected presidential election of 2016. Although much worse was yet to come including only the third impeachment of an American president, it was clear that our nation's most treasured values and enduring institutions were already being tested by a man who appeared to be the most disturbed, dishonest, and dangerous ever to hold the office.

I did not anticipate that this popular tourist destination would move me as deeply as it did. As I expected, even at this late time of the day, the grand monument was busy with tourists from all around the country and beyond. Nearly three million visit the site each year, with the busiest months being June, July, and August. The great diversity of visitors was immediately evident, people young and old, families with small children running through the grand columns of granite that frame the monument, people of every color, shape, and hue stood silent before the chiseled stone faces of Washington, Jefferson, Teddy Roosevelt, and Lincoln gazing solemnly to the southeast.

Like the American "experiment" that the monument celebrates, it is an unfinished work. The four imposing figures gaze dispassionately into the future they helped envision and create. Washington is rightly foremost of the group; if ever there was an indispensable man, our first president has a greater claim than any other. Tucked behind Washington's left shoulder, as if whispering in his ear, is the familiar visage of Jefferson. Even more discreetly tucked behind Jefferson in the natural recession of the rock is Teddy Roosevelt, almost as if the sculptor doubted whether he belonged in such august company, perhaps a concession to political imperatives of the time. Set a bit apart to the right of the three clustered on their shared promontory is Lincoln, who appears to occupy a promontory that is his alone, just as he occupies a singular position in our history. Second only to Washington, perhaps even his equal, Lincoln re-envisioned a "government of the people, by the people, for the people" and with superhuman effort renewed the hope that it would "not perish from the earth."

Located outside the tiny tourist town of Keystone, 24 miles southwest of Rapid City, the monument was designed, promoted, and executed by the famed American sculptor Gutzon Borglum (1867-1941), the son of Danish immigrants. He worked on the sculpture with a team of 400 laborers from 1927 till his death in 1941. It was completed by his son, Abraham. Borglum selected the four presidents to "represent the nation's birth, growth, development, and preservation, respectively. The memorial park covers 1,278.45 acres . . . and is 5,725 feet above sea level."[9]

Inside the handsome visitor center are plaques and displays that tell the arduous story of the monument's conception and challenging path to completion. It is a story of Borglum's vision and persistence as well as controversy and conflict. Originally projected to cost $500,000, it ultimately cost almost a million dollars, the bulk of it provided by Federal funds appropriated during the Great Depression.

On one of several posters in the visitors' center is the following quotation from President Calvin Coolidge:

It is natural that such a design should begin with George Washington, for with him begins that which is truly representative of America. . . . He stands as the foremost disciple of ordered liberty, a statesman with an inspired vision who is not outranked by any mortal greatness (August 10, 1937).

Other posters carry the familiar, inspiring words of those featured on the monument:

The preservation of the sacred fire of liberty and the destiny of the republican model of government are justly considered as deeply, perhaps as finally staked, on the experiment entrusted to the hands of the American people (George Washington, First Inaugural, April 30, 1789).

We hold these truths to be self-evident, that all men are created equal, that they are endowed by their Creator with certain unalienable Rights, that among them are Life, Liberty, and the pursuit of Happiness (Thomas Jefferson, "Declaration of Independence," July 4, 1776).

It is rather for us to be here dedicated to the great task remaining before us . . . that this nation, under God, shall have a new birth of freedom—and that government of the people, by the people, for the people, shall not perish from the earth (Abraham Lincoln, "Gettysburg Address," November 19, 1863).

We, here in America, hold in our hands the hopes of the world, . . . and shame and disgrace will be ours if in our eyes the light of high resolve is dimmed, if we trail in the dust the golden hopes of men (Theodore Roosevelt, March 30, 1912).

Reflecting on these lofty ideals, one cannot but wonder whether our bitterly divided nation will once again rise to the challenge that they describe. Will we call forth those better angels that Lincoln invoked in his First Inaugural as the nation plunged into a devastating war, a war whose scars continue to live even now so many years after Generals Grant and Lee reached a "Gentleman's Agreement" on April 9, 1865, at Appomattox? Such an achievement will require selfless leadership and moral courage of an order too-rarely evident among many who currently have charge of our nation.

Chapter Fourteen
From Rapid City to Bismarck

November 11, 1804: The Corps arrives at the Mandan village near present-day Bismarck, N.D., and constructs Fort Mandan as winter quarters, where they are embraced by the Indians and engage the French-Canadian trapper Touissant Charbonneau and, more importantly, his pregnant teen-aged wife Sacagawea, who played a critical role in the expedition's success.

Sunday, July 2, 2017, dawned bright and warm with a clear blue sky lightly brushed with cirrus clouds drifting like cotton candy in the wind. I got an early start with 8 a.m. mass at Our Lady of Perpetual Help Cathedral in Rapid City. The church is a 1960 modernist building, long and narrow with wood and marble finishes inside. A large replica of the familiar 15th-century Marian ikon for which the cathedral is named dominates the back wall above the main altar. It is mounted in an elaborate Byzantine frame. The original ikon has been in Rome since 1499 in the Church of St. Alphonsus where a weekly novena is prayed. The Rapid City cathedral is, of course, the seat of the local ordinary or bishop, but also serves as a parish church for many of the local Catholics. I had the impression of a thriving church community, but I did not tarry long after a few polite greetings as I left the church.

A small pleasure of being a Catholic is being able to walk into any Catholic church anywhere in the world, find a seat and participate in the mass. No credentials are required. Although Catholics are not known to be overly welcoming, they do not give any evidence of questioning your right to be there. It's a small thing, but something I prize. It gives me the opportunity to feel at home no matter where I find myself on any given Sunday.

After mass, I set out for Mobridge, SD, some 235 miles away. I can't recall now, and my travel notes are silent on my reason for putting tiny Mobridge (pop. 3300) on my itinerary rather than heading straight up to Bismarck. I did note, however, that a monument to

Sitting Bull sits on a bluff overlooking Lake Oahe, which dominates this section of north-central South Dakota. Dedicated by JFK in 1963, the massive "rolled-earth" dam that forms this largest of four Missouri River reservoirs in the state is some 245 feet high and 9,300 feet long. The popular recreational lake can hold up to 23.5 million acre-feet of water and offers 39 recreational sites along its more than 2,200 miles of shoreline from Pierre to Bismarck. Although the topography is radically changed, the Corps of Discovery camped along these grounds as they made their way up the river in 1804 and again on their return in 1806.

As I made my way across the rolling plains and grasslands of South Dakota, I gained a deeper appreciation for the majesty that Kathleen Norris so eloquently described in *Dakota: A Spiritual Geography* (1993), and I recalled with pleasure and gratitude her visit to Albright College in 2007 to offer the annual Hurwitz Lecture. As it happened, I was able to spend an atypical leisurely afternoon driving around the city of Reading with our distinguished guest, just the two of us visiting and chatting as we made our way up the winding Skyline Drive of Mount Penn (elevation approximately 1000 ft.) to the famed pagoda that overlooks the city. It is one of my happiest memories from those busy days.

About 85 miles northeast of Rapid City near the tiny unincorporated community of Mud Butte along Rt. 212, I came upon a little rest area with a historical marker to Ben Ash (Dec. 19, 1851-April 15, 1946). The marble plinth stands about six feet tall with an engraved map of the area from Bismarck to Deadwood. The inscription reads: "The Trail Blazers/ Here on 26 December 1875, Ben Ash, S.C. Dodge, Russ Marsh, Ed Donahue, and Stimmy Stimson on their trip from Bismarck through the Indian Country first sighted the Black Hills." In 1875-76, Ash and his companions blazed a trail from Bismarck to the Black Hills to accommodate the growing hordes of pioneers and fortune-seekers following the 1874 discovery of gold and other precious metals in the Black Hills.

In 1986, Ash was inducted into the South Dakota Hall of Fame as a "Champion of Excellence." There are now 741 others on this list. I was surprised to see that Kathleen Norris was not among them, so I dropped a note to the society suggesting that they consider her and promptly received a courteous and encouraging reply. Thus far, however, Norris has not been added to the list.

101

Ash is described as a "frontiersman, fearless law enforcement officer, cattleman, [and] trail blazer in the Black Hills." Born in Indiana, he moved with his family in 1859 to Yankton, then a new town in the Dakota Territory. The Ash family lived in one of four cabins that comprised the tiny town. As a young man he worked as a horse breaker and trader, becoming an assistant to the U.S. Marshall at the age of 17 and later served as a deputy marshal, then sheriff of Hughes County.

In 1873, Ash served under General George Custer as a wagon boss of 44 six-mule teams on the expedition that explored the Yellowstone Country in Montana. This was the historic venture that included the discovery of gold on French Creek in the Black Hills.

Later in his life, Ash settled near Pierre and was in the livery and grocery business. He subsequently bought a ranch, served for a time as sheriff, and ended his life as a wealthy rancher stocking cattle with a herd of up to 10,000 head bearing the "C Cross" brand. He is also an inductee of the National Cowboy Hall of Fame in Oklahoma City.[1]

The site of the solitary marker on the little wayside along Rt. 212 affords majestic vistas of the plains in every direction with little sign of humanity other than the Ben Ash memorial itself. The stone plinth is defaced by some sort of cryptic graffiti that suggests the mixed legacy of those intrepid pioneers trespassing as they were across land that the Native Americans considered sacred. It is not easy to travel through this territory without regular reminders of the tragedies and sometimes-unwitting cruelties visited upon those indigenous people as wave after relentless wave of pioneers swept across the land that Lewis and Clark had so boldly explored and claimed for their "Great Father" in Washington.

After my pause at the Ben Ash Memorial, I continued east and northeast toward Mobridge, some 150 miles up the road. Within the Standing Rock Reservation, just west of the river on a bluff overlooking Lake Oahe and Mobridge is a Sitting Bull Monument and on the same site a separate monument to "Sakakawea," the Indian woman who joined the Corps of Discovery during its 1804 winter stay with the Mandan tribe in North Dakota. She was one of at least two "wives" of a French-Canadian guide and translator named Toussaint Charbonneau, who lobbied assiduously to join the expedition. Sakakawea's language skill was key to Charbonneau being accepted. Not surprisingly there are multiple variant name spellings for the famous young Indian woman who played a crucial role in the success of the Corps. The spelling used here is what appears on the plaque honoring her at this site as "the most illustrious feminine representative of the Indian race."

This "Sakakawea" monument was erected in the 1920s with funds raised by local schoolchildren. The multiple monuments and statues to Sacagawea (now the more common spelling) all along the Lewis and Clark Trail, reflect the deep and broad impact this young woman has had on the imaginations of subsequent generations. As Stephen Ambrose records, she was one of Charbonneau's several Shoshone or Snake wives who had been captured around 1800 by a Hidatsu raiding party from a band that lived in the Rocky Mountains near the headwaters of the Missouri. Charbonneau had "won" them in a bet with the warriors who had captured them. At the time she and Charbonneau joined the Corps, she was 15 and six months pregnant. Her knowledge of the Hidatsu language was of greater value to the Corps than Charbonneau's guiding skills which proved to be uneven.[2]

The monument is a concrete obelisk, perhaps 30-feet high featuring a round, bas-relief brass bust of Sacagawea cradling a swaddled infant, her famed son, Jean Baptiste, who the explorers called "Pomp." Clark adopted, reared, and educated the boy after the expedition. On a separate concrete slab nearby is a bronze tablet with a detailed summary of Sacagawea's important role in the expedition's success. Although perhaps not perfectly accurate, it is a well-deserved tribute to this remarkable young woman's courage, strength, and skills.

Among many examples of Sacagawea's character recorded by Ambrose was one that occurred in May 1805 when a sudden squall struck one of the Corps' two pirogues almost overturning it while Charbonneau was at the helm. As Ambrose notes, it is unclear why the French-Canadian fur trader was in this critical position when Lewis had already described him as "perhaps the most timid waterman in the world." Through quick action and heroic effort, other members of the crew managed to save the craft from capsizing and limped to shore. Throughout this adventure, Sacagawea remained "calm, collected, and invaluable," according to Lewis. The next day, Lewis described her actions in his journal: "The Indian woman to whom I ascribe equal fortitude and resolution, with any person on board at the time of the accedent [sic], caught and preserved most of the light articles which were washed overboard."[3]

After the Corps' return, she and Charbonneau returned to the Mandan village near present-day Bismarck. They later lived at a fur-trading site called Fort Manuel located about 70 miles south of Bismarck in present-day South Dakota. It was here that the fort's clerk recorded her death of a "putrid fever" on December 20, 1812. She could not have been more than 25 years old when she died.[4]

Further down the gravel path on this isolated spot is the monument to Sitting Bull, Tatanka Iyotake, the great warrior and spiritual leader of the Hunkpapa Teton Sioux who resisted and heroically endured the incursions, violence, and persecution of the U.S. Government longer than many of his fellow natives. The monument is a seven-ton granite bust carved by the famed sculptor Korczak Ziolkowski, who started the mammoth Crazy Horse carving near Custer, South Dakota. Regrettably, my full day in the Rapid City area did not afford me time to visit this ambitious but yet-unfinished tribute to another heroic Native American.

This solemn sculpture of a grim, stern-visaged Sitting Bull looks east, as if in continued defiance of the forces that ultimately defeated him. It is a bust from mid-chest up to his round head with hair evenly parted and long braids lying against his chest. Two feathers stand at the crown of his head; his arms are folded across his chest cradling what appears to be a peace pipe. His prominent nose casts a shadow across his grimace, and his high cheekbones set off deep-set eyes that seem to project profound weariness. Engraved on the inset stone plaque in the base is the following:

TATANKA IYOTAKE
SITTING BULL
1831-1890

From the many photographic images available, it's clear that Sitting Bull usually wore a stern expression, but he appears to have been a good deal more handsome than this stone bust suggests.

Sitting Bull Monument near Mobridge, South Dakota

Nearby is a free-standing concrete slab with a triangular crest that resembles a tall tombstone. Set into it is another tablet of a complex, textured stone with swirls of pink and gray in its uneven surface. Engraved at the top is a bas relief image of Sitting Bull's head, festooned with two pairs of feathers, and his braids draped over a peace pipe. Below the sculpt of his head is an engraved summary of his life. It reads as follows:

1834-1890
SITTING BULL
TATANKA IYOTAKE

Sitting Bull was born on the Grand River a few miles west of Mobridge. His tragic end came at the very place he was born. He was shot when being arrested for his alleged involvement in the Ghost Dance Craze.

Sitting Bull was originally buried at Fort Yates, ND. On April 8 1953 surviving relatives with the aid of the South Dakota Memorial Association moved his remains to the present location and dedicated the Memorial Burial Site April 11 1953 [sic].

1876 – Victorious at the Battle of Little Big Horn
1877 – Sought asylum in Canada
1881 - Returned to the United States
1885 – Toured with Buffalo Bill's Wild West Show

It would be difficult to say which of the many tragic stories of the prolonged U. S. war against the Native Americans merits primacy, but surely Sitting Bull's is among a small number that should be considered. Sitting Bull's death in late 1890 was not the final chapter in America's longest war. According to Peter Cozzens in *The Earth is Weeping* that war ended the following month on January 15, 1891, when the Oglala chief and Ghost Dance leader Kicking Bear laid his carbine at the feet of General Nelson A. Miles, at Pine Ridge Reservation in southwest South Dakota.[5] Cozzens marks the beginning of the war on May 16, 1864, when a detachment of some 84 U. S. soldiers under the command of Colonel John Chivington opened fire without provocation on a band of Cheyenne led by Chief Lean Bear. In March of the previous year, Lean Bear had led a delegation of Indians to meet with President Lincoln in Washington. Lincoln and Lean Bear had pledged peace, and Lean Bear proudly displayed the medal and peace papers that Lincoln had given him as he rode out to meet the soldiers. As Cozzens puts it, "Lean Bear was just thirty feet from the soldiers when they opened fire. The chief was dead before he hit the ground."[6] The bloody struggle would continue for another 27 years and 8 months. Along with the grim legacy of slavery, it is the darkest stain on our history. And although rarely acknowledged by today's media in the wake of the 20-year American presence in Afghanistan, the sustained war against the native Americans is our nation's longest.

That dark chapter was succinctly described by an elderly Lakota chief who had watched events unfold from the Treaty of Fort Laramie in 1851 to the tragedy at Wounded Knee four decades later: "'The [government]made us many promises,' he told a white friend, 'more than I can remember, but they never kept but one; they promised to take our land, and they took it.'" [7]

After my visit to this somber, isolated site, I learned more about how it came to be. The surprisingly candid entry on the Mobridge city web site, records how Sitting Bull was killed on December 15, 1890, by an Indian policeman while attempting to execute an arrest warrant to prevent the revered tribal leader from participating in a Ghost Dance revivalist ceremony. As noted at the memorial site, his bullet-riddled remains were originally buried without ceremony in a grave near present-day Fort Yates, North Dakota, about 55 miles up the river.

The Mobridge website records how "the tragedy of his death has been compounded by the story of his remains." In 1953, an enterprising group of Mobridge businessmen aiming to attract tourists, collaborated with one of Sitting Bull's descendants by marriage, Clarence Grey Eagle, to obtain an opinion from the Bureau of Indian Affairs that authorized them to relocate Sitting Bull's remains to the site near Mobridge. It is a sad irony that Clarence Grey Eagle was the son of one of the Indian police officers who were involved in the attempted arrest of Sitting Bull, which led to his death. In April of that year, under cover of night, this group secretly removed what they took to be the great chief's remains from the Fort Yates site and re-buried them near Mobridge. In fewer than five months, South Dakota dedicated the Sitting Bull monument at the site of the relocated remains. The sculptor Ziolkowski boycotted the ceremony in protest of what he perceived as South Dakota's Governor "exploiting the ceremony for political and economic gain against the wishes of Sitting Bull's descendants."

Not surprisingly, citizens of Fort Yates continue to claim that the party from Mobridge failed to disinter the actual remains, and thus there are now two competing monuments to Sitting Bull, a grim reminder of the way in which Sitting Bull was torn between two competing and irreconcilable visions of his beloved land and people, his valiant defiance and ignoble defeat.[8]

I left the Sitting Bull monument in a somber mood despite the lovely day. It was 86 degrees at 3:10, with low humidity and a gentle breeze as I headed across the river to Mobridge. I made my way to the modest storefront Chamber of Commerce Visitor Center on Main Street to find the "pop-up" display on the Lewis and Clark expedition. The display was well done for its modest scale, featuring a series of fabric panels held up in spring-tension triptychs by fiberglass rods. Each of the dozen or so colorful panels featured photographic images accompanied by carefully researched and well-written scripts focused on the Lewis and Clark adventure as well as what they found in the area when they reached it on October 8, 1804. This included brief descriptions, with excerpts from the explorers' journals, of prairie dogs, mule deer, antelopes, and white-tailed jack rabbits, as well as local flora that included Prairie Turnip, Buffaloberry, and Sagebrush.

After enjoying this modest diversion and realizing I might have been wiser to head straight on to my hotel in Bismarck, I explored the little town a bit. The Main Street is a reminder of the Old West model of a variety of store fronts along either side of a wide thoroughfare with ample space for parking on both sides of the street. Mobridge feels larger than its small population and displays an obvious sense of pride and hospitality with a warm embrace of visitors who come to enjoy the history as well as the natural attractions of the big lake that the town borders.

Fanselow notes that Mobridge is known for its walleye and pike fishing, sailboarding, and the annual Sitting Bull Stampede Rodeo, July 2-4, which must have been going on during my visit, although I saw no evidence of it.[9]

Down Main Street toward the river one finds a pleasant riverside park with more historical markers on Lewis and Clark including an account of their adventures with grizzly bears and their friendly encounter with the Arikara Indians nearby. As Ambrose records, the Arikara welcomed the Corps with warmth including offering their wives for intimacy to several of the men. Clark's slave, York, was particularly an object of wonder and fascination. He, too, enjoyed the favors of a welcoming native woman.

I departed Mobridge around 3:30 and headed for Bismarck, another 115 miles up the road. About 27 miles up SD 1806 along the western shore of the river, I came upon Kenel, an unincorporated community in Corson County just below the North Dakota state line. According to the 2020 census, the population was 146. A post office called Kenel was established in 1914 and remained in operation until 1963. The community was named for Father Martin Kenel, a local priest.

I cannot recall what caused me to pull off into this little community but surmise that I must have seen a sign for Fort Manuel. Just east of the town up a poorly maintained dirt road bounded by tall grass that also grows in the median of its narrow track, I came upon the badly neglected historic site of Fort Manuel, which was established as a trading post in 1812 by a fur trader named Manuel Lisa. For me, its primary significance is the site where most historians agree that Sacagawea died in December 1812.[10]

Not another soul was at the lonely site that sits on a slight rise in a grassy field. There are several replica cabins spread out on the knoll and a rusted, pitted historical marker stands alone. It is so badly damaged that it was difficult to make out its message, but thanks to the South Dakota State Historical Society, I later found this entry:

> #391 Fort Manuel
> "August 8, 1812 to March 5, 1813
> The war of 1812 was not started when Manuel Lisa, a Spaniard, who had become an American Citizen, started from St. Louis on May 8, with men and supplies to start a fur trade post, located to trade with Aricara, Mandans and Yanktonaise on the Upper Missouri. Among his passengers were Touissant Charbonneau and his Shoshone wife, Sacacawea. ON [sic] the 9th of August they had arrived 'at a beautiful prairie bluff with several bottoms of fine timber around'. They started trade and a fort. By November 19th they had 'hung the great door at the entrance to the fort . . . saluted by seven guns and those rounds of musquestry, made the tour around the fort and baptized the same MANUEL". [sic] On Sunday, December 20th Luttig, the factor made this entry in his journal: 'This evening the wife of Charbonneau, a Snake squaw, died of a putrid fever. She was a good and the best woman in the fort, aged about 25 years she

left a fine infant girl'. This was the famed Sacacawea of Lewis & Clark's journey to the Pacific.

The Fort was not destined for a long life. Most of the Indians were allied to the British and on March 5, 1813, attacked and burnt the Fort. Lisa dropped down river with what he could salvage and re-established at the Old Loisel, 1802-1809 post, at the Big Bend."

Erected: 1965

Location: Corson County, BIA road – 2 1/2 mile north of Kennel [sic][11]

Having paid my respects to the memory of the remarkable young Sacagawea, I retraced my route to the highway and proceeded on to Bismarck.

At a leisurely pace, I reached my Holiday Inn around 5:45. At the Inn I discovered to my dismay that I had made an error in the reservation and that it had been for the night before. The innkeeper was gracious not to charge me for the no show and, even better, had no trouble providing me a room, despite it being high tourist season. Relief and gratitude were my appetizers for a very pleasant dinner of a Greek salad at nearby Mackenzie River Pizza Grill and Pub.

When I got to my room around 9 p.m., I was feeling my years. I had driven 390 miles. My trip total to that point was 2981.5 miles, and Fort Clatsop was still 1400 miles up the road.

Note: The **Sioux** are a confederacy of several tribes that speak three different dialects, the **Lakota**, Dakota, and Nakota. The **Lakota**, also called the Teton **Sioux**, are comprised of seven tribal bands and are the largest and most western of the three groups, occupying lands in both North and South Dakota.

The **Hunkpapa** (Lakota: Húŋkpapȟa) are a Native American group, one of the seven council fires of the Lakota tribe. The name Húŋkpapȟa is a Lakota word **meaning** "Head of the Circle."[12]

Chapter Fifteen
From Bismarck to Williston, North Dakota

April 7, 1805: The Corps departs the Mandans in their two pirogues and six small canoes that they had constructed on site. They send the 55-foot keelboat back down river to St. Louis loaded with items collected in the previous year's explorations.

Monday, July 3, 2017, dawned bright and clear, another warm summer day on the Great Plains, as I left my hotel for an early tee time at Hawktree Golf Club, just six miles north. I had been in touch with the course pro, who had given me a reasonable rate when I told him about my cross-country trip and plans for a book. He also promised to try to link me up with some local golfers. It was my good fortune to meet two brothers-in-law on the first tee, and they welcomed my company. So similar in size and appearance, these two beefy North Dakotans could have passed for brothers. They surely once would have been tough to encounter on someone's defensive line, but they proved to be cordial and patient company on this difficult but beautiful links-style golf course. We teed off around 8:30 a.m. CDT.

Designed by native son Jim Engh, Hawktree opened in 2000 and immediately captured national attention with *Golf Digest* rating it No. 2 among "Top New Affordable Courses" in 2002. In 2007-08, Hawktree was No. 24 on *Golf Digest's* top 100 "Greatest Public Golf Courses," and No. 1 in the state 2011-2017. *Golf* magazine rated it No. 62 on its top 100 in 2007, and it ranked no. 56 on *Golfweek's* 2007 list of "America's Best Modern Courses." It clearly merits these accolades as well as the typical 4-to-5-star ratings that golfers give it on various golf web sites.

With only 80 acres of irrigated turf, the course is self-described as "eco-friendly"; it is a stunning collaboration of the natural plains setting, the rolling hills, and the seemingly ever-present threat of Burnt Creek winding through the course and coming into play on at least 10 holes. Three ponds are additional challenge. Measuring more than 7000 yards from the tips, with a rating/slope of 75.2/137, we played from the less-daunting tees called "Hawk," which measured just over 6400 yards, 72.1/130. The course offers six tee options for men, three for women, as almost all golf courses still describe them. I am always pleased to see courses where the tees are ranked according to handicap. There are some women golfers who should never play the so-called "men's tees," and there are some men who should always play the so-called "women's or ladies' tees." Perhaps one day the USGA will step up and insist that all its member courses adopt a non-sex-based way of describing their tees. To be fair, I should note that the Hawktree score card does suggest handicaps for each of the six tees.[1]

After finishing my round and losing at least nine balls, I realized I should have played one of the more forward tees. Even then, I may have fared no better because I was not playing very well that day, and it's a course that demands accuracy and heartlessly punishes the lack of it. In addition to the holes where water is a challenge are the abundant stretches of high grass not far off the fairways. Finding errant balls in that knee-high obstacle was almost worse than counting them lost, as pitching the ball out of the thick vegetation was a formidable challenge. To round it all off, the course is wickedly punctuated by bunkers filled with natural black coal sand that seem always to be just where they can do the most damage, particularly on tough approaches to the smooth, rolling greens. It is an admirably well-maintained course, reflecting the pride that its proprietors have justly earned in this memorable achievement.

Having told my companions about my writing project, I shared with them the questions I hoped they would consider answering, took their emails, and followed up with the questions in writing. After sending another email in late December, I was delighted to receive a thoughtful response from one of my Hawktree golfing partners. Getting golfers and others to respond to my questions was challenging. Indeed, I ultimately received only fourteen responses. Apparently, many of those I met were reluctant to put their thoughts on paper. I'm not sure what to surmise from that reluctance, but clearly that dimension of my project proved to be the most difficult.

This correspondent, however, was not shy and offered comments that reflect values and concerns widely shared: "The thing I value the most would be the opportunity to succeed. My military experience showed me this is not everywhere nor should it be taken for granted. If you truly work hard with good morals you can be successful in life. Some feel they are deprived but it is usually more because they feel owed versus willingness to earn."

He described two issues that worried him. First was the power that he believes the media have over our lives and "the fiction they present." Observing that "the truth can be manipulated without consequence," and "it is ruining our system." Specifically, he cited racism and religion as "obvious targets where the minority can rule" because the majority are chastised to the point of self-destruction. His second concern was that welfare, Food Stamps, unemployment benefits, and what he described as "other government handouts" are "too easy for people that don't need it." Such abuse, he believes, is crippling our country.

With a magic wand, he would require "drug testing for welfare applicants," return corporal punishment to our judicial system, limit the number of appeals to prevent expenses, and require our prisons to become manufacturing facilities so that inmates could "earn their keep." He closed his note with an apology for "ranting" and cordially wished me a "wonderful New Years."

None of his concerns were new to me but reminded me that many who share them are in their daily lives much kinder and more generous spirited than one might infer from some of the harshness they appear to reflect.

After a quick lunch at the course, I headed into downtown Bismarck for a compressed tour of the capitol complex. I had clearly planned far too much for a single day, as I still had reservations that night in Williston, some 220 miles up the river.

The state's capital city, Bismarck, was the largest metropolitan area I had visited since leaving Omaha. The city population in 2020 was 73,435 with a metro-area population almost double that. It is an attractive, thriving government and commercial center with a well-groomed capitol complex featuring the tallest building in the state, the 19-story art deco capitol building itself, which is said to be visible from 20 miles away on a clear day. Also found here are the North Dakota Heritage Center, the North Dakota State Library, the

Governor's residence, the state office building, and the Liberty Memorial Building. Clearly, I could have spent the better part of the day touring this impressive complex.

On the grounds adjacent to the North Dakota Heritage Center is an impressive statue of Sakakawea, as it's spelled there. Renewed interest in the Corps of Discovery coincided with the Louisiana Purchase Exposition in 1904 and led to the North Dakota Federation of Women's Clubs in collaboration with the state Historical Society launching a fund-raising drive to erect the statue, which was unveiled in October 1910. The sculptor was Leonard Crunelle, a well-known Chicago artist. Crunelle used as his model a descendant of Sakakawea known as "Mink" or "Mink Woman," a Hidatsa woman whose "proper name" was Hannah Levings, according to the historical marker at the statue. Mounted on a large stone base, the imposing statue shows a handsome woman with strong features gazing westward and carrying a baby wrapped in a blanket sleeping peacefully on her back.

"Sakakawea" by Leonard Crunelle, Bismarck, North Dakota

114

In conjunction with the Lewis and Clark Bicentennial, the state legislature honored Sakakawea by commissioning a replica of the statue to be placed in the U. S. Capitol statuary hall in 2003:

> In selecting Sakakawea as the subject of this statue, the state legislature chose to honor her as a "traveler and guide, a translator, a diplomat, and a wife and mother" and to recognize that "her indomitable spirit was a decided factor in the success of Lewis and Clark's . . . expedition." Their choice appears to agree with the sentiment expressed by William Clark in a letter to Sakakawea's husband almost two centuries ago: "your woman who accompanied you that long dangerous and fatiguing rout to the Pacific Ocean and back deserved a greater reward for her attention and services on that rout than we had in our power to give her."[2]

Nearby is an imposing sculpture of a bison fabricated in steel rebar. Entitled simply "Buffalo," the sculpture shows a bison in midstride with its front left hoof raised while the other three touch the base. "The front half, including the head, is textured with metal bars to represent animal hair. The rear half is smooth, and has cut-out gaps across the surface, forming swirling patterns." It was dedicated on September 12, 1986.[3] The sculptor was Bennett Brien, a Native American artist from the Turtle Mountain Band of Chippewa Indians.[4]

This beautiful work of art is a solemn reminder of the mighty bison herds that once ranged across the American West by the thousands and were almost eradicated by uncontrolled hunting as the indigenous people were pushed off their native plains and herded into reservations where they were forced to take up farming and abandon the hunting rituals that defined their culture for centuries before the white men arrived.

I departed the capitol complex, crossed the river, and drove a few miles south to visit Fort Abraham Lincoln State Park, a 1006-acre multi-use historic, recreational, and cultural site that includes a fine reproduction of a Mandan village known as On-A-Slant. Established in 1907, the park is the oldest in North Dakota and includes campsites, cabins, trails, and historical replicas of the Mandan village that was once located there as well as its use as a U. S. Army fort. Its handsome stone visitor center was built by Civilian Conservation Corps laborers during the Great Depression.

The Corps of Discovery camped in the vicinity on October 20, 1804, and again on their return trip on August 18, 1806. In his journal, Clark referred to "the old (deserted) village of the Mandans."[5] Subsequent archaeological studies show that the Mandans occupied this site from about 1650 to 1750. By the time, the corps arrived in 1804, the Mandans had relocated about 60 miles north, where the corps would build a fort and spend a bitter cold winter.

Fort Abraham Lincoln was built by the U. S. Army in 1872 and occupied through 1891, when it was abandoned. The famed (or infamous, depending on who's telling the story) Seventh Calvary under command of Lieutenant Colonel George Armstrong Custer arrived in the fall of 1873. From here Custer led expeditions into the Black Hills where he discovered gold on sacred Sioux lands. The subsequent gold rush and escalating conflicts with the native peoples ultimately led to the end of the Sioux way of life. It was also from this site that Custer led his troops to the disastrous Battle of Little Big Horn, where he and 265 others were killed by Sioux and Cheyenne warriors led by Sitting Bull and Crazy Horse. Included in the historic site is Custer's House and other exhibits that explain the events leading up to the battle. I did not have time or interest to visit these sites, my primary focus being the restored On-A-Slant Village.

Although excavations show as many as 75 sturdy earth lodges once occupied this thriving Mandan village of seven or eight acres, today there are five well-maintained replicas that gave me an excellent sense of how these native people lived. The lodges themselves were constructed of large logs placed against a central post and radiating out from a center height of 10 to 15 feet to a diameter from 20 to 40 feet. Over these structures, the Mandan women, who primarily constructed and owned the snug lodges, placed a thick mat of willows and then a layer of grass and a layer of earth. A well-constructed lodge lasted about ten years. I enjoyed walking through the site with a few other late-afternoon visitors.

While touring this impressive site, I learned about a Native American woman named Regina Whitman Schanandore, also known as Eagle Plume Woman, who played a key role in the restoration of On-A-Slant Village which occurred soon after her death in August 1998. A well-known local storyteller, she shared her love for her native Mandan and Hidatsa culture to all who would seek her as a speaker. At age 73, she began writing a biweekly column, "From My Lodge to Your Lodge," for the *Mandan News*. From 1993 to 1998, she worked as an interpreter at the village, sharing stories of growing up Mandan on the Fort Berthold Indian Reservation. She lobbied tirelessly to see her dream of On-A-Slant Village restored. Shortly before her death she learned that U. S. Senator Byron Dorgan had been successful in securing National Park Service funding for the restoration. I hope and trust that this admirable woman would be pleased with the result.

After my short visit, I headed upriver to the Lewis and Clark Interpretive Center on U. S. 83, just north of Washburn. It is a handsome, frontier-style, wooden and stone structure sited on the bluffs overlooking the river to the west. Near its entrance is an imposing steel sculpture of Lewis and Clark conversing with Mandan chief Sheheke-shote (White Coyote). Each of the figures stands about 12 feet tall. Entitled "The Mandan Winter," it is the work of local artist and master welder Tom Neary. This chief welcomed the Corps of Discovery to winter among them and pledged the tribe's help as they were able in the following words: "If we eat you shall eat, if we starve, you must starve also" (November 1, 1804).

White Coyote proved true to his words as the tribe shared their provisions through a brutally cold winter. As the nearby historical marker records, the Corps of Discovery might not have survived the winter if not for the hospitality of the Mandan and Hidatsa. In his journal of December 8, Clark recorded several cases of frostbitten feet and, "in the case of York, a frostbitten male organ," as Julie Fanselow primly describes it.[6] Clark's actual entry reads as follows:

> The thermometer stood at 12 degrees below 0, which is 42[degrees][sic] below the freesing [sic] point . . . . Several men returned a little frost bit, one . . . with his feet badly frost bit. My servents feet also frosted &- his P-s [penis] a little.[7]

Although Clark's math was off two degrees, there is no doubt about the painfully cold winter. Even this rugged adventurer could not bring himself to spell out "the male organ"!

117

Given the time of day and the miles I yet had to travel, I breezed through the well-appointed center giving it far less time than it deserves. As Fanselow justly acknowledges in her guide, the center provides an excellent overview of the entire expedition, abundant artifacts representing almost all the Native Americans that the Corps encountered, and excellent interpretive materials on the winter of 1804-05. Among other impressive materials is "a full set of prints by Karl Bodmer, the Swiss artist who documented life along the Missouri River in the 1830s." The originals are in the Joslyn Art Museum in Omaha. This fine center is well worth a more leisurely visit than I gave it.[8]

As I left the building and was walking across the grassy perimeter to view the grand vista of the rolling hills and the river to the west, I was foolishly not looking where I was walking and stepped on the tail of long brown and gold snake which sent a quivering shock up my leg and quickly slithered away but not so far that I couldn't capture a couple of good photos. I sent them to a friend who is a biologist at Gettysburg College and a specialist in reptiles. He responded promptly that my pulse-quickening encounter was with a relatively harmless Bull Snake (*Pituophis catenifer sayi*), the largest of the nonvenomous snakes in the U.S. and common to the Plains. My snake was between three and four feet long. I later learned that they can grow to eight feet. Perhaps my unwanted encounter was with a youngster! It was a good reminder that I should pay closer attention to where I was stepping on my voyage of discovery.

Just a couple of miles upriver from the Interpretive Center is another interpretive center and a volunteer-built replica of Fort Mandan, as Lewis and Clark named their primitive quarters for the winter, which they built and occupied in early November. It was here that the French-Canadian fur trader Charbonneau and Sacagawea joined the Corps. On February 11, Sacagawea gave birth to her first child, a son, Jean Baptiste.

After the bitter winter, the Corps departed Fort Mandan on April 7, 1805; a contingent of eleven men took the keelboat back to St. Louis loaded with specimens collected in the first leg of the voyage. The remainder of the Corps, thirty-three persons, including Sacagawea's baby, proceeded up the river in six newly built canoes and the two pirogues with which they had begun their journey from the falls of the Ohio.[9]

As I drove into the leafy complex and past the small interpretive center toward what is called "Seaman's Point," overlooking the river, I saw the huge sculpture of Lewis's beloved Newfoundland dog, Seaman. Another steel sculpture by Tom Neary, the six-foot tall figure, weighing 1400 pounds, shows Seaman sitting on his hind quarters with front legs extended holding up his huge head as if on lookout duty, which was a task he routinely performed during the long journey. Over his massive shoulders, the broad sweep of the Missouri flows toward the sea.

"Seaman" by Tom Neary, Washburn, North Dakota

Seaman figures often in the journals, especially those of his master. Lewis's love for the dog was deep, but Seaman's ultimate end is uncertain. It is generally assumed that he returned with the Corps to St. Louis in 1806, but after that the record is cloudy. Details of Seaman's story are recorded on a nearby historical marker that suggests Seaman lived out his days near Meriwether Lewis's grave at Grinder's Inn on the Natchez Trace about 75 miles west of Nashville. It was here that the intrepid explorer, suffering from mental and spiritual illness, bedeviled by creditors, and haunted by feelings of failure took his life on October 11, 1809.

It was about 4:40 p.m. (MDT) when I left Seaman's Overlook and headed for Williston by way of Minot about an hour north of Fort Mandan via U. S. 83. Although not the most direct route, it was the speediest. A more interesting route would have been along the winding path of the official trail on ND 1804, but it would have added at least an hour of travel time and likely provoked frustration at all that I did not have time or daylight to stop and visit. I arrived at Minot about 5:40 p.m., took a little break, and then proceeded to Williston, still some 120 miles away. I arrived at the Grand Williston Hotel about 9 p.m., very tired after this long and eventful day. I knew little about Williston; it was merely a waypoint on my path.

Although happy to have reached my lodging for the night, there was immediately something about the "Grand Williston" that was off-putting. Its barren, battered parking lot was virtually empty and this during high tourist season. There were a few semi-trucks parked around the perimeter. I checked in hoping to find someplace nearby for dinner. As I found my way to my room, I had the feeling of being watched but the place seemed almost empty. I encountered not another guest during my entire stay.

I had a forgettable dinner at a nearby place called The Williston Brewing Company and paid more than $35 for what I cannot remember. All I recall is feeling eager to make it through what proved to be a restless night despite my fatigue. I had driven 293 miles.

It was not till January of 2019 that I got some inkling of what may have raised my hackles about the Grand Williston. In *Time* magazine's January 17 issue was a lengthy article with photos of the exploding problem of sex trafficking centered in Williston as the oil boom disrupted the life of the town. Included in that story is the following: "Then we pull into the parking lot of the Grand Williston Hotel, once notorious for the broken lock on its back door that allowed johns to come and go unnoticed by front-desk personnel."[10]

I don't think of myself as particularly perceptive, especially to what is not right in front of me. My wife would endorse that assessment as she has more than once described me as "obtuse." To take some of the sting out of that harsh judgment, she has always added that it's a trait I share with most men. If that's true, men must be an endless source of amusement, shock, and dismay among the women who must watch us stumble across unseen hazards (like the big snake I stepped on at the Interpretive Center near Washburn) and other phenomena that appear obvious to them.

If the horrors of sex-trafficking were indeed the source of my discomfort at the Grand Williston, it would be an uncharacteristic intuition. It might simply have been that the inn was an "off-brand" and among the cheapest places I stayed on the road. It was tired, worn, and a bit seedy, nothing "grand" about it aside from the pretension of it being so named. Although I tried to economize on my journey, I most often stayed at the reliably clean and comfortable places in the more affordable brands of Hilton and Marriott. I also found good lodging at Holiday Inn Express and some of the Best Westerns on my route as well as several very comfortable independents.

Before leaving Williston, I should mention that "The Links of North Dakota," about 28 miles east of Williston near the tiny town of Ray (pop. 500) is a highly regarded course, ranked by *Golf Digest* as number two in the state, behind Hawktree. Although I did not see it, the pictures on the website and elsewhere show a genuine links-style course along the shore of Lake Sakakawea, which was created by one of the many dams on the Missouri River.

Designed by award-winning architect Stephen Kay, The Links opened in 1995 to rave reviews. Operating on a thin budget, Kay did an impressive job of working with the terrain as it was. Among many accolades, soon after opening, *Golf Digest* rated it #2 in the country among "best new affordable" courses and described it as "one of the purest expressions of links-style golf." In 2020, *Golfweek* ranked it #1 in North Dakota and #35 in the nation. This is one I really regret missing.[11]

Chapter Sixteen
Fourth of July Trek to Great Falls, Montana

June 2, 1805: The Corps reaches a major fork near present-day Loma, Montana, about 50 miles northeast of Great Falls; its robust size causes them to question the correct course. After exploring the northern branch, which they name Marias River, the captains take a vote. All members of the crew vote for the northern branch, but the two captains overrule them and proceed on what proves to be the correct route.

Fort Union Trading Post National Historic Site, Williston, ND

After a "free" breakfast at the Grand Williston, I left the inn around 8:45 on the Fourth of July and headed southwest to the confluence of the Yellowstone and Missouri Rivers. My plan for Independence Day was to drive more than 400 miles to Great Falls, Montana, covering in a day a section of the Lewis and Clark Trail that took the Corps of Discovery from April 25 to June 13, 1805.

It was the first time that I could recall not being with family and friends for the traditional celebration of this national holiday. It seemed best to immerse myself in solitude rather than hover around as an outsider while others celebrated the vision and courage of our Founders.

As I arrived at the Missouri-Yellowstone Confluence Interpretive Center, some 24 miles southwest of Williston on ND 1804, I reflected on the mixed legacy of westward expansion that the Lewis and Clark expedition had ignited. It is neatly symbolized by two significant historic sites near the confluence. The Interpretive Center does a good job of reflecting this mixed legacy with artifacts and artworks of the Native American culture that the Corps found there and references to two important forts nearby:

> The Missouri-Yellowstone Confluence Interpretive Center (MYCIC) held its grand opening in August 2003. The $2.2 million center tells the history and prehistory of the area near the confluence of the Missouri and Yellowstone Rivers and includes a 2,000-square-foot permanent exhibit, *Trails, Tracks, Rivers, and Roads*. The 8,600-square-foot facility was built with local, state, and federal funding. It attracted more than 24,000 visitors from all 50 states and 20 countries its first year.[1]

The Center, a modern round structure, sits on a slight rise overlooking the great expanse of the fertile plains that stretch away for miles from the two rivers. When Lewis first arrived, he noted that "the whole face of the country was covered with herds of buffalo, elk, and antelopes . . . so gentle that we pass near them while feeding without appearing to excite any alarm among them; and when we attract their attention, they frequently approach us more nearly to discover what we are."[2] Other than the interpretive center, the entire area is undeveloped, a glimpse of the sweeping wilderness that Lewis and Clark encountered in 1805. Long before their arrival, however, it was a favored hunting ground for Native Americans who traveled from all directions to harvest the abundant wildlife that Lewis described.

Nearby is the Fort Buford Historic Site, built in 1866 and named for Major General John Buford of Gettysburg fame. It became a major supply depot for military field operations during the sustained war to subdue and "civilize" the Native Americans. The site includes a stone powder magazine, the post cemetery, and a large officers' quarters, which houses a museum. Like many of the forts established throughout the West, it was charged with protecting the ever-increasing waves of immigrants and the development of railroads. It was here that Sitting Bull finally surrendered in 1881. The fort was abandoned on October 1, 1895, almost five years after the last resisting Oglala Chief Kicking Bear had surrendered his arms at Pine Ridge Reservation on January 15, 1891.[3] I did not loiter long at this melancholy reminder of the relentless war that ultimately all but destroyed the spirit and culture of America's original inhabitants.

Fort Union Trading Post, less than four miles up the river along ND 1804 and straddling the North Dakota/Montana state line, tells a happier story of the white man's early exploration and settlement of the region. The National Historic Site is a careful, research-based reconstruction of the fort-like post that was built in 1828 by John Jacob Astor's American Fur Company, an international business which he had launched in 1808. The impressive complex was rebuilt on the exact same spot as the original after 1966 when the National Park Service acquired the land, at the time merely a grassy plain. The trading post is bounded by a sturdy 18-foot palisade that runs 240 feet east to west and 220 feet north to south. At its center is the handsome replica of the Bourgeois House, where the post's chief field agent lived and took his meals with others.

A vibrant trading center for 39 years (1828-1867), at its peak the post employed more than 100 people. They included skilled craftsmen, traders, hunters, interpreters, and common laborers. The sustained, mutually beneficial success of this commercial venture gives one a glimpse of what might have been. Multiple Indian tribes actively traded furs for goods from back East and Europe. The furs included buffalo, beaver, fox, otter, and others. Each of the parties to the trading was confident that they had the better of the others. The Indians thought the whites overvalued the furs. For example, nine buffalo robes equaled one gun, one of the most valued items. In addition, the whites brought blankets, cloth, pots, cups, knives, beads, and other items that were useful to the tribes.

Over time, the white traders took Indian wives as white women were virtually absent on the upper reaches of the Missouri. These marriages were both economic and personal bonds, further cementing the cordial relations between the new arrivals and the Native Americans who had lived on the Plains for hundreds of years. It was not until after the Civil War with the coming of hordes of pioneers that the cordiality turned to conflict as the Indians rightly saw their way of life threatened. The U. S. government bought Fort Union in 1867, dismantled it and expanded Fort Buford. An era of peaceful and mutually beneficial cooperation was ending.

Fort Union is a well-done glimpse back in time. It has the curious distinction of straddling the North Dakota/Montana border. One enters the complex in Montana in the Mountain Time Zone, but after parking my car, I walked back across the North Dakota border to find myself back in the Central Time Zone. According to my logbook, I left there about 10:25, which must have been 11:25 Williston time.

Wishing to avoid a rather small backtrack to get on U.S. 2, my primary route across the state toward Great Falls, I set out on MT 327 diagonally cross country toward Bainville. The road was unpaved but firm, dry and well graded. It ran along a rail line across some magnificent country that I was able to enjoy in splendid isolation. Independence Day, indeed!

I had this 15-mile stretch of unpaved road all to myself, followed only by the billowing dust that I kicked up. It took less than a half hour to reach Bainville, a tiny town of an estimated 314 souls located just south of U.S. 2. Although I did not tarry, their web site, which I consulted later, is impressive. Although clearly not a wealthy place, their civic pride is nicely reflected in this declaration:

> In the Town of Bainville, we are defined less by boundaries on a map than by the sense of shared values our residents hold dear. Small town values, guided growth, preservation of historical, cultural, and natural heritage are just a few of the core principles that make Town of Bainville a wonderful place to call home.[4]

They appear to have an active Town Council that meets monthly, a volunteer fire department, a public school system—the "Mighty Bulldogs" (K-12), three houses of worship (Lutheran, Catholic, and an independent, nondenominational congregation known as Faith Fellowship), a senior center where lunch is served on Tuesdays and Thursdays ($5 for those over 60, $9 for those under), and the Pioneer's

Pride Museum, which features a 1929 fire truck (admission free). The range of activities and services is impressive for such a small place. When I checked their website on April 7, 2020, the town appeared to be sheltering in place like much of the rest of the country in response to the Covid-19 pandemic.

About an hour west is the town of Wolf Point where I stopped for lunch at a McDonald's. Although I tried to avoid this largest of fast-food places on my trip, there was something comforting about this choice on the Fourth of July. Not surprisingly, it was not very busy as most folks were likely preparing or already enjoying cookouts with their friends and families. I was reminded of the early days of my marriage when my wife and I had left our home and families in Atlanta to live in South Bend where I pursued graduate study at Notre Dame. We were married only a little more than a year and were homesick, utterly on our own in what seemed at the time an alien culture, another world. We would assuage our homesickness by having dinner at McDonald's occasionally. Having worked at our local McDonald's when I was in high school, there was an illusion of being home as we enjoyed the perfect uniformity of their French fries and cheeseburgers. Although a strategy that involves more risk, I more often ate at locally owned and operated places that in some way reflected the culture of whatever town I was in. The results were, for the most part, at least satisfactory.

In May 1805, Lewis and Clark passed through the area that became the city of Wolf Point. The origin of its name is a matter of debate outlined in detail on its website. Some say the name came from a nearby river with reference to the abundant wolf population in the area. Others claim reference to a landmark that appeared to resemble a wolf. The most popular story was provided by a Pony Express rider named William Bent, a nephew of Kit Carson, who claimed that "Wolf Point got its name from the fact that one winter the wolfers killed such a large number of wolves that they froze before the skins could be removed. The frozen carcasses were piled near the river to wait the coming of spring and the pile was so high, it became a landmark for all the country around."[5]

Incorporated in 1915, Wolf Point is the county seat of Roosevelt County, has a population of some 2700, and is in the center of the Fort Peck Indian Reservation. It boasts of being home to the annual Wild

Horse Stampede in the second weekend of July, which claims to be the oldest rodeo in Montana.[6] I just missed it!

The city's *Wikipedia* entry notes that William Least Heat-Moon wrote of an uncomfortable night he spent in Wolf Point in *Blue Highways: A Journey into America* (1982), which I had read the year after my journey. I had to look up the passage. Heat-Moon happened to visit Wolf Point during one of the fierce rainstorms that are not uncommon on the Great Plains. The streets were filled with muddy water, and the rain drummed throughout the night on the thin metal roof of his battered van. Recalling the story of the frozen stacks of wolf carcasses, he noted that wolves were never again seen in the area, and wryly observed that after his one night there, "I couldn't imagine man or beast contending for the place."[7] I imagine the folks in Wolf Point's Chamber of Commerce are not too pleased that this literary reference is in its *Wikipedia* entry.

Heat-Moon also ruefully commented on the eradication of the buffalo in this area and throughout the plains: "And so the American Bison, a symbol to both red and white, disappeared even faster than the way of life it engendered."[8] I was pleased to learn that in 2012 an effort to restore the American Bison was initiated when 63 of the creatures were transferred from Yellowstone National Park to Fort Peck Indian Reservation and released on a 2100-acre preserve. In November 2014 an additional 136 American Bison from Yellowstone were added to the Fort Peck herd, and the preserve was enlarged to 13,000 acres. Fort Peck Fish and Game authority has a goal of 1000, which scientists regard as the minimum required for sustainable restoration. I hope Heat-Moon is pleased with this effort and others like the one at Custer State Park, which I had visited a few days before.[9]

Fort Peck Indian Reservation is home to some 10,000 Native Americans, including the Assiniboine, Nakota, Lakota, and Dakota peoples. It stretches more than 100 miles east to west and has a total land area of more than two million acres. Some 6000 Native Americans live on the Reservation in a self-governing community and own almost half of the reservation land. It is the ninth largest Indian reservation in the U. S.[10]

After my brief stop in Wolf Point, I headed west to find the Fort Peck Dam Interpretive Center and Museum, which Fanselow describes with admiration in her guide. I cannot recall how I went wrong, but after fumbling around the lake and crossing the dam, I somehow failed to find the place. The dam and lake alone, however, were worth the busted play. The earth-filled dam is more than 21,000 feet long, 3500 feet wide at its base, and 250 feet high. The lake thereby created has a storage capacity of nineteen million acre-feet of water and a surface area of 249,000 acres. As Fanselow observes, "[t]he lake stretches about 150 miles west, more than the distance . . . between Pittsburgh and Cleveland." Its shoreline is almost 1600 miles, more than the length of California. I could not begin to explore this great inland lake, but I did see enough to admire the achievement of the thing even as I recognized that it completely changes the landscape that Lewis and Clark first saw in 1805. How I missed the Interpretive Center and Museum remains a mystery, but after wandering about and admiring the area, I realized that I still had almost 300 miles to Great Falls.

At about 1:45 p.m., I made my way back to U. S. 2 near Glasgow (population 3600) and headed west. My next stop was a little crossroads called Loma where the Marias River flows into the Missouri. My high-speed pace across northcentral Montana on a warm, clear day was pleasant enough. The successive miles of sweeping prairies, some covered in grass for cattle grazing and some under active cultivation offered a variety of vistas that made me feel like an ant crawling across a picnic table.

Loma was some 220 miles away in Chouteau County, the largest wheat-producing county in Montana. In 2015, it produced 19.5 million bushels of wheat, two and a half times more than the next county in the state. Although miles of wheat fields dominated my view across the state, one of the more memorable images was of massive fields of bright yellow flowers shining in the summer sun. I discovered only later that this was canola, a Montana cash crop that is increasingly important in the state, but I also learned that North Dakota and Minnesota dominate production of canola in the U.S. (84 percent in 2019.)

Planting canola in the U. S. began in 1988, following Canada, which introduced the crop in 1974. Acreage devoted to canola in the U. S. has increased dramatically since 1991 from fewer than 300,000 acres to more than two million in 2017, yielding some 7.2 billion pounds.

"Not only does canola provide high-value canola oil and meal, it benefits other crops like wheat in rotation by breaking up pest and disease cycles as well as provides ideal habitat for pollinators," according to the U. S. Department of Agriculture.[11]

Agriculture is the biggest business in Montana. In 2015, its economic impact was $4.6 billion, more than $1.5 billion greater than the next largest business, travel. It's interesting to note, however, that agricultural impact has been declining, down from $5.3 billion in 2013. In 2015, there were 27,500 farms in the state. Although this includes smaller farms, the average acreage exceeds 2000, and there are hundreds that are much larger.[12] Given the severe winters, the growing season is only about six months and for many crops only about three. Montana farmers surely work hard in these conditions but are blessed with fine soil in many parts of the state. About 65.8% of the land is pasture and range; only about 28.5% is cropland.[13]

In my trek across the state, I saw a lot of pasture, range, and cropland in this sparsely populated state of just under 1.1 million, an eight percent increase since the 2010 census. That's about seven souls per mile, making Montana 44th in population density among U.S. states. It is the fourth largest state, following Alaska, Texas, and California. At 147,000 square miles, Montana dwarfs the larger states east of the Mississippi. The largest is Florida with more than 65,700 square miles. Pennsylvania has only 46,000 square miles.

Shifting nationwide population had a substantial impact on congressional seats following the 2020 census. Until then, Montana was one of seven states with only one U.S. Congressman. Alaska, Wyoming, North Dakota, South Dakota, Vermont, and Delaware were the others. It was not always so; the state had two congressional seats up until reapportionment following the 1990 census. It was one of five to gain a seat after the most-recent census. Texas gained two seats while Montana, Colorado, Florida, North Carolina, and Oregon each gained one. Since this is a zero-sum game, seven states lost a seat: California, Illinois, Michigan, New York, Ohio, Pennsylvania, and West Virginia. It would be California's first such loss since it became a state in 1850. The ancient art of gerrymandering will certainly be deployed as this significant shift in congressional representation occurs. Predictions are always risky, but it appears that blue states have lost to red states in this reshuffling of Congressional seats.[14]

Montana's top ten agricultural products follow in order: Beef cattle (2.6 million head or about 2.5 per person), wheat (fourth in the nation), hay (11th in the nation), barley (565,000 acres in 2017), lentil (top producer in the U.S.), dry peas (41% of U.S. production), sugar beets, dairy, hogs, dry edible beans.[15] Behind such a list lies hours of toil, sweat, frustration, and anxiety, busted knuckles, aching backs, and broken hearts. Although not immediate, there were enough farmers in my family that I am not tempted to romanticize their hard life. God bless those who feed us!

I made my way across the so-called Hi-Line (U.S. Highway 2) from Glasgow to Havre, some 160 miles, in about two and a half hours. Along the way, I passed through the tiny towns of Hinsdale (pop. 217), Saco (pop. 197), Malta (pop. 1997), Dodson (pop. 124), Harlem (pop. 808), Zurich (pop. 55), and Chinook (pop. 1203). The landscape was mostly rolling plains, quite majestic, but eventually somewhat monotonous. Even beauty becomes stale with overexposure. From Havre, I headed southwest on U.S. 87 toward Loma and then on to Fort Benton.

Just before reaching the confluence of the Marias River and the Missouri, I came upon a historical marker with the heading "A Missouri Crossroads." It reads as follows:

The Missouri River once flowed northeasterly through this valley to Hudson Bay. During the Bull Lake Ice Age, an ice dam near Loma diverted the river into its current channel. This channel began filling with glacial sediment, preventing the river from returning to its original course when the dam finally broke about 70,000 to 130,000 years ago. Several sections of the highway between Loma and Havre follow Big Sandy Creek, which is located in the old river channel.

From this point there is also a panoramic view of the drainages of three major Montana river systems.: The Teton, Marias, and Missouri. To the southwest, the Teton and Marias Rivers merge near Loma before joining the Missouri River about a mile downstream. In the background are the Bear's Paw Mountains to the east, Square Butte and Round Butte to the southeast, the Highwood Mountains toward the south, and the Little Belt Mountains in the southwest.

Because of the geography, this area was the crossroads for many events important to Montana history. The Lewis and Clark Expedition passed through here in 1805. They were followed by fur traders, the steamboat, the Great Northern Railway and the homesteaders.[16]

Arriving at this point on June 2, 1805, Lewis and Clark were surprised to discover a substantial river flowing from the north. At that time of year, still swollen with spring rain and snow melt from the nearby mountains, the unknown river was almost as wide as the Missouri. Their Indian friends from the previous winter had not mentioned such a river, so the explorers faced a dilemma. Which of the two was the Missouri? They spent the next several days exploring both the northerly river and the southerly one. The captains became convinced that the southerly river was the true Missouri, but the entire remainder of the Corps was convinced that the northern river was the correct route. Although Lewis and Clark maintained firm military discipline, they also routinely consulted with their men and gave them opportunities to weigh in on important decisions. In this instance, the two captains overruled their dissenting Corps but without complaint.

Some passages from Lewis's journal make clear how momentous this decision was:

> To mistake the stream at this period of the season, two months of the traveling season having now elapsed, and to ascend such to the rocky mountain or perhaps much further—and then be obliged to return and take the other stream would not only loose [sic] us the whole of this season but would probably so dishearten the party that it might defeat the expedition altogether.[17]

Just down the road from the historical marker is a small, covered observation deck with helpful interpretive signs marking what is now called Decision Point. It offers a commanding view of the area where the Corps of Discovery spent nine days trying to determine which of the two rivers was the Missouri. This area's visual beauty is beyond description, from the sweeping curves of the river set against lofty white cliffs, to the rugged Great Falls that Lewis discovered on June 13. Lewis charmingly acknowledges the difficulty of describing the beauty of the falls: "I wished for the pencil of Salvator Rosa or the pen of Thompson that I might be enabled to give to the enlightened world some just idea of this truly magnificent and sublimely grand object" (June 13, 1805).

After admiring the stunning panoramic views from the observation point, I headed down the road to nearby Fort Benton. Although quite small (est. 2018 pop. 1,443), Fort Benton, founded in 1846, merits more time than I had to give as the day was waning along with my energy. In its few blocks are monuments, memorials and museums that recall the days of its glory as the "oldest continuously inhabited settlement in Montana." Describing itself as "the birthplace of Montana," it is a National Historic Landmark among many other historic designations. In its heyday, it was the world's innermost port as the terminus for steamboat traffic up the Missouri. From 1860 till 1887, most of the freight for the Northwest U. S. and Western Canada was unloaded on the levee along the town's riverfront. It is named for the colorful Missouri Senator Thomas Hart Benton, an avid proponent of "Manifest Destiny," who authored the first Homestead Act. He served in the Senate for 30 years, one of the first two U. S. Senators elected after Missouri achieved statehood. It seems a felicitous naming since Fort Benton stands as an important symbol of America's rapid expansion west.

The steamboat era grew and expanded through the 1880s, becoming the principal means for trade as well as transportation of homesteaders and other travelers. As Fanselow notes, "Fort Benton has many claims to historical fame, but perhaps none so mighty as its reign during the steamboat era, when as many as ten steamboats a day tied up at its waterfront. In its heyday, Fort Benton also boasted what was known as 'the wildest block in the West,' jam-packed with bars, dance halls, and brothels." The trip from St. Louis on a steamboat took about two months, a stunning pace when compared to that of man-powered boats such as those that the Corps of Discovery had used. Passenger fare on a steamboat averaged $150, a considerable sum in those days. In 1867, a busy year, Fanselow notes that some 1500 people reached Montana by steamboat. The peak of river traffic was 1879, "when forty-seven boats carried 9,444 tons of cargo up the river."[18]

132

"Explorers at the Marias" by Bob Scriver, Fort Benton, Montana

I paused to admire the handsome official Montana Lewis and Clark Monument overlooking the river. Entitled "Explorers at the Marias," the massive bronze sculpture was created by Bob Scriver (1914-1999) to commemorate the country's bicentennial in 1976. It features Sacagawea with her infant swaddled on her back seated at the foot of Captain Lewis, who is gazing west through a long telescope while Clark, at his left side, holds his rifle in his right hand and takes a

133

reading from a square compass that is said to have been modeled after the actual one he used. Fanselow records that the sculptor researched the project for a year to ensure the greatest accuracy possible in the "equipment, clothing, body features, and faces." She notes that Sacagawea's baby is wrapped snugly in a blanket tied to his mother's back because the pack board on which she had previously carried him had been lost overboard a few days earlier. The "heroic-scale" monument is one-sixth larger than life-sized, weighs 2.5 tons, is 21 feet high, and sits on an 85-ton granite base.[19] Scriver, from Browning, Montana, was a highly regarded artist of the Old West and an authority on Native American culture. He regarded his Lewis and Clark sculpture as the best of his creations. One of the finer sculptures on the trail, it alone is worth the visit to Fort Benton, but I do wish I had given myself a half day to see the other historic sites. Indeed, if one wished to explore this historic and beautiful area, Fort Benton would be a strong contender for a base camp.[20]

The last leg of my long Independence Day trek was 40 miles to the Best Western Plus Hotel (now Heritage Inn on Fox Falls Road) in Great Falls. Traveling up U. S. 87 at a brisk pace, I arrived around 7:30 p.m. It took the Corps of Discovery eleven grueling days to portage the five formidable falls they encountered on June 13, 1805, some 18 miles, a distance they would normally have covered in an average day. Altogether, they spent more than a month in the Great Falls area, more than any site other than their two winter camps.

At day's end, I had logged 459.1 miles. My trip total since leaving Gettysburg was 3733.9. Fort Clatsop, the Corps' winter 1805-06 quarters and my ultimate destination at the mouth of the Columbia, was only 805 miles away, but my route included several detours and diversions that would push my arrival back to July 15.

Chapter Seventeen
Great Falls, Montana

June 13, 1805: Captain Lewis reaches the foot of The Great Falls and laments his inability to describe "this sublimely grand spectacle . . . the grandest sight I ever beheld."[1]

When I arrived at the Best Western Plus in Great Falls, I was road weary and having one of those moments wondering why I had thought this arduous journey was a great idea. I had also forgotten why I had selected Great Falls as a destination. Although the inn I had selected was adequate, it was a bit tired, not up to the standard of the Best Western Plus in French Lick, Indiana. For some reason, I recall that the luggage carts were too long to fit straight in the small elevators, just a minor annoyance, but one of those small things that makes one wonder what else the proprietors have failed to notice. I had dinner at the inn, served by a very pleasant young woman in a mostly empty restaurant as the hour was late.

Back in my room after dinner, I consulted Fanselow to refresh my memory on the importance of Great Falls in the Corps of Discovery's journey. Leaving aside the two brutal winters they had endured, it was the most physically demanding challenge they had yet faced. Reading Fanselow's account of the portage and Ambrose's excellent chapter on "The Great Portage: June 16-July 14, 1805" restored my confidence in my judgment. I was looking forward to a day of sightseeing and immersion in this spectacular stretch of the Missouri with the five falls that were such a formidable obstacle to the "undaunted courage" of the intrepid explorers.

I left the hotel after breakfast on the morning of July 5. It was another beautiful, clear, blue-sky summer day that promised a warm sun in a cloudless sky. My first task was to find a pharmacy where I could purchase a battery for my glucometer. My brief experience at a nearby CVS felt like a good omen for the day. I quickly found a rack filled with various batteries and, to my surprise and delight, the first bubble pack I touched contained the specific battery I needed—not my typical experience on such a mission. Perhaps listening to Mary Chapin Carpenter singing "I Feel Lucky" as I pulled into the parking lot set the tone.

The clerk, who wore a little plastic nameplate inscribed with "Franky," was warm and friendly. Since she asked what brought me to Great Falls, I briefly outlined my project. She seemed genuinely interested and there were no other customers to be served, so I shared the three questions I had been posing to others. To the first, she responded without hesitation, "freedom, for sure, but so much more." As for the second, she simply said she was not worried about much of anything. She explained it in personal terms related to her daily work: "For every troubled or troubling person, a good soul comes in." (I hoped I was one of the latter.) Then she asked me if I were "religious." When I affirmed that some might so describe me, she asked if I knew about a book and movie called "The Shack" and encouraged me to check it out. "God is out there," she assured me. We wished one another a good day, and I left feeling buoyed by our conversation. God has a way of turning up in unexpected places, perhaps more often than most realize as we fumble obtusely through our daily lives.

As I told "Franky," I had not heard of *The Shack* but thanked her for her recommendation. I made a note of it in my daily log and filed it away. The film had just come out earlier that spring (2017). Not until I was writing this account did I look into the book and its Canadian author, William Paul Young.[2] I finally read *The Shack* a few weeks before completing this book and can see how many have found it a deeply moving experience. Before reading it, I found on YouTube a brief "book tour" interview from the 700 Club, not my regular fare although I have long been familiar with it and its famous (or some would say infamous) founder, a fellow W&L alumnus, the evangelist Pat Robertson. Originally written as a gift for his six children, *The Shack* was self-published at the urging of friends in 2007 and became a word-of-mouth *New York Times* bestseller in 2008. By 2010 it had sold more than 10 million copies and been widely recognized as a "life changer."

During a brief tour of downtown Great Falls, I saw a fine sculpture of the famed local son and cowboy artist Charles M. Russell (1864-1926) outside the museum named in his honor. Although the people of Great Falls are justly proud of the C. M. Russell Museum, I did not invest the time to visit, as it represented a substantial detour from my primary focus. As with many other places along my journey, Great Falls merits more time than I had allowed. (See note at end of chapter.)*

I made my way to the Lewis and Clark National Historic Trail Interpretive Center, which is perched dramatically on the western bluffs overlooking the river. Of the many impressive such sites along the trail, this was the best I would see. Fanselow writes glowingly of the $6 million center, opened in 1998 and upgraded in 2003, as "one of the nation's most compelling and comprehensive looks at the expedition and its legacy."[3]

As I walked into the center, a huge, black Newfoundland dog greeted me warmly. I enjoyed petting the dog and having my picture made with him as I sat next to him on the floor. It was the closest thing to a hug I had had in quite a while, and I realized I missed our little dog. I spent the next couple of hours admiring the many exhibits housed in the 5500 square feet of the center. These include a striking, life-sized diorama of the men laboring to pull a loaded canoe up a steep, rocky hill that runs from the lower level up to the main floor near the entrance. The canoe, at least 30-feet long, was mounted on small wheels that the men had carved from cottonwood trees at their base camp below the falls.

One of the recurring themes in the journals is the importance of cottonwood trees. Ambrose notes what a welcome sight these large, shady trees are to anyone who has canoed on the upper Missouri River: "They provide shade, shelter and fuel. For Indian ponies, they provided food. For the Corps of Discovery, they provided wheels, wagons, and canoes." He goes on to quote the Lewis and Clark scholar Paul Russell Cutright's tribute: "Of all the western trees it contributed more to the success of the Expedition than any other. Lewis and Clark were men of great talent and resourcefulness, masters of ingenuity and improvisation. Though we think it probable that they would have successfully crossed the continent without the cottonwood, don't ask us how!"[4]

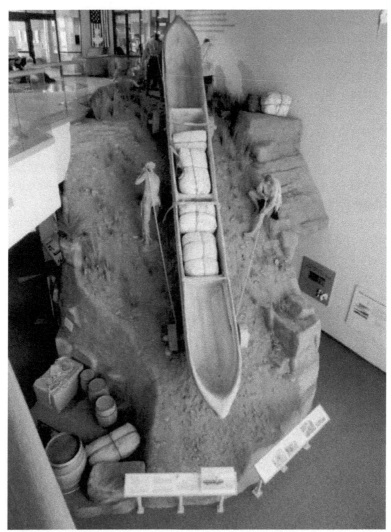

The Lewis and Clark Interpretive Center, Great Falls, Montana

In his journal entry of June 23, 1805, Lewis described the laborious portage as so exhausting that the men were "obliged to halt and rest frequently for a few minutes. At every halt these poor fellow tumble down and are so much fortiegued that many of them are asleep in an instant . . . some are limping from the soreness of their feet, others faint and unable to stand for a few minutes, with heat and fatiegue, yet no one complains. All go with cheerfullness."[5] This passage illustrates nicely the random variations of Lewis's spelling, almost as if he's proudly showing how inventive he can be in spelling the same word!

The first floor includes a small theatre where I viewed the 30-minute documentary film created especially for the center by Ken Burns and Dayton Duncan. It is based on the excellent four-hour, PBS documentary, "Lewis & Clark: The Journey of the Corps of Discovery," (1997). Another film produced by Gray Wariner, "Lewis and Clark: Confluence of Time and Courage," focuses on the portage; it is a 20-minute excerpt from a longer film originally produced for the U. S. Army Corps of Engineers in 2004.[6]

On the lower level is the center's main exhibit entitled "Journey Through a Crowded Wilderness," which presents the Lewis and Clark story from two perspectives: the Corps of Discovery's and the Native Americans'. As Fanselow observes, "Here, more than anywhere else along the trail, native contributions to the expedition are given their due, and the captains are gently taken to task for not fully appreciating the tribes they encountered."[7] Of course, Lewis and Clark were products of European education and experience. Like all of us, they brought their biases with them, and like most who followed them, they could not be expected to comprehend the complex social, political, and spiritual cultures that they encountered. The murderous conflicts that followed were perhaps inevitable.

After immersing myself in the exhibits inside the center, I walked out on the grounds to enjoy an interpretive trail leading down to the river. I left a bit after noon to get lunch at the nearby Montana Club, which one of the center's staff had recommended. This proved more than satisfactory.

In the afternoon, I drove down the eastern side of the river to Morony Dam, a large (883 feet long by 94 feet high) hydroelectric dam that was completed in 1930. It is located at the lower point of the five falls that the Corps of Discovery encountered in 1805, near the base camp they established for the grueling 11-day portage up an elevation of more than 600 feet from the first of the falls to the last; this includes 187 feet of vertical plunges and 425 feet of riverbed descent.

A historical marker outside the Interpretive Center notes the ready power source that the falls represented to early settlers: "Five dams now lasso the river and regulate its water levels and current" where the five falls once thundered before the amazed eyes of Lewis, who first encountered them on June 13, 1805, and felt defeated in his effort to describe "the grandest sight I ever beheld." Although still a grand sight, it is undoubtedly a much tamer one than Lewis and his compatriots encountered. Only Crooked Falls appears much as it did when Lewis first saw it.

From downstream up to the present-day community known as Black Eagle, across the river from Great Falls, these are the falls:

Big Falls, also confusingly known as "Great Falls," 87 feet.
Crooked Falls, also known as Horseshoe Falls, 19 feet.
Rainbow Falls, 44 feet, 6 inches.
Colter Falls, 6 feet, 7 inches.
Black Eagle Falls, 26 feet, 5 inches.

It doesn't require much imagination to understand how Lewis quickly realized that these obstacles would require portage. He walked up the northeast side of the river to what is today known as Smelter Hill, not far from where I had lunch and near the community of Black Eagle. From that lofty perch he determined that the south side of the river would be the least difficult to portage.

The other four dams upstream from Morony are shown on the helpful interpretive sign overlooking the river at the center:

Ryan Dam was built on top of the Great Falls (or Big Falls) in 1915. Cochrane Dam was completed in 1958. Rainbow Dam was built on Rainbow Falls and submerged Colter Falls in 1910. Black Eagle Dam, the first hydroelectric dam in the state, was built in 1880.[8]

I later discovered that the five dams at Great Falls represent one third of the 15 "mainstem" dams on the Missouri River. There are another 21 substantial dams on the various tributaries of the great river, but in total there are 17,200 dams of varying size and scope along the river's basin. Most of these are smaller irrigation dams, but surely "lasso" is a charming understatement for how men have harnessed the power of this mighty natural resource, the longest river in the country.[9]

On the second day [June 14, 1805] that the expedition camped near the series of falls, Lewis discovered Black Eagle Falls. In his journal, he described the last of the five falls: "I arrived at another cataract of 26 feet . . . below this fall at a little distance a beautiful little Island well timbered is situated about the middle of the river. in this Island on a Cottonwood tree an Eagle has placed her nest; a more inaccessible spot I believe she could not have found; for neither man nor beast dare pass those gulphs which separate her little domain from the shores."[10]

That charming island in the river is now accessible by a suspended footbridge that gave me access to this little park from which I could view the nearby Black Eagle Dam just upstream and the rushing waters of the river on either side of this grassy, wooded retreat. No sign of an eagle, but it was a peaceful, pastoral detour.

On the southwestern bluffs overlooking the river is a pull-off with a sign explaining how Smelter Hill across the river came to be named:

> In 1891, the Boston and Montana Consolidated Copper and Silver Mining Company constructed a massive smelter complex on the hill overlooking the site of the nest. The smelter processed copper from Butte until 1918 when the Anaconda Company converted it into an electrolytic copper and zinc refinery.
>
> Three communities, Little Chicago, Little Milwaukee, and North Great Falls, developed in the shadow of the 506-foot smokestack at the top of Smelter Hill. Men from all over North America and Europe came to work in the complex at Black Eagle, as it was known by 1916. A truly cosmopolitan community, all worked together in the plant, maintained their ethnic diversity and rubbed elbows in the vibrant business district along Smelter Avenue. Although the refinery shut down in 1980 and the stack razed two years later, Black Eagle remains a working-class community proud of its rich history.

Now the third-largest city in Montana, Great Falls was the largest until 1970 when it was eclipsed by Billings and later by Missoula. Nicknamed "the electric city," its population in 2017 was estimated at 58,638 (60,422 in the 2020 census). The cultural diversity described in the historical plaque above has apparently dissipated as the 2010 census shows a racial makeup that was 88.5% Caucasian, only 1.1% African American, 5.0% Native American and less than 1.0% each Asian, Pacific Islander, and other. Hispanic and Latino people were 3.4% of the population.[11] Of course, most European immigrants who worked in the smelter complex were Caucasian, so their descendants surely contribute to a rich cultural mix that reflects the legacy of thousands who settled all across the West through the 19th and well into the 20th centuries.

At the end of this beautiful and interesting day, I made my way back to my hotel for a well-earned night's rest. Although I had walked a great deal, I had only driven 74.9 miles, a welcome respite from the previous day. My total mileage was 3808.8.

*C. M. Russell Museum Complex is an art museum located in the city of Great Falls, Montana, in the United States. The museum's primary function is to display the artwork of Great Falls "cowboy artist" Charles Marion Russell, for whom the museum is named. The museum also displays illustrated letters by Russell, work materials used by him, and other items which help visitors understand the life and working habits of Russell. In addition, the museum displays original 19th, 20th, and 21st century art depicting the American Old West and the flora, fauna, and landscapes of the American West. In 2009, the *Wall Street Journal* called the institution "one of America's premier Western art museums." Located on the museum property is Russell's log cabin studio, as well as his two-story wood frame home. The house and log cabin studio were designated a National Historic Landmark in 1965, and added to the National Register of Historic Places in 1966. In 1976, the listing boundaries were amended to account for moving the house.[12]

Chapter Eighteen
Discoveries at Helena and Golf at Old Works

July 27, 1805: The Corps reaches the Three Forks of the Missouri in southwest Montana, 80 miles east of Anaconda and 70 miles southeast of Helena, now the state capital. After multiple frustrating failures, they meet the Shoshones, Sacagawea's tribe from which she had been kidnapped by a Hidatsa war party five years earlier.

State Capitol, Helena, Montana

Thursday, July 6, dawned bright and beautiful, promising to be another great day for touring a segment of the Lewis and Clark Trail into the soaring mountains for which the state is named. I was also looking forward to a round of golf at the Old Works in Anaconda some 180 miles southwest of Great Falls by way of Helena, the state capital.

Eager to get on the road, I left the hotel around 7:20 a.m. Given my 1 p.m. tee time, I took I-15 along the river rather than the more leisurely old U. S. Route 91, a Great Depression-era road that runs more closely alongside the twists and turns of the river through some of the most spectacular scenery on the trail. The views along I-15 were sufficiently grand to satisfy me.

Until I reached Helena, my route was close to that of the Corps of Discovery, which they traveled in mid-July 1805. Knowing that they were approaching the point where they would need to find passage across the mountains, their overarching interest was in locating Sacagawea's Shoshone people from whom she had been abducted five years earlier. After some false starts, they were ultimately able to secure horses and a guide from the Shoshones. It helped greatly that Sacagawea's brother was a chief. Without this assistance, their grueling passage across the Rockies might not have been completed before another winter intervened.

Soon after leaving Great Falls, the rolling plains that had characterized my Fourth of July trek across Montana gave way to a variety of impressive mountain ranges. Within a half hour, I reached the area known as The Gates of the Mountains. Lewis described it in his journal entry of July 19, 1805:

> This evening we entered much the most remarkable clifts that we have yet seen. These clifts rise from the waters edge on either side perpendicularly to the hight of (about) 1200 feet. Every object here wears a dark and gloomy aspect. The towering and projecting rocks in many places seem ready to tumble on us . . . . From the singular appearance of this place I called it *the gates of the rocky mountains.*[1]

I reached the beautiful state capital around 9:20, grabbed a coffee at a Starbuck's, and proceeded to tour the downtown with my primary focus on its capitol, which sits on ten acres of landscaped grounds overlooking the downtown. Established in 1864 after gold was discovered nearby, Helena is the county seat of Lewis and Clark County. Its population of 32,000 makes it the fifth least populous state capital in the country and the sixth largest city in Montana.[2]

I later learned that after Montana became the nation's 41st state in 1889, an election was held to determine the site of the permanent state capital. There were seven candidates on the ballot; in the first round of voting, Helena and Anaconda received the most votes, but neither had a majority. Helena prevailed in a runoff two years later.[3]

It is one of those small decisions that in retrospect had momentous consequences. Both Helena and Anaconda are tucked away in the mountains far from the geographical center of this large state. Neither seems a logical or convenient site for the state capital, but the stark contrast between tiny Anaconda, with a population of fewer than 10,000, and the bustling affluence of Helena reflects both the legacy of the wealth generated by the gold rush of the 1860s as well as the more enduring economic boon of the state's government.

The capitol, which is listed on the National Register of Historic Places, is built of Montana sandstone and granite in a Greek neoclassical design, like so many of its U. S. counterparts. It is crowned by a copper-covered dome with a female statue that was until recently known as Lady Liberty.[4] The main section of the capitol was dedicated on July 4, 1902, after a somewhat shaky start that included the termination of the original planning committee because of corruption and the suicide of the state's chief architect. Its two additional wings were completed in 1912.[5]

I later learned of an intriguing story with a Pennsylvania connection associated with the statue of "Lady Liberty." Apparently commissioned by the original capitol planning committee, the imposing, 17-foot copper-sheathed, bronze sculpture of a robed woman carrying a torch and a shield arrived by train a few years after the committee had been disbanded and all its records destroyed. Local officials correctly assumed it must have been ordered for the new capitol, so it was installed on September 1, 1901, but with no knowledge of the sculptor.

It was not until 2006 that the rest of the story unfolded following an email from a Pennsylvania woman named Alice Nagle. She had been going through her deceased grandfather's papers and found records of a sculpture he had done for the state of Montana. She wrote the Montana Historical Society to ask if her grandfather's sculpture still "graced the dome."[6]

Her grandfather was, in fact, a well-known sculptor named Edward J. Van Landeghem. Born in Belgium in 1865 and trained at the Academy of Fine Arts in Brussels, he and his wife immigrated to the U. S. in 1899 and settled in Philadelphia. Some of his other commissions include a statue of the Virgin Mary at The Catholic

University of America in Washington, D.C.; a George Washington statue for the Masonic Hall in Lansdale, Pa.; and a bas relief entitled "Washington's Greatest Moments of Despair," which is in the Valley Forge Memorial Chapel Museum.

Little is known about how Van Landeghem, who died in 1955, received the commission for Montana, but Nagle informed the historical society officials that he had named her "Montana." In a formal ceremony later in 2006, the sculpture was officially dedicated as "Montana" to the delight of many in Montana, but especially women of the state who were quick to point out the important role that courageous women have played in the state's history, noting with pride that women in Montana secured the vote six years before the nation extended that right to all women with ratification of the 19th Amendment in 1920.

In 2014, "the Montana Capitol Restoration Foundation in cooperation with the Montana Historical Society released its ninth annual Christmas ornament, this year displaying 'Montana,' the statue that sits atop the Capitol dome, and highlighting the artist who created her yet remained cloaked in mystery for more than a century." Nagle and her daughter were present to receive their own ornaments in a ceremony hosted by the Montana Historical Society. The ornament includes Van Landeghem's name etched on its back.[7]

Anyone visiting the capitol will notice an imposing equestrian sculpture directly in front of the building on an eight-foot-high granite base. The bronze figure represents Thomas Francis Meagher (1823-1867), one of the more colorful and controversial characters in Montana's history. Created by Irish-born Chicago sculptor Charles J. Mulligan (1866-1916), the sculpture is described "as much a tribute to the many Irish immigrants who made Montana their home as it is to Meagher himself. The Meagher Memorial Association raised $20,000 . . . for the statue, which was dedicated on July 4, 1905, before a cheering crowd of over 1500."[8] ("Mulligan," really? Yes, really! Seems very fitting for the golfing dimension of my trip, but whether the Chicago sculptor required any do-overs in crafting the Meagher sculpture, I have been unable to discover.)

Born in Waterford, Ireland, Meagher was a leader in the Young Irelanders' ill-fated 1848 revolution to free Ireland from British rule. During those heady days when revolution was in the air across Europe, he is credited with having introduced the now-familiar tricolor flag of Ireland after having visited France to study its revolution. Since most of the Irish people were suffering from the famed "potato famine," the envisioned revolution in Ireland never gained momentum. Meagher and his associates were arrested, convicted of sedition, and sentenced to death, but in response to public outcry Queen Victoria instead exiled them to Tasmania where he lived for four years before escaping on a small boat.

With the help of American whalers, he found his way to the U. S. and ultimately to New York City, where he became a lawyer, journalist, and popular orator. In the Civil War he became a brigadier general and recruited what became known as the Irish Brigade, composed primarily of Irish immigrants from New York, Pennsylvania, and Massachusetts. That connection caught my eye because of the heroic role the unit played at the Battle of Gettysburg under the spiritual care of Father William Corby, who went on to become the second president of Notre Dame. Meagher, however, was not in command at Gettysburg. As it had in the battles of Antietam and Fredericksburg, the heroic Iron Brigade, although reduced to the size of a regiment (about 600 men), suffered terrible losses at Gettysburg. It earned the dubious distinction of having been the third most injured unit in the Civil War.[9]

After the Civil War, President Johnson named Meagher territorial secretary of Montana, where he later served briefly as acting governor. A controversial figure for many reasons, but not the least for being a Catholic and an Irishman, he died under mysterious circumstances at Fort Benton when he was only 44 years old. He was there awaiting a shipment of arms to supply a state militia he had raised to combat Native Americans who were growing increasingly hostile to the incursions of settlers on their traditional lands. The still-disputed cause of Meagher's death, when he either fell or was pushed from a steamboat docked at Fort Benton, range from suicide to murder to illness related to delirium tremens. His body was never recovered. Historians still debate the issue. Surely, few men have lived as full a life in such a short time.[10]

I left Helena a little before 11 a.m. and headed south to Anaconda. This route, west on U. S. 12, then south on I-90, took me well away from an important leg of the Lewis and Clark expedition some 80 miles east of Anaconda. In his journal on July 22, Lewis joyfully notes that Sacagawea "recognizes the country and assures us that this is the river on which her relations live, and that the three forks are at no great distance."[11] The Corps did, indeed, arrive at the Three Forks of the Missouri a few days later.

When they arrived at what is now known as the Three Forks of the Missouri, they had no difficulty deciding which fork to follow upstream to the southwest. They named this fork the Jefferson in honor of the president, "the author of our enterprise," as Lewis noted. Another stream, running south, they named for Secretary of State James Madison, and the third fork, running southeasterly, they named for Albert Gallitin, Jefferson's Secretary of the Treasury, who also had supported the expedition.[12]

In his journal, Lewis poignantly recorded that their camp proved to be the precise spot where the Hidatsa had attacked Sacagawea's family five years before, killing four men, four women, and four boys, before taking Sacagawea and several younger women captives. He observed that "I cannot discover that she shews any immotion of sorrow in recollecting this event, or of joy in being again restored to her native country; if she has enough to eat and a few trinkets to wear I believe she would be perfectly content anywhere."[13] Surely this revealing observation tells us more about Lewis's failure to understand the Native American's utterly alien culture than about Sacagawea and her people.

It was here that one of the most fortunate events of the expedition occurred. When the Corps was finally able to make contact with Sacagawea's people, who were understandably more than a little skittish about these unexpected guests, they discovered that one of the tribal chiefs was Sacagawea's brother. This happy chance certainly contributed to the Corps' ability to trade for the much-needed horses and secure a guide who would lead them across the mountains and down to the Snake River on the western side of the Great Divide. It is worth noting that when Sacagawea did encounter her brother, she showed great emotion, joy mixed with tears.

Golf at Old Works

I arrived at the Old Works golf course around noon where Vince Van Meter, the sales and marketing manager, welcomed me to this extraordinary work of vision and imagination carved out of a Super Fund clean-up site in 1994-97. It is Montana's only Jack Nicklaus signature public golf course, is rated the No. 2 golf course in Montana by *Golfweek* magazine, and for many years was ranked by *Golf Digest* as one of the 100 best public courses in the country. Any golfer traveling in the area would want to experience this beautiful, challenging layout.

Its history sets it apart and reflects the enterprise of a little town with lofty ideas as well as the creativity and competitiveness that characterizes Nicklaus as a player and designer of world-class golf courses. The site had once been a massive copper smelting operation that dated back to 1883 when an Irish immigrant named Marcus Daly purchased land in the area to build a smelter for the copper being mined in nearby Butte. Eventually, the enterprise grew to three large smelters that processed thousands of tons daily. The Old Works site closed in the early part of the 20th century and became an abandoned waste site until 1983 when it was designated a Super Fund site. The last smelter in the area closed in 1980 in response to falling copper prices. Since the Anaconda community was dependent on this major employer, its closure was devastating to the small community.

In 1989, visionary local citizens came up with the idea of creating a "world class" golf course on the Old Works site and managed to capture Jack Nicklaus's imagination. Through collaboration among the community, ARCO, and state and Federal agencies, the audacious dream was realized when the course opened in 1997.[14]

When Nicklaus returned in 2016 for a 20th anniversary celebration of Old Works, he commented with satisfaction on the extraordinary challenge that the site presented: "This was one of the most significant projects that I was ever involved with from the standpoint of all of the things it created out of a virtual wasteland, and it was a toxic wasteland." He noted that a conventional cleanup of the site would likely have cost ARCO "at least $45 million." The final cost for creating Old Works was "about $22 million," but could have been half that if not for the daunting requirements of the EPA, including "14-foot-deep 'baskets' under all 18 greens, to ensure that toxic materials wouldn't rise to the top."[15]

Although the course incorporates many historic relics of the copper smelter, it is hard to envision it once being a wasteland. The 18-hole, par 72 track wanders through high mounds of slag and remnants of flues and ovens that once steamed with liquified copper. One of the most memorable features is the use of black slag in all the bunkers. Not only do the bunkers provide a striking visual contrast to the well-maintained greens and rolling fairways, but they are a pleasure to play. Unlike conventional white sand found at most courses, this fine-grained material is as smooth as silk and resists a buried lie.

With five sets of tees, the course plays from 5290 to 7700 yards. The generous fairways are bordered by native grasses, and Warm Springs Creek, once a toxic stream, now crystal clear, winds through the course and fosters a healthy trout population. At the edge of the course, one cannot miss the old smelter stack that stands more than 585 feet, large enough to contain the Washington Monument! It is, in short, a visually striking and pleasing aesthetic experience, as all good golf courses should be. The pleasure is enhanced by knowing its dark history.[16]

It was my good fortune to play my round with a Canadian who had driven down from his home in Calgary. An agent with our northern neighbors' internal revenue service, he provided good company as we navigated the challenges of a course where no two holes are alike. We had good conversation and completed our leisurely round in about four hours. The multiple impressive visual attractions of the course deserve one's attention.

I made the mistake, quite clear in retrospect, of playing the "Copper" tees. Although the score card suggests these middle tees are for those with a handicap of 10-19, they play 6776 yards with a rating/slope of 71.9/125. Although considerably easier than the back tees (Slag) at 76.1/136, the Copper tees proved more than I could handle. I would have been wiser to play the next tees up, "Limestone," at 68.2/120, 6144 yards. I have since learned that playing more forward tees enables me to have a much better chance of reaching greens in regulation with something less than a seven iron. It is definitely more fun. Too many golfers let their egos get in the way of a more enjoyable experience.

After my round at Old Works, I found my lodging for the night, the Marcus Daly Motel on West Park Street in the town's central shopping district. This little gem of an old-fashioned motel felt like a throwback to an earlier time; although not lavish, it was perfectly comfortable, providing a clean, neat, well-appointed overnight stay that was quiet and felt secure. I had a pleasant chat with Fay, a co-owner, who welcomed me at check-in. She made me feel as if I were an old friend or long-lost family member. As I recall, she described herself as an immigrant from central Europe who had been in the U. S. for quite some time. She clearly took pride in her motel. If all my accommodations had matched the Marcus Daly, I would have no complaints. The price was hard to beat at just $80 and change.

I think Fay recommended a place for dinner called Donivan's, on East Park Street within easy walking distance of the Marcus Daly. I had a delicious salmon on a cedar plank for dinner in the historic restaurant and pub that is dedicated to the town's history of copper smelting. It was a relaxing end to a very pleasant day. As I strolled back through the town after dinner, I took some pictures of architectural details on various buildings. Anaconda has many charms. I'd like to return. At day's end, I had driven 190.7 miles. My trip total was 3,999.6 miles since leaving Gettysburg on June 20.

Window on West Park Street, Anaconda, Montana

Chapter Nineteen

Across the Mountains to Lolo Pass and Coeur d'Alene

August 13, 1805: The Corps meets with the Shoshones and discovers that Sacagawea's brother is Cameahwait, the tribal chief. They trade for horses and "Uncle Toby," who will guide them across the Bitterroot Mountains.

My destination on July 7 was Coeur d'Alene, Idaho. The most direct route from Anaconda is via I-90, a 270-mile drive to the northwest, but that was not my plan. Although I had left the Corps of Discovery route, which was well south of mine, I decided to try a more rustic route through the Bitterroot National Forest to Hamilton, Montana, south of Lolo on U. S. 93. Although, this route through the forest looked more direct, it was via Montana Route 1, 25 miles of which was unpaved although well-graded, and then the misleadingly named Skalkaho Highway, a two-lane blacktop that leads down into the Bitterroot Valley to Hamilton. The total mileage of this "more direct" route may have been a couple of miles less in driving distance; it was at least an hour longer in travel time because of the conditions. Was it worth it? Definitely. A spectacularly beautiful trek through fields and forests, waterfalls, and wildflowers of other-worldly beauty, it is one of my most-treasured memories from this trip.

Soon after leaving Anaconda, quickly ascending into the mountains, I came upon a rustic wooden historic sign hanging on a log frame mounted in a sturdy rock and mortar base overlooking the row upon row of peaks to the west. It commemorates what was known as the Atlantic Cable Quartz Lode, oddly named in 1867 for the recently laid second transatlantic telegraph cable. Three prospectors who were searching for their horses that had wandered off stumbled upon gold in a nearby creek, and that led to further exploration. A small mining camp called Cable City quickly grew up around the site; in 1880 miners discovered a particularly rich lode of only some 500 feet buried deep in the mountain; it soon produced more than $150 million in current dollars. In 1889, the so-called Butte "Copper King," William A. Clark, paid $10,000 for a single nugget said to be the largest ever found in Montana.

My scenic route over the mountains to Hamilton, was 80 leisurely miles through the Beaverhead/Deer Lodge National Forests, then into the Bitterroot National Forest and across Skalkaho Pass at 7258 feet where the lacey falls that bear the same name come splashing down the mountainside and rush under the road that I traveled, dropping steeply hundreds of feet below where I stood. "Skalkaho" is a Salish word meaning "many trails." The road, following an ancient Indian trail, was built in 1924 to connect the mining operations in these mountains with the settlements in the Bitterroot Valley to the west. Although it added time to what would be a long day, the pristine wilderness felt like traveling back in time.[1]

For the first time, I saw an exotic wildflower known as Bear grass or Turkey beard growing on tall stalks in the shade of evergreens alongside the road. Other common names are Bear Lily, Pine Lily, Elk Grass, and Squaw Grass, none of which do justice to the lacy cone-shaped, delicate white flowers that bloom on its tall stalks, some reaching up to three feet. A member of the Lily Family, its scientific name is *Xerophyllum tenax*. Native Americans made good use of the plant, weaving its tough leaves into garments, baskets, and ornaments; they ate the roasted rootstock. I didn't realize at the time that I was lucky to stumble upon these delicate flowers as they bloom only once every five to seven years. These sturdy plants play an important role in the fire ecology of the regions where they grow: "It has rhizomes which survive fire that clears dead and dying plant matter from the surface of the ground. The plant thrives with periodic burns and is often the first plant to sprout in a scorched area."[2]

Xerophyllum tenax.

My two-hour ramble across these mountains, led me to an important campsite known as Travelers' Rest near Lolo, just southwest of Missoula. It took the Corps of Discovery some 46 days to travel, mostly by water, from Three Forks to the same spot arriving there on September 10, 1805. Their maddeningly tedious route up the twists and turns of the ever-narrowing Jefferson River then further up the equally serpentine and narrowing Beaverhead River brought them at last to Lemhi Pass at what is now the Idaho/Montana line where they finally met with Sacagawea's people and secured horses as well as their Indian guide, Toby.

From the Lemhi Pass on the Continental Divide, the Corps of Discovery proceeded up through the Bitterroot Mountains to find the historic passage over the Rocky Mountains through Lolo Pass. It was a grueling passage across rocky, uneven ground. During this 160-mile trek, the Corps got a foretaste of the challenges they would face crossing the more arduous trail down the steep, western slopes of the Rockies in search of the Columbia River. Along the way, Lewis wrote in his journal a prescient observation about the Native Americans as he reflected on the values they had in common:

> Among the Shoshones, as well as all the Indians of America, bravery is esteemed the primary virtue; nor can any one [sic] become eminent among them who has not at some period of his life given proofs of his possessing this virtue. With them

there can be no preferment without some warlike achievement, and so completely interwoven is this principle
. . . that it will in my opinion prove a serious obstruction to the restoration of a general peace among the nations of the Missouri.[3]

After more than two weeks of grueling travel in the Bitterroot Mountains, the weary troop arrived on September 9 at what is today known as Travelers' Rest State Park, an interesting and well-interpreted site. The Corps would spend three days here in 1805 preparing to cross the mountains and would again camp here on their return trip in June 1806. Based on extensive archaeological research done in 2001-2002, this well-kept state park claims to be the only archaeologically verified precise site where the Corps of Discovery camped. The evidence is based on an excavated latrine that contained elements of mercury, not a naturally occurring element in this area.

Among the Corps' various medical supplies was Dr. Rush's Bilious Pills, known among the men as "Thunderclappers." These popular and powerful purgatives contained mercury. According to the journals, two of the privates (Goodrich and McNeal) were subjected to this treatment in 1806. The archaeologists found a trench that met the criteria of an Order of Encampment in a military manual developed by Baron von Stuben, the Prussian military officer who served in Washington's army. In the trench, where the two privates likely spent more uncomfortable time than they might have wished, were traces of mercury. In an odd foreshadowing, my most distressing experience on the trail occurred later that very night in Coeur d'Alene.

I spent an hour or so at the site, toured the Visitor Center and walked a well-marked self-guided trail through a portion of the 51-acre park which includes a stretch of the clear, rushing waters of Lolo Creek. Although I spotted only a few, the park claims to be home to some 125 different species of birds as well whitetail deer, river otter, beaver, and fox. For thousands of years, this site was used by the Bitterroot Salish as a gathering and trading site. The U. S. Government forcibly removed the Salish from the area in 1891, just one of the many tragic indignities inflicted on the Native Americans as the whites overran their lands. The native people, however, still regard it as an important ancestral homeland.[4]

Although neglected for many years, Travelers' Rest was spared any development and remains much as it must have appeared to Lewis and Clark when they named it in 1805. Now managed by Montana State Parks, vital support is provided by the nonprofit volunteers and members of Travelers' Rest Preservation and Heritage Association, which is always seeking new members: http://www.travelersrest.org. The National Park Service recognized it as a National Historic Landmark in 1960, and it was added to the National Register of Historic Places in 1966.[5]

Although Coeur d'Alene was still 170 miles north, I left Travelers' Rest and headed west up U. S. Route 12 into the Bitterroot Mountain range to reach Lolo Pass about 30 miles away. At 5,233 feet, this high point straddles the Montana/Idaho state line and offered me spectacular views across the difficult terrain that the Corps of Discovery crossed in the early snow and bitter cold of September 1805. The portage at Great Falls was exhausting work in brutal heat, but I'm pretty sure the men of the expedition would have rated their descent through the Bitterroot Mountains as the greater ordeal.

On top of the bitter weather and the treacherous terrain, there was little or no game to be found. They were forced to slaughter one of their horses for food before straggling into the hospitable arms of the Nez Perce Indians along the Clearwater River some ten days later. As if the terrain and weather were not sufficient challenge, "Old Toby," the guide that the Corps had recruited from the Shoshones, proved unreliable and lost the trail more than once along the way.

When the Corps arrived among the Nez Perce, they were weak and sick. It appears that the Indians intended to slaughter these intruders but were persuaded to spare them by the intercession of a woman named Watkuweis, who had been sold to a white trader and lived for a time among the whites in Canada before returning to her home. "These are the people who helped me," she told the warriors among her tribe. "Do them no hurt." As Ambrose observed, "First Sacagawea, now Watkuweis. The expedition owed more to Indian women than either captain ever acknowledged."[6]

Lolo Pass is the highest point of the historic Lolo Trail from the Bitterroot Valley in Montana to the Weippe Prairie in Idaho. It was often used by the Nez Perce and was known by that name before French traders named it Lolo, probably a nickname for Lawrence, around 1812. Highway 12, a well-maintained but very curvy road completed in 1962, now crosses the pass and runs parallel to the old Indian trail but at lower elevation along the narrow, rushing Lochsa River. The river, bounded by steep cliffs was certainly not considered navigable by the explorers of 1805, nor did the terrain allow them to follow its path.[7]

Having reached the summit of the pass, I stopped briefly at the rustic visitor center and rest area that is located there. It includes restrooms and interpretive exhibits about both Lewis and Clark as well as the Nez Perce.[8]

I then backtracked and returned to I-90 to complete my trek to Coeur d'Alene through some spectacular mountain vistas, especially through the Lolo National Forest as I approached my second crossing into Idaho for this day. Coeur d'Alene is only about 60 miles beyond the Idaho/Montana border, another great mountain vista with stunning views in every direction. Nearby I found a historical marker describing Silver Valley, another rich mining area where more than 1.2 billion ounces of silver have been extracted. Only a few active mines remain, and land reclamation is a work in progress.

It was around 4:30 Pacific Time when I reached my hotel, a nice, if pricey, Holiday Inn Express. I had toyed with the idea of staying at the famed resort, but my budget prevailed. I had traveled 370.7 miles since leaving Anaconda that morning, only 100 miles more than the direct route, but it felt longer.

French traders, who explored the area in the late 18th and early 19th centuries, dubbed the local Native Americans they found in the area "Coeur d'Alene," meaning "heart of an awl" for their hard-driving trading practices. The charming city of some 50,000 that has now grown up along the north shore of the lake is considered a "satellite" of Spokane, Washington, just 30 miles to the west.[9]

Near my hotel, I found "Bardenay," an attractive and unusual place for dinner which claims to be the nation's first full-service restaurant distillery. Having no reservations on a busy night, I ate at the bar. It is an Idaho boutique chain, with additional locations at Boise and Eagle, each specializing in a different array of liquors distilled on site.

I didn't make a note of what I ate but recall an enjoyable dinner with a couple of glasses of wine and good service. Happy to be off the road after a day of deep immersion in Lewis and Clark, I was looking forward to golf the next day at the famed Coeur d'Alene resort course. As noted above, I awoke at some point that night with extreme gastrointestinal distress. Without elaboration on the grim details, let's just say it was a night I would not want to repeat. It ended with my groggily becoming aware that I had passed out and was lying staring at the side of the toilet. It was my closest brush with serious injury on the entire trip. Unfortunately, whatever assailed me that night took about three days to depart.

Chapter Twenty
Golf at Coeur d'Alene

September 11-22, 1805: With their Shoshone guide, the Corps crosses the Bitterroot Mountains encountering early snow and brutally difficult terrain; they cover 160 miles on foot and horseback in 11 days, arriving nearly starving among the Nez Perce along the Clearwater River near present-day, Lewiston, Idaho.[1]

By-passing the Lolo Trail down the western slopes of the Bitterroot Mountains to where the starving Corps of Discovery met the Nez Perce tribe meant that I missed one of the most interesting sections of the trail. That grueling passage offers several interpretive sites along the way, but having read of the course at Coeur d'Alene, I could not resist this golf Mecca with its famed floating island hole. This was a definite bucket list item, and I might never again be so close to the famed resort.

After my turbulent night, I did not feel in top form as I headed for the golf course, but ever hopeful, foregoing the planned round of golf didn't enter my mind. I had spoken in advance with Andy Mackimmie, the head pro, who gave me a 9:30 tee time on July 8 and assured me that he'd pair me up with other players. Andy expressed interest in my project and greeted me warmly when I arrived that morning in the well-appointed pro shop. He also kindly gave me a helpful discount on the not-unreasonable green fees for such an elegant resort.

My playing partners were a pleasant couple visiting from Chicago, both teachers and good golfers. I enjoyed their company and given their interest in my project, I had expected to hear from them by email, which they had given me without apparent reluctance, but even after a second prompt, I never did. I certainly don't take that personally, nor do I fault them for not responding. As the tenor of our public discourse grows increasingly toxic, I see more folks reluctant to be drawn into conversations that might lead to political controversy. This cannot be good for our country, as vigorous, ideally respectful, debate is a cornerstone of democracy.

This meticulously maintained course and the entire resort invite hyperbole, which is easily found in the many reviews in print and on-line. A good example from *Golf Digest* is posted on the resort website: "is what every resort should be. It's not just upscale, it's posh. You aren't just pampered here, you're spoiled. It's not just an escape, it's an experience."[2] In April 2017, the same magazine published a glowing review that had nary a discouraging word. I had not seen the piece before setting out on my trip, so it had no influence on my decision, but reading it subsequently made me wonder if it was paid advertising.[3]

From the moment of my arrival, the commitment to service excellence was evident. I couldn't help but contrast the gracious pampering that I experienced with the painful challenges that the Corps of Discovery had faced just some 175 miles south in September 1805. What would they think of what has become of the pristine wilderness they encountered? Happily, the natural beauty of this spot, fewer than 100 miles south of the Canadian border, has been lovingly preserved, not exactly in its original condition but even with the pristine beauties of the course itself, one has ample opportunity to admire the soaring natural beauty that invites wonder at every turn. Indeed, leaving the golf aside, just seeing this place is worth the trip.

As for the basics, the par 71 course is not long, playing 6,803 yards from the tips (Gold) to a very friendly 4,448 yards from the forward tees (Mauve). My partners and I agreed on the Tan tees, 5,914 yards (68.2/116). Designed in 1991 by Scott Miller, a Jack Nicklaus disciple, it encompasses about 200 acres, lovingly and creatively carved out of the slopes of an evergreen forest that borders the 25-mile-long lake for which it is named. As others routinely note, Miller showed his skill in numerous ways, but tucking this elegant design into a relatively cramped space without making it feel at all cramped is one of its impressive features. Another is the clever contouring of the course that makes it rare to see golfers on other holes. One of its more forgiving features is fairways that, although relatively narrow for a "family-friendly" resort course, often slope from the edges toward the center, thus giving many a golfer a much "friendlier" bounce than an errant tee shot might otherwise receive.

The lake is visible from almost every hole, and either it or the little creek that rambles through the course make water a frequent hazard, but never unfairly. The owner of the course, Duane Hagadone, who grew up locally, reveals his passion for gardening in the abundance of wildflowers, annuals, and perennials that adorn the course, including some 30,000 bright red geraniums in artful clusters around many greens. Bent grass is the playing surface from tees to greens.[4]

Golfers staying at the resort (which I heartily recommend) are whisked from the hotel across a narrow inlet on a mahogany taxi boat and arrive at the course where they are greeted by their forecaddie. Their clubs have already been loaded on their plush golf cart, which features state-of-the art GPS as well as heated seats among other amenities. The practice area features a driving range where players warm up by hitting floating balls out into the lake. The chipping and putting areas are generous in size and in meticulous condition. If desired, a massage therapist from the spa will give you a pre-round neck and shoulder massage. Yep, it is an experience! My personalized, four-color bag tag with an image of the famed floating green is still hanging on my golf bag alongside my annual USGA tag and my old one from The Berkshire Country Club in Reading, where I was a member for 12 years while serving Albright College. It's a silly habit, but these tags feel like good luck charms.

My partners and I were assigned an affable young woman named Jessie as our caddie, and she worked hard to make our round as successful and pleasurable as possible. Given the state of my digestive tract, my expectations were low, but I started somewhat promisingly with a respectable bogey on the first hole, a 500-yard par five that played longer. I followed that with a double bogey on the par-4 second hole, sadly not the last of the day, but I gained confidence after a birdie on the next hole, a 114-yard par 3.

Even if I could recall all the rest, I would resist reviewing them. Not only does my game not merit such detail, but I find either listening to or reading such detailed renditions from other golfers just about the most tedious experience of golf. No one really cares, I am tempted to say! I suppose I am obliged, however, to recall my experience on number 14, the signature island hole.

I am told it's the only floating-island hole in golf. It's controlled by an elaborate, computer-driven set of cables that move the island each day. The caddie gives the players the actual and the effective playing distance to the hole and offers any other counsel that one might deem helpful. From 150 yards, where we teed up, the iconic hole appears more like a two-car garage door than its reputed 15,000 square feet. Despite all the help, I managed to put my first ball in the water (short) and my second in the bunker that guards the front of the green, also short. We boarded the little ferry and trundled over to the island where I did manage a halfway decent sand shot and then two-putted for double par. I wish I could say it was my only triple of the day. I finished with 94, about my then-average score, as it turns out.

As we completed our round, I was feeling a little less queasy and grateful for the good company of my new Chicago friends but most impressed by the spectacular beauty, the immaculate conditions, and the superb service at Coeur d'Alene. I later ran across a review that seems a good way to conclude:

> I want to applaud the designers of the Coeur d'Alene Resort Golf Course for striking such a **wonderful balance between fun and challenge**. Throughout the course, you see little things they did to make the course friendlier for the amateur player. At the same time, no one is coming out here and posting a low score without real skill. It's a balance that many courses shoot for but few achieve.[5]

I had an early tee time the next morning at Circling Raven, just down the road, so I consulted masstimes.org and found that St. Pius X Catholic Church nearby had a Saturday vigil mass at 5 p.m. After mass, still feeling queasy and a little lonesome, I found an Applebee's, which I thought might give me the illusion of being in my own neighborhood back home on a Saturday night. It didn't, and I didn't stay long. As I waited for my dinner, I noted the following in my day log: "I'm not sorry I've done this. Who knows what will come of it? But I would never be away from home again for so long. I don't want to be single!" At day's end, I had added only a few additional miles to the 4398.8 since leaving home.

About a week after my memorable visit to Coeur d'Alene, Andy Mackimmie sent me a thoughtful email reflecting on the questions I had been posing. "Looking back at our nation's history," he wrote, "I've always been impressed with the resilience and perseverance of the American people," reflected in solving problems through technology, exploring new frontiers, and responding to challenges like the two World Wars and 9/11. "The American spirit in my mind is progressive, always moving forward to create better lifestyle opportunities, not only for our country, but for humanity in general."

As for what worries him, he wrote, "I am concerned our government needs to . . . plan better for global environmental changes. I understand there are non-petroleum based renewable energy resources in development, however, I worry it may be too little too late with politics and money getting in the way."

If he had a magic wand, he would remove "all the politics and individual selfishness out of the government. I feel far too many decisions are made by wealthy corporate individuals with only their self-interest in mind instead of looking at the impact their decisions potentially have on future generations."

It's a great wish, but I hope this thoughtful young man recognizes it as fanciful. I expect he does; his including it as a "magic wand" wish strikes me as perfectly in tune with the question itself as well as the "go for it" spirit of golfers who dare.

Chapter Twenty-One
Circling Raven and Lunch with a Mountain Man

October 6, 1805: The Corps proceeds down the Clearwater River in five canoes they had carved during their stay with the Nez Perce; it is the first time they have traveled downstream since leaving St. Louis.

In 1858, General George Wright's cavalry troops had been engaged in what have been called the Northwest Indian Wars. On September 7th of that year, the soldiers . . . captured about 900 horses belonging to the local tribes located in the areas of Coeur d'Alene, Idaho and Spokane, Washington. As a show of power and to quell the potential for uprising

Wright ordered the herd corralled near the banks of the Spokane River and then killed. Wright also ordered food caches destroyed, thus leaving the tribes with little food or the ability to travel to gather more, as the winter approached.

Several years ago, after conferring with Coeur d'Alene Tribal member and historian, Cliff "Circling Song" Si John about the event, the sculpture was conceived which I have entitled, "Rise of the Schitsu' Umsh", honoring the resilience and resolve of the Coeur d'Alene Tribe of Indians in overcoming the low point in their nearly ten thousand year occupation of our region. The sculpture, depicting four horses rising out of the bones of their murdered ancestors, are being urged upward from the earth by the spirit of legendary tribal prophet, Circling Raven.

During the years since that event, the tribe has not only retained its proud culture and distinctive community, but has risen back to prosperity and health, to the enduring benefit of our region as a whole, and serves to communicate the powerful message that death and destruction need never have the final word. –Kevin Kirking, sculptor[1]

L ocated only about 30 minutes southwest of the Coeur d'Alene
Resort by way of a scenic drive down U.S. 95, Circling Raven
Golf Course outside Worley, Idaho, is a visual feast from the
landscaped drive onto the property, where I first saw the hotel, casino,
and spa that are part of the complex, to the elegant warmth of its well-
stocked, stone and timber pro shop, to the sweeping scale of the 18-
hole, par-72 course itself. This beautiful course is expansively laid out
across some 620 acres of rolling Palouse grasslands and evergreens,
punctuated with wetlands, ponds, and grand vistas of the Cascades to
the west. Opened in 2003, the course was designed by Gene Bates,
another Nicklaus disciple.[2]

"Circling Raven has garnered numerous honors since opening,
including being rated a Top 100 Resort Course, Best in State, and a
Top U.S. Casino Course. Its golf shop has won national and regional
awards for its excellence and its variety of products, displays, and
performance."[3] The August 2009 issue of *Golf Digest* ranked the
course No. 17 in "America's 100 Greatest Public Courses by Price,"
and noted that it was No. 61 in its "Greatest Public Courses for 2009-
10."[4]

Circling Raven made my list partly because it was convenient to
the resort course at Coeur d'Alene but also was listed among the top
100 by *Golf Digest* in 2016, when I was planning my trip. More
recently, the course won first place on Golf Advisor's "Golfer's
Choice 2020" rating of Idaho's best public courses. In its report on
that recent accolade, *The Golf Wire.com* notes the impressive
amenities off the course. These include a 25-acre driving range and
generous short-game and putting green, its award-winning golf shop
and the Twisted Earth restaurant and bar in the clubhouse. The resort
itself includes a full-service spa, more than 300 hotel rooms and
suites, bars, restaurants, lounges, and eateries as well as opportunities
for cultural immersion and more. The casino recently completed a
multi-million-dollar renovation. For several years, the course has
hosted the Circling Raven Championship as an official qualifying tour
event of the LPGA, (as of 2022 sponsored by Epson).[5]

In March 2019, the course announced plans for extensive
renovations under Gene Bates's direction: "We are advancing the golf
experience at Circling Raven for the next 15 years, with its condition,
playability and aesthetics," said Bates. "Each phase of the master plan

will be implemented such that the course will be available for play the vast majority of time." Bates's scope of work is expected to include renovating, removing and/or adding bunkers; leveling existing tees as well as creating new ones; re-grassing greens with a new bent grass variety; exploring the addition of new holes adjacent to the practice area; expanding the practice facilities; and identifying an area for destination golf accommodations.[6] As of September 2022, the improvements have included renovation of the first and tenth tees, expanding the practice putting area, and "tweaking" the 25-acres practice area, according to course publicist, Dan Shepherd.

The entire complex was developed and is owned and operated by the Coeur d'Alene Tribe. On a knoll near the entrance is a fine sculpture of the tribal chief and spiritual leader for whom the resort is named. Mounted on horseback and carrying a lance festooned with feathers, he wears an elaborate headdress and gazes across the terrain.

This image, which is also the logo for the resort, reflects the indomitable spirit of the indigenous people who have occupied these lands for thousands of years. Like most Native Americans, the Coeur d'Alene were almost eradicated by the relentless efforts of the whites who began invading their lands not long after Lewis and Clark's epic journey. Between military actions and disease, about 90 percent of the tribe was killed by mid-century. Although most of their millions of acres of land were ultimately taken from them, the tribe has endured and found ways to flourish through such enterprises as Circling Raven. One cannot but be impressed with such a spirit in the face of continued challenges. Circling Raven is much more than a golf course, hotel, spa, and casino. It is a monument to the tribe's enterprise, courage, and vision as well as a graceful tribute to the sacred land that they have long inhabited and loved. On the tribe's website, the following is found:

> The modern Coeur d'Alene Tribe is the sum of uncounted centuries of untold generations. In the tribe's own ancient language, it is called Schitsu'umsh, meaning "Those who were found here" or "The discovered people." In this remains a land abundant in beauty and resources, a legacy of leadership, and a lineage that continues from the time immemorial. The Coeur d'Alenes are who they always were and who they will always be.[7]

I arrived around 7:15 on another clear summer morning that promised a warm, pleasant day on the course. In the pro shop I met young Matthew Nosbaum, the assistant golf professional, who welcomed me with interest in my journey and my project. He set me up with another single player, George, a 71-year-old Greek immigrant who told me proudly of being father to 7- and 8-year-old boys with his second wife and a 48-year-old from his first marriage. We were then joined by a father and son who owned a garage-door business in Wenatchee, Washington, some 200 miles west. It proved to be a congenial group on a very challenging course that accurately boasts of an ingenious variety of holes gracefully spread out across the expansive terrain. Although there were other players out this day, we rarely saw them.

A detailed, appreciative review in *GolfCourseGurus.com* by Billy Satterfield offers a complete overview of the course:

> I fully admit, I have a love affair with Circling Raven . . . . The crown jewel of Gene Bates designs, Circling Raven features solid holes, a stout challenge, and no gimmicks. Often compared to the Coeur d'Alene Resort due to the close proximity, the courses couldn't be more different . . . . CDA Resort is a "feel good" resort course and Circling Raven is a "players" course. You'd love to play the CDA Resort every couple of years just to have the experience, but you'd like to have Circling Raven as your home course to play as much as possible . . . . With a drivable par 4, GPS carts, massive clubhouse, split fairway par 4, and one of the toughest par 3s you'll ever meet - Circling Raven offers something for everyone.[8]

On the course website, one can enjoy a YouTube video done in 2009 by Tom Davidson, who was then Circling Raven's Director of Golf: https://www.youtube.com/watch?v=B0WniiMK0Gw.

From the tips, the gold tees, the course plays almost 7200 yards with a slope and rating of 74/144. Happily, my group selected the somewhat less daunting white tees at 6108 yards, 69.2/131. As with most of the others that I played on my journey, I would have been happier if I had played the next tees up, in this case, the red tees, at

5389, 70.4/128, but that wisdom lay a couple of years later for me. The forward green tees measure 4708, 66/116, a considerably more forgiving layout for ladies, youth, beginners, and wise golfers who know their limitations.

Although I posted one of the worst scores on my journey (102), it was a thoroughly enjoyable experience. The company was relaxed and agreeable; even though all were better players than I, they never made me feel unwelcome as I struggled to achieve a few bogeys. I managed to post only one par on the short tenth hole (298 yards from the white tees), but my most memorable achievement was a birdie on the daunting par 3 thirteenth, which plays 200 yards from the white tees, 253 yards from the gold! More important was the sheer beauty of this memorable course. Like Billy Satterfield, I would love to play Circling Raven on a regular basis.

Lunch in St. Maries, Idaho

We finished up around noon, having made good time despite my struggles, and I headed south for a late lunch date with the cousin of a Gettysburg friend who lives near the little city of St. Maries (2020 population 3219, up from 2618 in the year of my visit), about 30 miles south through the scenic, evergreen hills of the St. Joe National Forest, some 868,000 acres of game-rich land through which the St. Joe River runs north into Coeur d'Alene Lake. The river is popular among whitewater enthusiasts in the spring and is also popular among trout fishermen.

St. Maries dates its origins to Joseph Fisher who built a sawmill there in 1889. In 1908, the railroad arrived; the city was established in 1913 and soon thereafter named county seat of the newly formed Benewah County.[9] Styling itself as the "Hidden Jewel of the Gem State," St. Maries appears to be a thriving little community that attracts outdoor enthusiasts all year-round.[10]

I met Jim Bennett at Casa de Oro, a little Mexican restaurant perched on a hill overlooking the St. Maries municipal golf course, a charming par-35, nine-holer that appeared to feature substantial terrain changes over its 2665 yards. It clearly would have presented much less challenge than Circling Raven as its longest hole is a 420-yard, par 5. Tempting, but I had miles to go before sunset and was continuing to feel queasy.

Jim is as close to a real mountain man as I would encounter on my trip. After 25 years of service, he retired from the Idaho Department of Natural Resources. He's married to a woman who brought five children to the match, and they live on a small farm tucked into the hills nearby. He describes his livelihood now as "subsistence farming," cultivating hay as a cash crop. Each year he heads up into the hills to harvest an elk that will feed them through the winter. The elk will weigh in at around 500 pounds, obviously too large for even a big man to drag out of the woods, and Jim is not physically large.

He described his bloody process for getting his elk back to his modest home, a double-wide trailer. He field-dresses the elk on the site of the kill, cutting portions and strapping them to his body in segments of 50-60 pounds, which he then carries back to his home. After several trips, I imagined him looking as bloody as the carcass he was butchering in the woods. He acknowledged that if someone came upon him trekking his prize through the woods, they might be shocked at his appearance. But I'm pretty sure that the art of field-dressing an elk is not a deep mystery in this area. From a few YouTube videos that I later viewed, it's not as messy as I imagined. A skilled hunter with a sharp blade can field-dress an elk in a matter of minutes.

Jim was very interested in my project, and we had a lively conversation over lunch. He focused primarily on the Native American perspective, which seemed especially fitting on the heels of my round at Circling Raven. Jim brought a book with him that I mistakenly thought was a gift. After an awkward moment, he explained that he brought it along so I could see it and so he'd not forget to talk about it. *Lewis and Clark Through Indian Eyes* (Vintage Books, 2007), is a collection of nine essays by self-described "Indian Writers" reflecting on the legacy of the expedition. The editor, Alvin M. Josephy, Jr. (1915-2005), was a popular historian of the American West who wrote or edited more than a dozen books on the subject. *Lewis and Clark Through Indian Eyes* was his last book, completed just before his death and published the following year. I bought my own copy after returning from the trip and have read and re-read it with admiration.

The nine contributors are an impressive group of writers who represent different tribes and a range of perspectives, some voicing hostility to the impact that Lewis and Clark had on Native Americans, others pointing out errors of fact regarding the great expedition, and

169

others pondering the mystery of inevitable conflict despite the good, if naïve, intentions of both Jefferson and his Corps of Discovery.

In preparing for the bicentennial commemoration of the great expedition, Josephy attempted to provide a corrective to the prevailing absence of the Native American perspective on Lewis and Clark specifically and on the larger, bitter story of suffering and betrayal as white men invaded the lands and nearly destroyed the diverse, proud cultures of the indigenous peoples. I was not surprised to find anger and grief in the nine narratives, lamenting as one writer put it, the shame of being "treated as aliens and intruders in their own country."[11] But it was also moving to see the repeated expressions of hope, of pride in their heritage and in their endurance.

One of the contributors was Gerard A. Baker, a Mandan-Hidatsa, who in September 2000 was named superintendent of the Lewis and Clark National Historic Trail. For the next four years, he was responsible for managing the trail and the traveling exhibit "Corps of Discovery II: 200 Years to the Future." In 2004 he was named superintendent of Mount Rushmore National Memorial. He closed his essay with a recurring theme in the collection: "I pray that the Lewis and Clark story will be only a stepping-stone to continue to bring out the truths of the Indian people and the story of our struggle and survival. We will never go away."[12]

The collection concludes with a lyrical meditation by the Pulitzer Prize-winning N. Scott Momaday, Ph.D., a Kiowa novelist, essayist, poet, painter, playwright, and professor, who received the National Medal of Arts in 2007, is a fellow of the American Academy of Arts and Sciences, and holds more than 20 honorary degrees:

> For the men who entered the unknown and returned, and for those who knew the land and watched from the heart of wilderness, nothing would be the same ever again. It was the most difficult of journeys, marked by extraordinary triumph and defeat. It was in the truest sense a vision quest, and the visions gathered were of profound consequence. All that we are, good and bad, was in it.[13]

In 2012 a United Nations special investigator, after spending nearly two weeks visiting American Indian reservations examining discrimination, "called on the US government to return some of the land stolen from Indian tribes as a step toward combatting continuing and systemic racial discrimination." His report described

> a history of dispossession of their lands and resources, the breakdown of their societies and 'numerous instances of outright brutality, all grounded on racial discrimination.
>
> And discrimination in the sense of the invisibility of Native Americans in the country overall that often is reflected in the popular media. The idea that is often projected through the mainstream media and among public figures that indigenous peoples are either gone or as a group are insignificant or that they're out to get benefits in terms of handouts, or their communities and cultures are reduced to casinos, which are just flatly wrong.[14]

The relative invisibility of Native Americans is probably more acute east of the Mississippi, where their numbers are much smaller than in the western U.S. Pondering this phenomenon as I worked on this chapter, I asked a golfing buddy if he had any idea how many Federally recognized tribes exist in the U.S. He took a wild guess with "maybe 20 or so"? He was as surprised as I had been when I learned that there are something like 570. There are 326 reservations, mostly west of the Mississippi, comprising 56.2 million acres or about 87,800 square miles. This may seem like a large amount of land for the fewer than one million Native Americans who reside there, but it is, of course, a tiny fraction of the lands that they once claimed as their own. Most of the reservations are relatively small tracts of land, but twelve are larger than Rhode Island. The largest, some 17.5 million acres, is the Navajo Nation Reservation in Northeast Arizona, Southeast Utah, and Northwest New Mexico. According to 2018 U. S. Census Bureau estimates, the total Native American population was 5.7 million, or less than 2% of the total. More than 75% live outside reservations. Inside the reservations, conditions have been compared to "Third-World Countries," with high poverty, disease, early mortality, and an epidemic of teen suicide. That such conditions exist within the borders of the wealthiest nation in the history of the world is a scandal that is invisible to most Americans.[15]

During the Obama Administration, several protracted class-action suits brought by many tribes were settled in a series of decisions that netted almost $5 billion in compensation to individuals and tribal trust accounts. The complaints at the heart of these suits documented abuses that date back into the 19th century. Whether the amounts awarded represent adequate compensation is beyond my capacity to judge, but at least the Obama Administration can claim a victory in attempting to resolve a protracted legal battle and render a measure of justice and compensation for this grim chronicle that is among the darkest in our history.

Chapter Twenty-Two
Of Missionaries and Massacres

October 10, 1805: The Corps reaches the Snake River and camps near present-day Lewiston, Idaho.

After lunch with Jim Bennett, I left St. Maries around 3:45 p.m. and headed south and west for Lewiston, Idaho, about a two-hour drive via Idaho Routes 3 and 12. The first part of my route was through the St. Joe National Forest. It was not the quickest route, but on Jim's advice, I took the more scenic way. His counsel was rewarding. It was another warm, blue-sky afternoon. As I emerged from the National Forest, the rolling hills were less heavily wooded and there were fine vistas in every direction. My route took me along the St. Maries River for about 45 minutes until I reached the tiny unincorporated community of Clarkia, where the river flows away from Route 3. Just before I reached the little city of Kendrick (est. population of 300), the Potlatch River began to run along the winding road. Near the city of Juliaetta at a lovely spot overlooking the river, I found a state historical marker entitled "Spalding's Mission." It reads as follows:

MARCUS WHITMAN AND HENRY HARMON SPALDING LED PRESBYTERIAN MISSIONARIES WEST IN 1836 TO ANSWER A NEZ PERCE CALL FOR TEACHERS.
Spalding began his mission and school nearby, [sic] but moved here in 1838.Believing in secular as well as religious teaching, he taught the Indians irrigated farming, brought in the Northwest's first printing press, and built saw and flour mills. But hostility slowly developed, and Spalding left after the Whitman massacre at Walla Walla in 1847. He returned with the gold rush to labor among his converts until his death in 1874. His grave is nearby.

That terse narrative on a subject about which I knew almost nothing piqued my curiosity, which I satisfied after my return home. It is, at the very least, another example of the platitude that the victors write the histories. Although the story of these earnest missionaries gives me no reason to doubt their good intentions, theirs is another early instance of the cultural disruption visited upon the native peoples in the wake of the Lewis and Clark expedition. I could not verify that the Nez Perce called for teachers within a generation of this tribe having offered life-saving hospitality to the starving Corps of Discovery as they emerged from the brutal trial of crossing the Bitterroot Mountains in the early fall of 1805. It could be true; there are multiple accounts from the Lewis and Clark journals and later records that the Native Americans regarded the whites with awe and attempted to appropriate their powers in multiple ways that included inviting the whites to have sex with their women.

Juliaetta, which is two miles from the Nez Perce Reservation, is a tiny "city," as it is called, of fewer than 600 citizens that was first settled in 1878 and incorporated in 1892 when the railroad reached that point. Its unusual name reflects the even-handed diplomacy of its first postmaster who honored his two daughters, Julia and Etta, with the clever coinage in 1882, and surely thereby avoided a family squabble. More importantly, the little city reflects, like scores of others, the stunning speed with which white settlers followed in Lewis and Clark's footsteps.

The Whitmans and Spaldings were among the first to cross the Rockies to bring their earnestly held faith to the indigenous people. Whether the Indians wanted it or not is apparently not a question that occurred to these pious pioneer-missionaries. Among their notable accomplishments, perhaps their greatest impact was that their two wives, Narcissa Whitman and Eliza Spalding, were the first white women to make the overland trip by sturdy mule-drawn covered wagons that contained all they thought they would need to establish homesteads in the Northwest. Narcissa Whitman's frequent letters from the trail describing their exciting and, from her perspective, exhilarating journey were published widely back East and played a significant role in encouraging other families to seek new lives in the West. It's also notable that the only way Narcissa could gain the needed church endorsement to achieve her dream of being a missionary to the Indians was to be married, which she promptly arranged with Marcus. They departed on their transcontinental journey the day after their wedding, and Narcissa became pregnant shortly thereafter, thereby demonstrating that even a pregnant woman could manage the rigors of the journey and achieving the distinction of delivering the first white baby west of the Rockies.

The Spaldings ultimately settled among the Nez Perce in Lapwai just east of present-day Lewiston. The Whitmans established their mission among the Cayuse tribe at Waiilatpu, Washington, eight miles west of present-day Walla Walla. Although the Spaldings appear to have had greater success, neither of the earnest missionary couples achieved what they had imagined. It appears that the Whitmans never converted any of the Cayuse to Christianity, and both displayed a profound failure to understand or appreciate the culture of the tribe among whom they lived for more than a decade. As the historical sign indicates, the Whitmans and a dozen other white settlers were killed by angry Cayuse, led by their chief, Tiloukaikt, in what is now called the Whitman Massacre, on November 29, 1847. The Cayuse's fury was fueled by the deaths of almost half the tribe and nearly all their children in a measles outbreak that the Indians blamed on the whites. Although the whites suffered from the disease as well, the number of deaths among the Indians was much greater. This "massacre" marked the end of the Whitman mission and the suspension of the Spaldings' as well.

Marcus Whitman's most lasting impact is very likely his return trip back East in 1842 to persuade the American Missionary Board to continue the Cayuse mission. Having succeeded in the effort that ultimately cost him his life, he helped lead the first "Great Migration" of some one thousand pioneers up the Oregon Trail. From then on, the Whitmans spent more time serving the new settlers than the Cayuse, further fueling suspicion among the Indians. An important by-product of the large and growing influx of settlers was Britain's abandoning its claim to Oregon, which had grown increasingly tenuous as more Americans settled in the Northwest.[1]

Wondering about the deeper story behind the Spalding Mission and the "Whitman Massacre," I made my way into Lewiston where I planned to spend the night. It is beautiful country of rolling hills and farmland known as the Palouse, famed for its abundant wheat crops. The Potlatch River flows into the Clearwater where Idaho Route 3 joins Route 12. Following the Clearwater into Lewiston, I found my Hampton Inn perched on an imposing bluff overlooking the river just outside the city. It had become very hot, quite a contrast to the cool morning air twelve hours earlier in Coeur D'Alene.

After settling in my room, I discovered within a short walk Ernie's Steakhouse, which looked promising, rustic but clean and offering spectacular views of the Clearwater River and its surroundings. My experience was disappointing. First, I had the option of dining inside or on a covered patio overlooking the river. Inside, it was so cold that I thought my teeth would chatter; outside, it was so hot that I thought I my wine would be mulled before I could finish my dinner. Always preferring to be warm than cold, I sat outside, by far the more popular option. I ordered a glass of wine and "Ernie's Steak House Salad," which touted pit-smoked prime rib. The salad was more than disappointing. The "prime rib" consisted of small fragments of beef that looked like what had been scraped off a cutting board after the best cuts were long gone. It was dry, over-cooked, tough, and mostly just salty. I made a note to myself: "Lesson at age 67—don't order salad at a steakhouse. They are offended."

After dinner I made my way back to my hotel, feeling increasingly worse for wear. Although my hotel was not more than a quarter mile away, I had not realized how steep the hill was when I walked down to Ernie's. In the baking heat with a rumbling stomach, I labored back to my hotel with an uneasy sense that my gastrointestinal problems were yet to be resolved.

Chapter Twenty-Three
From Lewiston to The Dalles

October 16, 1805: The Corps reaches the junction of the Columbia River, the first white men on the river east of the Cascades.

Although I had planned to see more of the many appealing Lewis and Clark sights in the area, my stomach had other ideas. I spent most of the morning of July 10 in my hotel room responding unwillingly to the call of the wild. Feeling only slightly better, I left the hotel around 11:30 facing a long drive to The Dalles, Oregon, some 250 miles downstream. As with so many of the other sites on my journey, I wish I had had more time to spend in charming Lewiston, population about 32,000. One could easily spend a week or more using Lewiston as a base for exploring the region where so much of critical importance happened to the Corps of Discovery in September and October 1805. There are a multitude of landmarks, parks, interpretive sites, museums, and trails that commemorate this chapter of the voyage.

It's also worth noting that Lewiston's mild climate permits year-round golfing. As I experienced directly, some summer days can be very hot. Dry heat, yes, but an oven is also dry. It was a good thing I had not planned a round of golf in Lewiston; my distressed condition would surely have made it unwise even if I had. Fortunately, there are no renowned courses in the area. Indeed, given the weather, I was surprised to discover only four courses nearby, one private, two public, and a municipal. All looked good but not great, relatively short with low slope and high course ratings. The best of the four appears to be the private Clarkston Golf and Country Club, which is the oldest, dating back to 1937. From their website, it appears that nonmembers could get on the course with little difficulty, but they do not post green fees. Perched above the Snake River in Clarkston, this par 72 plantation-style course measures 6,650 yards with a slope of 138 and a rating of 72. This would have been my first choice. Next in line

177

would be the Lewiston Golf and Country Club, which is public and appears to have spectacular views and vistas. Located just south of downtown Lewiston, this par 72 track measures 6,728 yards from the tips, has a slope of 125 and course rating of 71.9. Although a much shorter course at only 5,861 yards, Quail Ridge south of Clarkston appears to be a well-maintained public course with impressive vistas west of the Snake River. It is a par 71 with a 114 slope and rating of 68.1, very likely the least challenging of the area courses.

As my trusty guide Fanselow writes, "Lewiston . . . is an educational center and major retail hub—and possibly the public art capital of the Lewis and Clark Trail."[1] In addition to the great natural beauty of the place where the Corps of Discovery finally began traveling downstream toward the Pacific, there was too much artwork for me to see in a few hours. I did, however, have two memorable tastes of the area's public art.

As a lifelong "collector" of college campuses, my first visit was to Lewis-Clark State College in the center of the city. (Not to be confused with Lewis and Clark College, a private, liberal arts college in Portland, Oregon, which traces its founding to 1867.) Founded in 1893 as Lewiston State Normal School to train teachers, the four-year public college now boasts an enrollment of more than 3600 students from 20 states and 30 countries. It received its current name in 1971. Although women outnumber men five to three, the college has a long history of a strong baseball program. The "Warriors" hold 16 national titles, have had 78 All-Americans, and 108 players drafted by major league teams. Among the 15 "Notable Alumni" listed on its Wikipedia page, all but two are major league players or coaches. Baseball clearly is a big deal here.

After parking on a tree-lined street nearby, I walked onto the campus shaded by large hardwoods. On the college's Centennial Mall visitors will find life-sized statues of Lewis and Clark conferring with the Nez Perce chief Twisted Hair, while his young son, Lawyer, examines trade items at his feet. Nearby a native woman is picking huckleberries and another woman is showing a little girl how to find camas roots. All the figures are in a deeply planted, shady garden area. A replica of the canoes that Lewis and Clark built for their downstream journey is nearby. A brass plaque on a stone at the edge of the garden identifies Doug Hyde as the Native American artist and Nez Perce descendent who crafted the figures. The work is entitled

"Hospitality of the Nez Perce." It was dedicated in 1993 in conjunction with the college's centennial celebration. A replica is on the statehouse grounds in Boise.[2]

Reflecting the continuing appeal of Sacagawea, the college's new $16 million, 60,000 square-foot Nursing Health Science Building, which was opened in 2009, is named Sacajawea Hall. (As noted earlier, the variant spellings of the Corps' indispensable lone woman on their journey are a defining characteristic of the trail.) On the plaza at the hall's entrance is an impressive bronze statue entitled "Sacajawea's Arduous Journey." The almost ten-foot-tall bronze monument depicts the young Indian woman holding a long staff as she cradles her baby "Pomp" on her back and climbs the rugged portage at Great Falls. The college website links her role in the Corps of Discovery to the "help and caring" that define nursing and health care.

"Sacajawea" by Carol Ann Grende, Lewiston, Idaho

The artist was Carol Ann Grende, a local woman who had a lifelong passion for the Lewis and Clark story. She also did the impressive Lewis and Clark sculpture at the Falls of the Ohio Visitors Center in

Clarksville, Indiana, which I had admired earlier in my journey. I learned after my return that she had died in March 2009 at the age of 53 from complications related to leukemia. Her beautiful Sacajawea monument in Lewiston must have been her last major work. Her obituary quotes her vision of Sacajawea: "I have seen her in my mind's eye, a woman of great strength and perseverance. In her face is great determination. Sacajawea is truly a culmination of my career and represents the perseverance we all must have to proceed on in times of trouble."[3] Her words take on special poignancy in light of the "troubles" that soon took her life, and the sculpture itself, like so many others along the trail, is a fitting symbol for the turbulent times in which we now live.

Following Fanselow's directions, I left the college campus and made my way north toward the confluence of the Clearwater and Snake Rivers where there is an interpretive center overlooking the Corps' campsite nearby on October 10, 1805. Fanselow notes that the explorers thought they had reached the Columbia River at this point, but it was still six days travel downstream. I would make it in a couple of hours.

The most striking object at this interpretive center is a large bronze sculpture entitled "Tsceminicum," Nez Perce for "meeting of the waters." This massive work by local artist Nancy N. Dreher was commissioned by the U.S. Army Corps of Engineers as an interpretation of Native American mythology with the central role of an Earth Mother. The monumental meditation in bronze reflects the interconnectedness and interdependence of all living things that is central to Native American spirituality.

"Tsceminicum" by Nancy N. Dreher, Lewiston, Idaho

It stands outside the entrance to the center and is, in effect, a wall of perhaps 20 feet in length and 10 feet in height. Kneeling at one end and greeting visitors is the image of a Native American woman with her hands resting on her knees palms up hovering over a spring of water that appears to run from her hands. Her calm, strong face expresses serenity. Her long hair flows directly back from her forehead as if in a strong wind and blends into the figures that are in bas relief behind her on both sides of the wall. She appears to be emerging from this exuberant display of local wildlife from beavers to moose, cranes to crows, bighorn sheep to eagles almost as if she is at the head of a rushing stream and pulling all these creatures along behind her, the very embodiment of energy and fecundity. As noted on a plaque at the end of the sculpture, the coyote presides over them all as the most important figure in Nez Perce legends.[4]

Given the miles yet to travel, I reluctantly skipped another notable site that also celebrates Sacagawea and reflects the small city's civic pride. Dating back to 1901, Pioneer Park on Fifth Street, four blocks north of Lewis-Clark State College, was once a popular community gathering place. It featured a bandstand where open-air concerts were regularly offered, and President William Howard Taft spoke from its stage during a campaign trip in 1911. At its center was a fountain featuring Sacagawea flanked by four concrete coyotes spewing water at the Indian woman's feet. Sadly, over time, the bandstand and the fountain fell into disrepair and became victims of vandalism. In

181

conjunction with plans for the state's 1990 centennial, a group of citizens raised funds to rebuild the bandstand, which had been demolished in the 1950s, and the fountain with a new bronze sculpture of Sacagawea and the four coyotes though no longer spewing water. With donated funds and labor, the project was completed with much fanfare in time for the centennial.[5] This project is but one of many that reflects the deep-rooted philanthropic spirit of American culture.

I departed Lewiston in the early afternoon heading west and southwest to The Dalles, Oregon, where I had overnight reservations at The Dalles Inn. Although my 257-mile route on U.S. 12 and Interstate 84 did not follow closely the Snake River, which the Corps of Discovery traveled in October 1805, I imagined what a great relief it must have been for the intrepid explorers to travel at long last downstream after their arduous journey from St. Louis to the source of the Missouri in the eastern foothills of the Rocky Mountains. The trip down the Snake in their five, newly carved canoes was some 140 miles to the Columbia at present-day Burbank, Washington, just south of Tri-Cities. With the increased presence of curious Nez Perce along the way, the Corps made this leg of the trip in only six days, arriving at the junction with the Columbia on October 16, 1805.[6]

The Snake River, erroneously named by white traders who mistook an Indian sign for twisted or weaving river, is the thirteenth longest in the U. S.—slightly longer than the Columbia—stretching for more than a thousand miles across portions of six states (Wyoming, Idaho, Nevada, Utah, Oregon, and Washington). Originating in a remote corner of southwestern Wyoming in what is now Yellowstone National Park, the Snake covers almost 108,000 square miles and is the largest tributary of the Columbia River, comprising about 41 percent of the Columbia River Basin.

Most of the Snake River's 20-plus major tributaries are in the mountainous sections of this winding river that flows through a wide variety of geographic regions and climates. The largest of its tributaries is the Clearwater River, which drains 9,000 square miles of northcentral Idaho. The Salmon River is its second-largest tributary and a reminder of the profuse fecundity of the salmon that once swarmed up the river each year to spawn and die.[7]

Salmon was a staple of the Nez Perce diet and was the principal nourishment that the Indians offered the starving Corps as they staggered out of the Bitterroot Mountains that late September of 1805.

The unhappy result was violent dysentery among all members of the Corps. Their weakened condition slowed them down and endangered their lives as the suspicious Nez Perce recognized the opportunity to slay the suffering explorers and seize their weapons and goods. As noted above, the Nez Perce Indian woman named Watkuweis very likely saved their lives.[8]

Although small consolation for my own continued intestinal distress, it was a curious coincidence to return to the Lewis and Clark Trail on the Clearwater and recall the Corps members' similar complaints at the same place.

Having traveled only 283 miles, I arrived in The Dalles, Oregon, around 6:30 p.m. on July 10, checked into the very modest, motel-style room at The Dalles Inn. On the desk clerk's recommendation, I strolled down to The Baldwin Saloon at First and Court Streets for dinner. The historic saloon evokes the spirit of early pioneers and fortune seekers in warm woods and brass with period art including an eye-catching painting of a nude woman reclining across the wall above the handsome bar. The restaurant dates back some 100 years and prides itself on an all made-from-scratch menu. Perhaps the charm of the place persuaded me that the worst of my distress had passed and so I enjoyed an excellent home-cooked dinner. Through no fault of the chef, this proved to be a mistake. I can happily recommend The Baldwin Saloon for good food and service in a warm and pleasant setting.[9]

After my late dinner, I made my way back to The Dalles Inn hoping for a good night's rest. I was not disappointed. The modest little motel was quiet and comfortable.

Chapter Twenty-Four
Columbia River Gorge and Mt. Hood

October 24, 1805: After navigating treacherous Class V rapids at Celilo Falls and The Dalles in their cumbersome, hand-hewn log canoes, the Corps reached today's site of The Dalles, Oregon, and rested at "Fort Rock Camp."[1]

Columbia Gorge, July 11, 2017

Although a small town of only some 15,000 inhabitants, The Dalles is the county seat and largest city of Wasco County. Archaeological evidence suggests that the region has been continuously occupied by humans for 10,000 years. Perhaps most importantly for visitors, it marks the eastern entrance to the magnificent Columbia River Gorge National Scenic Area, the first such region named by the U. S. Government.[2]

Even discounting for the characteristic exuberance of writers who are paid to attract tourists, the following passage doesn't seem hyperbolic as I reflect on my visit to the area:

> The Columbia River Gorge was designated a National Scenic Area — the largest in America — for good reason.
>
> You'd be hard-pressed to find vistas as stunning as these. At the western end of the Gorge, the view from Crown Point is a front-row seat to the mighty Columbia as it unfurls and cuts through the Cascade mountains. From there dozens of awe-inspiring waterfalls spill from basalt cliffs, lining the Historic Columbia River Highway, like the famous Multnomah, Bridal Veil and Latourell falls. The landscape seems to grow bigger, grander and brighter as it rolls east.
>
> Bring your sense of adventure because the Gorge is made for exploring. Walk along a waterfront, discover hidden waterfalls, follow the wildflowers at Rowena Crest or challenge yourself with a trek up Dog Mountain. Cycle the roads around The Dalles or in the Post Canyon Mountain bike network. And it's hard to resist water sports on the Columbia, especially when Hood River is known as the windsurfing capital of the world.
>
> But the Columbia River Gorge isn't just spectacular scenery. There's plenty of hand-crafted beer and farm-fresh dining too. Thanks to its unique geography, the Gorge boasts a world of wine — from pinot noir and chardonnay in the cool western hills, to tempranillo and syrah in the drier, sunnier east.
>
> See the Columbia River Gorge for yourself, and then you'll understand all the hype.[3]

The Dalles appears to be a healthy, bustling little community, aided certainly by the presence of the county's government offices. Like many smaller cities across the U. S., the largest employer is the Mid-Columbia Medical Center. Agriculture and tourism are primary economic drivers. Its most famed product is sweet cherries, which are shipped worldwide. Some 6000 acres of cherry orchards surround the town. Incorporated in 1857, it was once a major Indian trading center at the upper reaches of where early French explorers and traders from the West Coast and points north had penetrated before Lewis and

Clark's arrival in late-October 1805. By the 1840s American settlers had begun arriving in the area in substantial numbers as this was for a time the terminus of the famed Oregon Trail. The town's name is derived from the French word "dalle" meaning a sluice, referring to the series of formidable rapids that once characterized this stretch of the Columbia. All are now submerged under the deeper waters created by a series of dams.[4]

The Corps camped here for three days (October 25-27) on a high point of rocks that they cleverly called Fort Rock Camp. They had survived a perilous set of rapids and falls that the nearby Indians had judged to be suicidal. The Corps hired the Indians to assist in portaging their more valuable cargo and proceeded to take their cumbersome dugout canoes down the rapids to the amazement of the Indian observers who, Ambrose surmised, watched from the shores expecting their deaths:

> The natives, expert canoeists themselves, did not believe Lewis and Clark could do it in their big, heavy dugouts. They gathered by the hundreds along the banks to watch the white men drown themselves, and to be ready to help themselves to the abandoned equipment afterward. But, to the astonishment of the Indians, the Americans made the run without incident.[5]

After my return, I came across a bizarre footnote in the history of The Dalles. In 1984, the town was victim to the nation's first and worst instance of bioterrorism, perpetrated by followers of a charismatic, "new age" Indian cult figure named Bhagwan Shree Rajneesh who founded a movement bearing his name. Using salmonella bacteria, the perpetrators contaminated the salad bars of ten local restaurants. Some 751 people were made very ill but there were no deaths. The apparent purpose of the attack was to render local citizens incapable of voting so that Rajneesh's followers could gain control of local government. The long, complicated tale ultimately resulted in two of his followers being convicted of multiple charges and serving twenty-nine months in a minimum-security Federal prison before being released early for good behavior. Although Rajneesh, himself, was suspected of having orchestrated the attack, it was never proven, and he cooperated in the prosecution of his followers. In 1985, however, he was arrested and charged with violating numerous immigration laws; in a plea deal he admitted to making false statements, was fined $400,000 and was deported with no re-entry for five years. After being refused entry by multiple countries, he returned to his native India and took up his work at an ashram that he had founded there before moving to the U. S. He died at the age of 58 in 1990, but his movement continues under the management of the Osho International Foundation. The story is not exactly what comes to mind when one thinks of "the Wild West," but it does illustrate the complexity of a country born out of the desire to be free of "old world" constraints.[6]

My first stop on this sunny day was the Columbia Gorge Discovery Center and Museum just northwest (downstream) from The Dalles. It is perched on a hill overlooking the river and thus offers one of many spectacular vistas along the Historic Columbia River Highway. The Discovery Center offers a wide range of permanent and temporary exhibits that focus on the history, culture, geology, flora, and fauna of the area. It is very well done and merits more time than I could give it. The permanent exhibit devoted to Lewis and Clark focuses on the 30 tons of cargo the Corps carried across the trail that they carved across the continent from Pittsburgh to the Pacific. It is yet another way of appreciating the formidable challenges they faced in topography and weather.

Also memorable is the Ice Age exhibit that features a life-sized, 13-foot Columbian mammoth and other local wildlife of that pivotal geologic period in our continent's history. The Center's exhibit devoted to the indigenous people of the region features an impressive collection of woven baskets, the careful handiwork of the original Americans who arrived some ten millennia before European explorers "discovered" this land. One's appreciation for time and natural forces that shaped this beautiful region is deepened here. It is an excellent way to begin exploring this spectacular national treasure, surely one of the most breathtaking on my journey.

On a plaque at the Discovery Center, one finds this reminder of the tragic theme that is never far from the surface as one travels the Lewis and Clark Trail:

> *A Columbia Plateau Indian prophet said, "Soon there will come from the rising sun a different kind of man from any you have yet seen, who will bring with them a book and will teach you everything, and after that the world will fall to pieces."*

A helpful attendant at the Center suggested a route to tour the scenic area along the Historic Columbia River Highway traveling west toward Portland and then looping back east to Mount Hood. I left the center around 10:30 and headed west through the winding loops of the highway that runs about 75 miles from Troutdale, just east of Portland, to its terminus at The Dalles.

The spectacular highway, which was carved out of the daunting twists and turns, peaks and plunging valleys of the Columbia River Gorge between 1913 and 1922, was the first such planned scenic roadway in the United States. Featuring the most visually stunning stretches that I encountered in my trip, it has been recognized and celebrated with a listing, among others, on the National Register of Historic Places and as a National Historic Landmark. The American Society of Civil Engineers acclaimed it as a National Historic Civil Engineering Landmark, recognizing the substantial challenge of building the roadway over such rugged land. One of the many admirable dimensions of this experience is how the two-lane road reveals the challenges of building it while giving the traveler a sense of what the region looked like before the road existed.[7] It is, in short, an inexhaustible delight to travel. There are also many hiking trails of varying lengths and difficulty throughout the scenic route.

Among the many wonders of this section of the Columbia River is the dramatic range of weather. At the west end of the gorge, closer to Portland, the average annual rainfall is 75-100 inches; just 80 miles to the east, closer to The Dalles, one reaches the edge of The Palouse, the much-drier, grassland area where the annual rainfall is 10-15 inches per year. This wide-ranging weather supports a great variety of micro-habitats including at least 13 endemic wildflowers.

The dramatic features of the Gorge itself reflect a history that dates back to the Miocene Era, 17-12 million years ago, but it continued to be shaped through the more recent tumultuous geologic developments of the Pleistocene (2 million-700,000 years ago) and most recently by cataclysmic floods at the end of the last Ice Age, 15,000-13,000 years ago, which cut the dramatic, steep walls that define the gorge with elevations ranging from 4,000 feet to sea level.[8]

My first memorable stop as I made my way into the scenic area was a dramatic overlook known as Rowena Crest Viewpoint. This popular spot near the town of Mosier between The Dalles and Hood River offers dramatic vistas of the river and the gorge's precipitous features. Any visit to the area should include this point of interest.[9]

As I made my way further west, I stopped at several of the scores of lacy waterfalls tumbling down the heavily wooded cliffs that tower over the road's southern border. Among the more impressive are Multnomah, the tallest at 620 feet and most visited; Bridal Veil; and Latourell Falls. There are 77 falls along the gorge's historic highway.

I did not loiter long at Multnomah because of the crowd and limited parking. A bit further along the road I enjoyed a more leisurely visit to Latourell Falls, the third highest along the highway at some 224 feet. Located in the Guy W. Talbot State Park, the narrow falls drops straight down among hardwoods and firs to a basin that then drains under the highway and into a creek that flows into the Columbia just below.

This rustic retreat is one of many that came into public hands by the deeply rooted tradition of American philanthropy. An interpretive sign tells that these falls and the 125 surrounding acres of land were a gift from Guy Webster and Geraldine Talbot in 1929. Guy W. Talbot was the president of Pacific Power and Light Company at the time; he and his wife had lived on the land when they made the gift.

Many other sites along the scenic highway were also donated by private individuals or civic groups beginning soon after the completion of the road in 1915. These include Multnomah Falls, Chanticleer Point, Shepperds Dell, Crown Point, and Wahkeena Falls.

Most of these falls have picnic facilities and hiking trails. Additional gifts and acquisitions expanded the park over the years, most recently in 1984.[10] These natural treasures are now owned and maintained by the state of Oregon.

A couple of miles further west of Latourell Falls, the road begins rising in a series of tight loops to the magnificent Crown Point overlook and the site of the famed Vista House, which was constructed in 1918. Samuel Lancaster, who supervised the Columbia River Highway project as the assistant highway engineer for Multnomah County in 1913, had a vision of building an observatory on Crown Point as a respite and attraction for travelers and a tribute to the first explorers and settlers of the Oregon territory. Edgar M. Lazarus, a Portland architect, designed the octagonal shrine, a graceful beacon standing 733 feet above the river. The structure is an example of German "Art Nouveau." Native Italian craftsmen, who had built

189

retaining walls and bridges for the scenic highway, laid the foundation for what Lazarus called "a temple to the natural beauty of the Gorge."

Vista House is about 44 feet in diameter and 55 feet high with floors and stairs faced in Tokeen Alaskan marble. Most of the interior rotunda is light cream and pink Kasota limestone, including hand-carved drinking fountains. The exterior is faced with light gray sandstone. The domed roof was originally covered in matte-glazed green tile, later replaced by copper but then restored in a 2002 renovation.

On the pillars inside Vista House are a series of poems and prayers. The most poignant of the group is the one that serves to remind us of the vexed legacy between the Native Americans and the Europeans who invaded their treasured lands:

> We call upon the mountains,
> the Cascades and the Olympics,
> the high green valleys
> and meadows filled with wildflowers,
> the snows that never melt,
> the summits of intense silence,
> and we ask that they
> Teach us, and show us the Way.
> We call upon the forests,
> the great trees reaching
> strongly to the sky
> with earth in their roots
> and the heaven in their branches,
> the fir and the pine and the cedar,
> and we ask them to
> Teach us, and show us the Way.
> "Chinook Invocation"
> (Quoted in Edward Goldsmith, *The Way*, 1992)[11]

Goldsmith was a famed and controversial environmentalist, writer, and philosopher who died in 2009 at the age of 80. He was the founding editor and publisher of *The Ecologist,* a periodical that espoused a systems approach to environmental issues and ultimately became a highly influential publication. *The Way* was Goldsmith's "magnum opus," his effort to pull together all the diverse strands of his thinking and writing on environmental issues. He was a strong defender of indigenous peoples and a critic of uncontrolled development.[12]

The presence within Vista House of the "Chinook Invocation" taken from Goldsmith's book reflects the unavoidable dilemma faced by all who lovingly celebrate such natural treasures as the Columbia Gorge. It is but one example of the tragic irony that lies within the American story. The desire to embrace its beauties leads inexorably to the destruction of those very beauties. We can't seem to avoid breaking what we have loved.

Mount Hood, July 11, 2017

I left Vista House and headed southeast along U. S. Route 26, which leads to Mount Hood, some 50 miles away. This state road stretches almost 97 miles from Portland east around the south side of Mount Hood and north to Hood River. Most of this route is known as the Mount Hood Scenic Byway and merits that label. Very soon after leaving Vista House, I took a picture of Mount Hood's snow-covered peak gleaming in the summer sun and framed by a clear blue sky above the evergreens and vineyards along the way.[13]

Upon reaching the slopes of Mount Hood around 3 p.m., I was amazed to see skiers and snowboarders coming down the mountain as

I parked my car near the rugged old Timberline Lodge, a National Historic Landmark that was one of the many monumental projects financed by FDR's Depression-Era Works Progress Administration (renamed in 1939 the Work Projects Administration). On this pleasant summer afternoon, it was an odd sensation to take photos of skiers in full cold-weather gear come gliding down the slope that ends at the Lodge.

At some 11,240 feet, Mount Hood is Oregon's tallest peak and is classified as a "potentially active" stratovolcano, also known as a composite volcano, the most common type, because they are built up by the molten materials from eruptions over many years.

The last recorded volcanic activity here, classified as "minor," occurred in 1907. A somewhat more significant eruption had occurred just before Lewis and Clark arrived in 1805. Although the odds of a major event appear to be small, one cannot but recall the disastrous eruption of Mount St. Helens in 1980, where 57 individuals lost their lives. Other famous stratovolcanoes include Krakatoa in Indonesia, which erupted catastrophically in 1883, and Vesuvius in Italy, which erupted in AD 79 destroying the cities of Pompeii and Herculaneum, both claiming thousands of lives.[14]

Simon Winchester's *Krakatoa: The Day the World Exploded: August 27, 1883* (HarperCollins, 2003) is a fascinating account of that cataclysmic event. Although, as Winchester writes, the Krakatoa eruption was not likely the worst in earth's history, it was the first to occur at a time when the event, no matter how crudely understood, could be communicated almost instantly via telegraphic cables all around the world: "It was the greatest detonation, the loudest sound, the most devastating volcanic event in modern recorded human history, and it killed more than thirty-six thousand people."[15] When one visits Pompeii, as my wife and I did in 2012, and walks the haunted streets of that city frozen in time, one gets a sense of the disaster that a volcano can suddenly visit on humanity. It is a somber reminder of the usually neglected vulnerability that all humans share.

Timberline, one of six ski areas on the mountain, has a lift whose base is nearly 6,940 feet elevation; it is the only place in North America open for skiing all year round. Standing at the foot of that slope, I was reminded of stories my mother told me of taking my sister and me up into the mountains near Vernal, Utah, to play in the snow when it was midsummer. I was only two or three years old, so I have no direct memory of those excursions, just a small black and white photograph of my sister and me bundled up in snow suits taken by our adoring twenty-something-year-old mother. God rest her soul.

Experts say the odds of Mount Hood having an eruption in the next 30 years is between three and seven percent, hence its classification as "potentially active," but the mountain is informally considered dormant. The festive activity on the day of my visit was anything but dormant.[16]

Timberline Lodge, a 40,000 square foot, four-story log and stone structure, was built and furnished between 1936 and 1938 by local artisans and laborers, a rugged but graceful reminder of the visionary leadership that Roosevelt provided to a devastated nation. The project cost was $695,730 ($14.3 million in 2022); eighty percent of that went to the 100 laborers who made creative use of local and repurposed materials. President Roosevelt himself dedicated the imposing structure on September 28, 1937. Still publicly owned but privately operated, the Lodge is a popular tourist attraction drawing more than two million visitors each year. Among its more curious claims to fame is having served as the exterior for Overlook Hotel in Stanley Kubrick's popular horror film *The Shining,* based on Stephen King's novel of the same title. It is a curious coincidence that the film was released in the same year that Mount St. Helens erupted, perhaps illustrating that the human appetite for being scared stiff is not adequately satisfied by the real horrors of life.[17]

The initial appropriation for the WPA was $4.9 billion, about 6.7 percent of the 1935 GDP. At its peak in 1938, the great public works program provided jobs to three million men and women as well as the dignity of not merely being "on the dole." Between 1935 and 1943, 8.5 million were employed. The projects included parks, schools, roads, and more than 10,000 bridges. The largest single project was the Tennessee Valley Authority. As we look out across our nation's current infrastructure needs, the WPA's success should be a source of inspiration.[18]

Driving away from Timberline Lodge heading back to The Dalles Inn, I was struck by acres of brilliant purple wildflowers growing across the low, rocky hills at Mount Hood's base. I pulled off the roadside to admire and captured a couple of images of these bright, hardy summer blossoms. It was a moment of grace after a long, quiet day exploring this glorious natural treasure. When I got back to my room around 4:30, I had driven 192 miles. It was a good day of being caressed by majestic beauty.

Chapter Twenty-Five
Golfing in Bend, Oregon

November 2, 1805: The Corps passes Sandy River junction, the furthest point east reached by European or American explorers from the Pacific.

Crosswater Golf Club, Sunriver, Oregon

Wednesday, July 12, 2017, dawned bright and warm in The Dalles, promising to be another great day for golf in the high desert. It was already 77 at 8:30 a.m. After a light breakfast at the Inn, I set out for The Pronghorn Resort near Bend, about 130 miles south. My ultimate destination was Fort Clatsop near Astoria, where The Corps of Discovery finally reached the Pacific and spent a soggy, miserable winter of 1805-06. It is only 176 miles downstream and west of The Dalles, but I had planned my final golf detour in the beautiful, high-desert resort town of Bend.

When I was planning my trip, I discovered that Central Oregon is home to three championship public golf courses regularly ranked among *Golf Digest's* top 100: The Jack Nicklaus Course at Pronghorn Resort (#37 in 2020), Crosswater in Sunriver (#55 in 2020), and Tetherow in Bend (#71 in 2020). Although a substantial detour, I couldn't resist the attraction of this triple-header. It proved to be an excellent decision.

On July 6, soon after arriving at Anaconda, Montana, for my overnight visit and memorable round at The Old Works Golf Course, I called the Central Oregon Visitors Association (COVA) and had the good fortune to speak with Kristi Richter, Membership Group/Events Manager. Kristi could not have been more welcoming and helpful. She expressed keen interest in my project and offered her assistance, which proved to be considerable. Although Central Oregon boasts 30 courses, I told her of my hope to play the three among *Golf Digest's* top 100. She did not promise success but said she'd see what she could do and get back to me. To my delight, she exceeded my expectations by getting me tee times on all three at very attractive "media rates." I remain very grateful for her enthusiastic help.

Central Oregon offers much more than golf, and its visitors association does an impressive job of promoting its varied attractions. Founded in 1971 and supported by more than 450 member businesses, COVA plays a vital role in attracting more than 4.5 million overnight visitors annually. Indeed, tourism is the region's single largest industry, accounting for more than 9,900 jobs and an economic impact that exceeds $1.28 billion per year. It helps that this area is one of the most beautiful in our nation, but effective marketing cannot be undervalued. Anyone planning a trip to the area should start with its outstanding visitor's association: https://visitcentraloregon.com/about-cova/.

Driving down to Bend with Mount Hood looming over my right shoulder for most of the way was uneventful but offered another series of spectacular views across the high desert with the majestic Cascades off to the west of my route through a series of tiny towns like Maupin (est. pop. 441) about 40 miles south of The Dalles, on the Deschutes

River, which flows through Bend and forms a significant feature and hazard of the Crosswater Golf Course. Maupin is named for a late nineteenth-century settler, Howard Maupin (1815-1887), who had a farm and operated a ferry there.

The Deschutes is a major tributary of the Columbia River, flowing mostly due north from its source in the Cascades south of Bend to Miller Island east of The Dalles. The early nineteenth-century French fur traders named it *Riviere des Chutes* for the imposing Celilo Falls now submerged under Lake Celilo formed by The Dalles Dam, which the Army Corps of Engineers constructed between 1952 and 1957. For thousands of years, it was a major route for Native Americans who traveled along it to the Columbia. It was both a water route and an obstacle to early American pioneers as they lumbered across the Oregon Trail in their unwieldy covered wagons. Lewis and Clark camped nearby on October 22, 1805, and on their return journey on April 21, 1806. Miller Island, named for a settler who bought it in 1895, is now preserved as part of the Gifford Pinchot National Forest. Protected from development as a National Wild and Scenic River, the Deschutes is today a popular recreational attraction for fly fishermen and whitewater rafters. It is home to the Columbia River redband trout, known locally as the redside, which are abundant and prized for their large size. Among the many attractions of this region, the Deschutes stands out for its majestic beauty.

The thriving resort community of Bend is the Deschutes County seat with a population of about 100,000. The metro area includes almost twice that number of permanent residents, making it the fifth largest in Oregon. The fine shops, restaurants, and boutiques clearly cater to the millions of annual visitors.

Kristi Richter had arranged three-night's lodging for me at the Pronghorn Resort, which is 15 miles outside of downtown Bend. I arrived at the elegant resort a little before noon and checked into my "junior suite" with delight at the amenities, including a gas-log fireplace. It was surely the best lodging I had yet enjoyed on my trip. Among its many gracious features was a jar of fresh coffee beans with a grinder to make my own coffee each morning. The desert-inspired décor featured wood and stone finishes. I was impressed and grateful.

Pronghorn boasts two exceptionally beautiful championship golf courses that are emerald-green oases in the desert. The Jack Nicklaus Signature Course, opened in 2003, is public. The Tom Fazio

197

Championship Course is private, especially prized by those who have made Pronghorn their year-round home. Each course has been recognized by multiple golf publications and critics as exceptional golf experiences. The resort has an excellent website: https://pronghornresort.com.

When I arrived at Pronghorn, I was ready for some lunch and made my way to an outdoor snack bar overlooking the Nicklaus course. There I met a pleasant young man, a schoolteacher from Pittsburgh and graduate of Allegheny College, one of Pennsylvania's many, fine liberal arts colleges. He was spending the summer working on the morning grounds crew, which gave him free access to afternoons of golf. In an unaffected manner, he shared his story and his strong Christian faith with me. He was one of four children and had clearly had a challenging life guided by a devoted single mother. I shared with him my plans for a book and later that day sent him the questions I had posed for others along the trail. A couple of weeks later he sent me an email reflecting on those questions.

Not surprisingly, his strong faith was prominent in his responses. For what he most valued about being an American, he cited "the freedom and opportunity to grow and develop our faith and education." He wondered if his faith might mean more if it weren't free and if "being a Christian gave you no political or social gains," if one's life were in danger for being a Christian, as is the case in some places. Although not routinely reported by the U. S. media, persecution of Christians continues to grow. According to Open Doors, a British-based advocacy group, in 2019, 260 million Christians faced "high or extreme persecution" in one of the 50 countries on the organization's "World Watch List." The number of those who died for their faith declined substantially to 2,983 from the more than 4,000 in the prior year. Christians face the gravest threat in Nigeria. Other countries where the persecution is widespread include North Korea, described as the most repressive, China, and Indonesia.[1]

He also expressed his appreciation for the opportunity for anyone —regardless of income, race, or religion—to pursue one's passions and interests through education. His own challenging life experiences were reflected in that observation. From our visit over lunch, it was clear that meeting the financial challenge of higher education had not been easy. Although he did not say as much, I surmised that he, like so many others, had carried a substantial debt from college loans.

In recent years, a recurring story in the popular media has generated widespread concern about the so-called "student debt crisis." The numbers can appear daunting. Most frequently we see the total student debt figure, which in 2020 reached $1.64 trillion among almost 45 million borrowers. That figure is often compared to the total U.S. credit card debt, $587 billion in 2020. One is given the impression of college graduates staggering under a crushing debt load that prevents them from getting a good start in life, forcing them to defer investments or activities that earlier generations took for granted after earning their bachelor's degree.

There is some truth to the stories and disheartening examples can be found, but there is also a good deal of exaggeration generated by focusing on worst cases that are far from typical. For example, about 30 percent of college grads have no debt at all. For the rest, the average in 2019 was $29,900, which resulted in an average monthly payment of $200-$299. The average debt for graduates of public institutions was $25,550; for grads of private, nonprofit colleges it was $32,200. For graduates of for-profit colleges, the debt was almost $40,000. Of all graduates from colleges and universities at all levels, only about seven percent had debt exceeding $100,000, and many of these were graduates of professional schools that would lead to much higher incomes than those with only a bachelor's degree.

In my years as a college administrator, putting "the student debt crisis" in context was a perennial challenge. As one who graduated with debt, I have always felt it was the best investment I ever made. Although income potential should not be the only reason for going to college—and college is certainly not for everyone—it is a fact that the average lifetime earnings of those with a bachelor's degree are $1 million more than those who do not have this credential.

My young friend from Pittsburgh clearly understood the value of his education, but what worried him most about America today was "our disregard for God" and the resulting pain and suffering in the way we treat each other. He attributed "broken homes, drug addictions, bullying, exploitation, slavery—sex trafficking, increase in mental illness, and suicide" to the decline in religious faith across the country. Although difficult to prove the causality, his concerns were echoed by others I encountered in my travels and since.

As for his "magic wand," he hoped that all might "sincerely love Jesus . . . and our neighbors, foreign and domestic, as ourselves." I came away from my visit with this earnest young teacher feeling confident that he would contribute much to his students and to his community.

My tee time was around 1 p.m. with David Matich, the resort's group golf sales manager, who proved to be pleasant company for the afternoon round. David was a 29-year-old from Michigan and, despite being a much better golfer than I, made me feel right at home on the challenging course. From the tips, the course plays 7379 yards with a slope and rating of 75.2/151. He wisely suggested that we'd have more fun playing the gold tees at 6000 yards, 68.9/135. Even that was perhaps more challenge than I could handle at that time. After starting with three double bogeys, I was happy to card four pars and end with a 98. I wish I could find my way back to Pronghorn now that my post-retirement game has improved, but I am still quite capable of shooting in the high 90's on my home course.

After our round, David took me over to the signature 8th hole on the Tom Fazio course. It features a volcanic lava tube or cave between the tees and the elevated green. I walked into the dark cave and immediately felt the dramatic drop in temperature. It felt like a wine cellar as I looked out on the very warm afternoon just steps from the cave's entrance. It is a striking feature of this hole but also a great attraction for the resort. Pronghorn hosts all sorts of events in this unique geologic feature, including weddings, concerts, and elegant picnics.

I had a quiet dinner at the resort's up-scale Cascada restaurant, which claims its "inspiration" comes from local farmers and ranchers. It boasts an outstanding selection of regional craft beers, cocktails, and wines as well as spectacular views of the surrounding mountains from inside or on the patio. It was a very pleasant end to a completely enjoyable day. I felt pampered by the hospitality of everyone I met at Pronghorn and slept well in my comfortable room.

Crosswater Golf Club
Thursday, July 13, promised to be another warm, sunny day with a 61-degree temperature at 7:30 a.m. After a fresh cup of coffee in my room, I made my way over to the Trailhead Lodge for a delicious breakfast frittata and then headed out for Crosswater Golf Club at nearby Sunriver, about 15 miles south of Bend and a 40-minute drive from Pronghorn. I had a 10:09 tee time arranged with a warm welcome

by assistant golf pro Cody Johnson, who took a keen interest in my project and later responded thoughtfully to my questions.

The striking contrast between Pronghorn and Crosswater illustrates the range and variety of topography in Central Oregon's high desert. Although Crosswater sits at an elevation of more than 4000 feet, lush wetlands and thick evergreens framed by the nearby Cascade Mountains define the visual impact of this stunning course. The accolades for the course make a long list, which I'll not repeat here, but a few deserve mentioning. It certainly merits the frequent five-star ratings that individual golfers give it. Recalling this memorable test of golf is a pleasure that makes me long to return.

Designed by the award-winning architect Bob Cupp, Crosswater was recognized by *Golf Digest* as the best new course of the year at its opening in 1995. It continues to appear regularly on *Golf Digest's* annual top 100 list, coming in at number 50 in 2019. When it opened, it was the longest golf course in the U. S., measuring 7,683 yards.

I do not recall playing a more immaculately maintained course in my travels. From the reviews I read, the pristine conditions are the norm, but it surely didn't hurt that Crosswater had hosted the 50th PGA Professional National Championship less than a month before my visit (June 18-21, 2017). It was the fourth time that the Sunriver Resort, which includes Crosswater and two other championship courses, had hosted the PGA's showcase event for its professional members. Previous events were in 2001, 2007, and 2013.

Sunriver Resort is a residential community and resort operated by Hyatt. Its two other 18-hole courses are Meadows, designed by John Fought, and Woodlands, a Robert Trent Jones, Jr. design that "features dense forests of ponderosa and lodgepole pine, outcroppings of lava rock and an abundance of water." The Meadows, located near Bend, has hosted numerous USGA and NCAA events, including the NCAA Men's Division I championship. To complete this attractive golf mecca, Caldera Links is a "family-friendly" 9-hole track designed by Bob Cupp and Sunriver's own Jim Ramey. This little gem features bent grass greens and bluegrass tees with holes ranging from 60 to 185 yards. It is reserved exclusively for Sunriver Resort guests, Caldera Springs residents, and Crosswater Club members.[2]

Among its many accolades, in 2019 Crosswater was hailed as #2 overall for Best Courses in Oregon by the Golf Advisor Golfers Choice Award. Other tributes include Top 10 Destinations for Family

Golf by *Golf Digest* in January 2016 and top 10 of the best courses in Oregon in 2014 by *Golf Week*. In 1999 Crosswater was designated as one of only 150 U. S. Audubon Sanctuary golf courses. There are more than 15,000 courses in the U. S., about 43 per cent of the worldwide total.[3] It would be difficult to find a more appealing destination for a memorable golf vacation.

I am often struck by the creative genius reflected in a well-designed golf course. To be able to envision a graceful combination of art, science, and engineering in a terrain that once appeared to be a swamp or a wasteland is an admirable talent. Crosswater is one of the more striking examples I've had the privilege of playing. According to *Golf Digest*, the course was the site where John Wayne filmed scenes from his celebrated 1969 film "True Grit."[4]

I expect "The Duke" would be stunned by the transformation worked by Bob Cupp on some 600 acres of evergreen woodlands and carefully preserved wetlands that define the course today. The Deschutes and Little Deschutes Rivers flow in wide loops through the course and can come into play on seven of the holes. The design is described as "traditional heathland style" and features five sets of tees, the shortest of which measures 5723 yards. From the tips, the rating/slope is 76.6/146. The fairways and greens are well-maintained bent grass. I once again foolishly selected the so-called "Member" tees, which play 6550 yards (71.4/138). From these tees, the par fives range from 518 yards (no. 2) to 572 yards (no. 12) and include a par 3 of 204 yards. Quite a challenge for a guy whose average drive is 200 yards! I was pleased to shoot a 92.

Although Crosswater is technically a private golf club, it appears on the *Golf Digest* list of best public courses because resort guests can play the course for a daily fee. I was grateful for the privilege of playing the course.

Cody Johnson had arranged for his summer intern, a Mississippi State University student and aspiring golf professional to join me for my round. Unfortunately, he was tied up with a crew making a promotional video when I arrived, so he joined me on the back nine. It was one of only two times on my trip when I failed to have company for all 18 holes. Only once, on my return, did I play alone. One of the pleasures of golf is being able to walk on to a public course without a tee time and find another single, a twosome or threesome who will welcome your company. It's rare to be refused and when it happens, I always think I see something like embarrassment, even a tinge of shame in the refusal. Although it costs little more than a bit longer time on the course, this reflexive welcome always charms me.

The young intern was good company on the back nine. Despite his good example and helpful tips, I played more poorly with him than I had on the front nine. He was interested in my project and agreed to send me his thoughts on the questions I had been posing along the way. The day after my visit, he emailed me a thoughtful set of comments that reflected impressive maturity for such a young man. Reading his words gave me a surge of hope for our future.

He wrote that he most valued about our country the "selflessness that so many great Americans exhibit," and it was clear from his elaboration that he was thinking not just of those who make the headlines but of ordinary folks who routinely exhibit a willingness to be helpful to one another. He cited as an example the choice that so many make to serve in our armed forces, but he also expressed admiration for "neighbors and peers at work" who "are constantly willing to stop whatever they are doing to assist someone in need." Although he may not have fully realized that his experience reflected a privileged life not equally accessible to all, his spirit of gratitude was refreshing.

The security of personal information was his greatest concern: "The rapid increase of information technology has allowed the average person to access almost anything . . . our personal identities are composed of 'accounts,' Bank accounts, school ID accounts, social media accounts, work accounts, phone accounts. They have all become such an integral part of our lives that a failure or breach in one of them is devastating." His insightful remarks reflect well his being a member of the generation that has grown up on the Internet and the exploding pervasiveness of social media. Since 2017, this concern has only grown as social media has become ever-more intrusive and our national political leadership appears incapable of finding ways to moderate it.

In response to my question about what he would change with a "magic wand," he offered a keen insight that appears almost prophetic in hindsight as I write in what I may fatuously hope are the waning days of the Trump Era. Recognizing the importance of Freedom of Speech as "the first of our great [Constitutional] amendments," he trenchantly observed that "sometimes Americans just needs to shut up. The President of the United States does not need to be arousing strong emotions of people on social media. It is not the place for that! The constant bickering over "Black Lives Matter" and the LGBT community is pungent and repulsive. How can anyone be heard over the distressed mass of people shouting on the streets or typing in all caps on social media? Just shut up. Problems are solved by listening and thinking. In order to do so, one must refrain from picking up the microphone." I can only imagine what he came to think in the three years that followed his 2017 email. I was pleased to learn that he completed his college work and in December 2020 was working as a golf pro at a course in California.[5]

A couple of weeks later, I received an email from Cody Johnson responding to my questions. He expressed appreciation for the "opportunity to live an extremely healthy lifestyle" as well as "the ability to make so many decisions on how I choose to live my life. We may not feel like we have all that much freedom at times, but we are very fortunate to have the opportunities that we do." His source of worry about America today was a bit cryptic: "I feel we as a general public have completely lost sight of the things that really matter." Such a comment begs for further exploration, but that was beyond the scope of my design. Indeed, I can imagine having had many, lengthy conversations with several of the folks who were kind enough to respond to my questions, but time and energy constrained me.

His succinct response to my "magic wand" question was not quite as cryptic, but it too tempted me to ask for more. He simply wrote, "Distribution of wealth and power, and conservation of the planet and all of our resources." I assume that he meant a more just and equitable distribution of wealth and power as well as greater concern for the environment, but I don't wish to put words in his mouth. His thoughtful, generous, and gracious manner in our relatively brief time at Crosswater gives me some confidence that I'm not far off the mark.[6]

Tetherow Golf Club
My last full day at the Pronghorn Resort had come too quickly, but I resolved to make the most of it. I was up early and returned to the Trailhead Grill for breakfast, which may have been my only option on the property. Although Pronghorn is an attractive, full-service resort, it sits in isolation about 15 miles from Bend. One does not dash out

for a quick bite off site without planning 45 minutes to an hour of travel time.

My tee time at Tetherow was not till 1:50 p.m., so I set out on foot to explore the residences surrounding the resort. There are many impressive homes scattered around the perimeter of the two golf courses, all of them showing creative designs that reflect the desert and the feel of the region, with lots of stone and timber elements. There are four distinct residential "communities" at Pronghorn. These include The Estates, with homes ranging from $500,000 to $3.5 million; Four Peaks, smaller homes with slightly lower price tags; The Villas, "Tuscan-inspired" houses just off the 17th fairway on the Nicklaus course; and finally, "The Residences," which are townhouses privately owned but managed by Pronghorn as rentals for a portion of the year. The latter are three-to-four-bedroom units ranging from 2000 to 2600 square feet. One listing was for $489,000 for a four-bedroom, four-bath home of 2565 square feet. For those seeking shorter stays, the Huntington Lodge offers a wide variety of options including the gracious suite where I stayed.

After almost four miles of walking through the warm morning's dry desert air, I returned for a delightful massage at the resort's spa followed by some time in the sauna. If being relaxed before playing golf is as important as most say, I was there!

After dropping by the pro shop to pick up my re-gripped driver, I headed toward Bend, picked up a quick lunch at a Wendy's and then found my way to Tetherow. The course is four miles southwest of downtown Bend at the edge of the Deschutes National Forest, a 1.6 million-acre, year-round recreational wilderness attraction that is nestled along the eastern slopes of the Cascades. Spanning a variety of landscapes and ecosystems, the elevations range from Lake Billy Chinook at 1,950 ft. to the South Sister's summit at 10,358 ft. More than eight million visitors annually find their way there to camp, fish, hike, hunt, ski, mountain bike, and admire the beauty.[7]

Tetherow showed me again how different the high desert golf courses can be. It is quite unlike either the Nicklaus course at Pronghorn or Crosswater just a few miles south along the Deschutes River, which runs along the south side of the Tetherow property as it flows into Bend. Recently named a top 10 course in Oregon by *Golf Digest*, Tetherow's distinctive 18 holes were designed by the award-winning Scottish architect David McLay Kidd, who also designed

Bandon Dunes and Castle Course at St. Andrews. Tetherow reflects Kidd's philosophy of design which he describes as follows:

> How can we create a course to be as natural as possible, as seamless as possible, as sustainable as possible? . . . [He] likened it to birthing a child for adoption. When we give birth, but Mother Nature adopts, how can we make sure the new mother accepts the child and raises it as her own? It cannot be done when the course starts off at odds with nature herself! . . . Fun golf exists for the average golfer where choices exist. A narrow fairway littered with hazards offering a single strategy of play might be thrilling for the low handicapper, but not so appealing for everyone else . . . [the] hazards on a golf hole should not punish the average golfer trying to make par or bogey, but in fact, guard the hole from the attacking golfer attempting to make birdie or better.[8]

It is a challenging and austerely beautiful links-style course with firm, fast-running fairways and some of the most difficult greens I've ever played. Thick, high grasses and other gnarly vegetation lurk all around the edges to punish errant shots. Of the three courses I played in the area, Tetherow has the greatest elevation variety by far. The combination of altitude, which it shares with the other courses, and the firm, sandy fairways gave me noticeably greater distance on all the shots that landed in the fairways.

Tetherow is named for a 19th-century pioneer named Solomon Tetherow (1800-1879). Originally from North Carolina, he led a wagon train into the Oregon territory in 1845 along with his wife and at least ten children. Three more were born once they reached Oregon; ten of their fifteen children lived to maturity. He settled and lived out his life near Monmouth, Oregon, outside present-day Salem. Apparently, his name has local resonance, as Tetherow's fine-dining option is named Solomon's in his memory. It is one of three dining options at this appealing resort perched on the hills overlooking Bend. One of his sons penned an affectionate portrait of his father:

> Sol Tetherow was born in Tennessee in the year of 1800. He was married to Ibbie Barber and they had 15 children, ten lived

to reach old age and three of the children were born after they came to Oregon.

Sol Tetherow crossed the plains coming to Oregon in 1845, locating in Dallas, Oregon, Nov. 16, 1845. He bought Sol Shelton's squatter's rights to a section of land, or traded him a brindle ox named Bright for his square mile. Dallas is now located on that claim.

In 1847, Mr. Tetherow found a claim on the forks of the Luckimuate River more to his liking, so he moved his family there.

Of the ten children raised to man and womanhood, only one is living at present time, Sam Tetherow of Dallas. Martha Burns, a sister, passed away Jan. 17, 1924 in Portland. Sam Tetherow was nine years old, when his father started for Oregon and can remember many incidnets [sic] of the trip. Nearly three thousand people came across the plains in the year 1845.

The wagon trains were divided into different groups. Sol Tetherow was captain of one group. Nearly two hundred families of this emigration left the road at Hop Springs near Fort Boise an took what was said to be a short cut off to Oregon. They got off the trail in Malheur county and had all sorts of grief. Stephen Meek was their guide. It was a member of this party that found gold near the head of the Malheur River, afterward called the Blue Bucket Mines.

Early in their married life an outbreak of the plague caused them to lose their first two children: A son Amos was born Jan. 21, 1827 and a daughter Matilda was born Oct. 30, 1832, both of these children were born in Platte Co. Missouri. No other records have been located regarding where they are buried.[9]

The University of Oregon library in Eugene has a copy of the journal that Tetherow kept during his migration to Oregon.[10] I came across a PDF that includes a typed transcription of the journal in a document at the University of Oregon library (F880.L58), but for the life of me,

I can't figure out how to capture the hypertext link to this document. Anyone interested enough to pursue this sidetrack in my narrative should be able to find the 25-page document by simply Googling "Solomon Tetherow."

Entitled "Captain Sol Tetherow/Wagon Train Master" by Fred Lockley, the document includes on its cover the following description of its contents: "Personal Narrative of his son, Sam. Tetherow, who crossed the plain to Oregon, in 1845, and Personal Narrative of Jack McNamee, who was born in Portland, Oregon, in 1848, and whose father built the fourth house in Portland."

This naturally led me to discover Fred Lockley (1871-1958), who was a newspaper columnist, a rare book dealer, and the author of books on Oregon and Pacific Northwest history. His is another interesting story of how restless, adventurous, enterprising characters made their way across the country and gave it the shape it has today.[11]

His narrative regarding Solomon Tetherow is a fascinating oral history, primarily based on his leisurely interviews with Sam Tetherow when he was 88, his parents' last surviving child. Although only nine when his family crossed the plains to Oregon, he recalled the journey vividly.

I knew none of this history when I arrived at Tetherow Golf Course on Friday, July 14. As I drove up Skyline Ranch Road overlooking the course, I knew before I got out of my car that I was in for a treat. Grant Zimmerman, the group golf sales manager, welcomed me warmly and apologized that he would not be able to join me for the round of golf as he had hoped. He gave me a very generous discount and paired me up with an amiable young man named Zeb Weld who would be my caddie and would play a few of the holes along with me.

Zeb suggested we play from the Sage tees which measure 6106 and are rated 69.6/127. This proved to be a good decision. I managed to get away with only one triple bogey on #16, the number two handicapped hole and the longest par four. I carded three birdies (#2, #17, #18), a rare accomplishment for me. The strong finish gave me a 91. In a follow-up email with Zeb, I expressed my wish that I had played better—as always! He kindly observed that fewer than ten percent of those who play Tetherow break 100, "So good on you." He earned what I hope was a generous tip.

My birdie on 18 stands out in my memory mainly because it seemed so unlikely. The par five slopes uphill into a prevailing westerly wind back toward the resort. It was late afternoon as we were finishing, so the sun was moving down the western sky creating a little hazy glare. I had just scored an improbable, lucky birdie on the previous hole, a par 3 that played only 124 yards. I fully expected the typical way that golf courses (and our minds) pay us back after an unearned birdie. My drive on the 464-yard, par five left me about 220 yards uphill to the green. My drive was among the best of the day, and I got great downhill roll on the firm, fast fairway because the hole slopes down from the tees, then starts sloping uphill from where my ball stopped on the left side of the fairway.

Zeb reminded me that I'd get good roll if I hit the fairway, so he encouraged me to go for it. I did not entertain the thought that often comes into my head on such a decision: "what's the worst that can happen?" As every golfer knows, the worst can be very bad indeed. Nevertheless, I pulled out my three wood, a club I hit infrequently because I find it so hard to hit it pure. I have much better results with my five wood and normally trade the slightly less distance for the greater likelihood of hitting it well. Perhaps my low expectations helped me relax because I took one easy practice swing, stepped up and hit the ball as well as I ever do. It had that sweet feel and sound that every golfer knows and longs for. The ball leapt off the club heading uphill with the slight draw I needed from my lie on the dog-leg-left hole. Because of the elevation and the glare, I couldn't see where the ball landed, but I knew it had to be close to the green. Zeb simply said, "that was a good one."

When we reached the green, I don't know who was more surprised to discover my ball resting on the three-tiered green, not close to the hole but close enough to hope for birdie and feel pretty sure of par. With good help from Zeb and 17 previous holes to get used to the speed, I hit my first putt up to within about three feet and sank the birdie, again with good counsel from my young caddie. It was a deliciously memorable end to a great afternoon of golf, and I immediately began replaying the holes that kept me from breaking 90: "the woulda, coulda, shoulda holes."

As I was working on this book, I ran across an entertaining review of Tetherow entitled "Why Tetherow Golf Club is the Most Polarizing Course in Oregon" by Sean Ogle. It's a good read, giving ample credit to the difficult greens and the challenge of tight lies on the fescue fairways, but I agree with his conclusion: "It's one of the most scenic courses I've ever played, and it passed the true test of a good course in my book: It made me want to run right back out and play another 18."[12] Ditto!

Several months after I had returned from my trip, Zeb sent me a thoughtful email responding to the questions I had asked him to consider. For what he most valued about our country, he spoke admiringly of its first inhabitants and their relationship with the land. "I value the land that was preserved and the ability to go into the woods and mountains. To stand on some of the same lakesides as native peoples. I enjoy the opportunity to daydream about a day in someone's shoes here hundreds of years ago."

His response to what worried him late in 2017 looks prophetic in light of subsequent events, particularly the violent mob's assault on the U. S. Capitol on January 6, 2021, just a couple of weeks before I was writing these lines. (More on this topic in my closing chapter.) He spoke of hearing people "joke about the end of days and how violent people say they would be if things starting crumbling. I'm worried," he continued, "that there could be people that would want to take your life in order to survive themselves." He continued his brief apocalyptic reflection by commenting on the weapons now available that would make it difficult to protect one's family "like my parents did when I was growing up."

The combination of anxiety and perhaps just nostalgia for what appeared to be a simpler past may reflect his relative youth and the necessary loss of innocence that comes inevitably as one reaches adulthood, especially if one has enjoyed a relatively secure and happy childhood. Whatever the cause, his comments were touching and genuine. In the ensuing years, the increasing frequency of violence in our streets, the toxic divisiveness and coarseness of our public debates, the increased polarization of politics through echo chambers of social media and partisan "news" channels that make no effort to present a "fair and balanced" account of national and world events, the recent disheartening experience of the presidential election of 2020, and the violence that followed it combine to make this thoughtful young man's concerns appear prophetic.

Finally, for his magic wand, he dreamed of restoring the landscape "to what it was 300 years ago and change the way we build our industries and homes." He expressed his belief that "a little more interaction with nature . . . would change the outlook of some people."[13] My appreciation for the afternoon in the company of this thoughtful, courteous young dreamer was deepened by his email. I wish him well.

I completed my memorable round at Tetherow wishing I could come back and play it again the next day. If I ever get back to Bend, it will be tough deciding where to stay. The resort at Tetherow would certainly be on my short list. Although Pronghorn and Sunriver Resort are lovely, Tetherow is more conveniently located just outside Bend. On the other hand, Sunriver Resort offers a range of accommodations and access to all four of its impressive golf courses. A difficult decision, but I'd surely want to play the Nicklaus Course at Pronghorn, Crosswater, and Tetherow again. One could have a fine week or more of great golf in Bend.

Leaving Tetherow, I headed into town looking for dinner. I had made no plans but trusting to luck worked well this time. I saw a relatively new steakhouse called Bos Taurus, immediately got a seat at the comfortable bar, and visited with Eric, the bartender, as I enjoyed an excellent steak dinner. Upscale and a bit pricey, the quality of the food and service paired with the charm of its post-industrial décor made it a memorable experience. I would return. Conveniently located on Minnesota Ave. in the heart of Bend's thriving downtown, Bos Taurus was a great way to end my last day in this golf mecca.

Chapter Twenty-Six
The Last Leg: On to the Pacific!

November 7, 1805: Captain Clark records "Ocian in view! O! the joy." He notes that the Corps has traveled 4,142 miles from the mouth of the Missouri[1].

Replica of Fort Clatsop, Astoria, Oregon

The delightful detour to Bend left me with about 260 miles to reach Fort Clatsop on a bluff overlooking the Columbia River near Astoria, Oregon, founded in 1811. It was here that the Corps of Discovery spent a wet, miserable winter of 1805-1806. According to their journals, it rained 94 of the 106 days of their tedious stay, December 7-March 23. Fortunately, my weather on July 15 was much better, another warm, sunny day.

After breakfast, I left Pronghorn Resort around 8:45 a.m. and made my way northwest toward Salem, Oregon, traveling through the beautiful wilds of the Willamette National Forest to Interstate 5 and then almost due north arriving at Fort Clatsop National Memorial and Visitor Center around 2 p.m. I had traveled 5557.5 miles since leaving my home in Gettysburg on June 20. Clark had noted in his journal on November 7, 1805, "Ocian [sic] in view! Oh! The joy." He then added, "Ocian 4142 Miles from the Mouth of Missouri R."[2] I checked my own mileage to discover that I had driven 4,555 miles since arriving in St. Louis on June 23. Although my journey bore little resemblance to the grueling experience of the Corps of Discovery, I shared the joy. The mighty Pacific stretched out before me in splendor.

Julie Fanselow observes accurately that "Fort Clatsop is among the very best interpretive sites along the Lewis and Clark route."[3] Although not the largest, nor the most visually impressive on arrival, it is well done. In my two hours of admiring the Visitor Center's exhibits, the hiking trails, a living history demonstration of tanning hide, and the impressive replica of the tiny fort that the Corps built, I gained a deep sense of the life they lived in those 106 days—absent the constant rain.

"Arrival" by Stanley Wanlass, Fort Clatsop Visitor Center, Oregon

Upon entering the Visitor Center, an impressive, life-sized sculpture entitled "Arrival" by Stanley Wanlass commands one's attention. Shining in the afternoon sun through the tall windows behind it is the image of Meriwether Lewis standing with arms outstretched as if in a benediction with William Clark kneeling in front of him recording events in his journal. A Clatsop Indian is crouching over Clark and holding a starry flounder as if to represent the hospitality that these Native Americans extended to the Corps. Alongside them is Lewis's beloved dog, Seaman, the sturdy companion of their arduous travels. Limited edition replicas of the work are available for $2400 in the Center's gift shop. This detailed tribute to the courage and endurance of the intrepid explorers is yet another reflection of the way in which the Lewis and Clark expedition has captured the admiration and imagination of so many over the years. It was dedicated on September 9, 1983.[4]

Among the exhibits is a full-size canoe like the ones that the Clatsop tribe crafted to navigate the turbulent waters of the Columbia. Clark described and sketched these high-bowed canoes with admiration, noting their superiority to the rough-hewn craft that the Corps had hacked out of fallen timber after crossing the Bitterroot Mountains. This sleek canoe reminded me of a darker moment in the expedition's saga. As the Corps was preparing to depart in March 1806, they attempted to trade with the Indians for two of their canoes. Their stock of trade items was depleted, and Lewis thought the price the Clatsop chief demanded was exorbitant. Nevertheless, he was able to strike a bargain for one canoe by handing over his prized uniform coat. He complained in his journal, "I think the U' States are indebted to me another Uniform coat, for that of which I have disposed on this occasion was but little woarn [sic]."[5]

Despite his best efforts, he could not reach an agreement for the second needed canoe. In an uncharacteristic moment of weakness, Lewis instructed his men to steal one. He recorded a weak rationalization that reflects his uneasy conscience in the matter: "We yet want another canoe, and as the Clatsops will not sell us one at a price which we can afford to give we will take one of them in lue [sic] of the six Elk which they stole from us in the winter."[6] As Ambrose noted, Lewis did not record that the Clatsops had paid for the stolen elk with dogs, which were much prized by the men for food.

The sordid deed was done with Lewis acknowledging that it "set a little awkward" in light of the Clatsop's generous treatment of the Corps throughout the difficult winter. As if to make some amends, Lewis presented the chief with a certificate affirming his good conduct and "friendly intercourse" during their stay. Although he had no other option, on the morning of their departure, Lewis formally conveyed to the Clatsop chief "our houses and furniture." Of the chief, Lewis wrote in his journal, "He has been much more kind an [sic] hospitable to us than any other indian in this neighbourhood."[7]

On the grounds near the Visitor Center is a handsome bronze sculpture of Sacagawea with her baby swaddled on her back. Standing about five-feet tall, it is one of the many artistic tributes to this remarkable woman who played an indispensable role in the success of the journey. The artist was Jim Demetro, who now lives in Puerto Vallarta, Mexico, where he has a studio and teaches.[8]

I learned later that the sculpture I saw was a replacement of an earlier one, a gift, that had been installed in June 2004 in conjunction with the Lewis and Clark bicentennial. Local papers record the sad tale of that statue having been stolen and sold for $200 of scrap metal in January 2008. The culprit was apprehended and sentenced to 50 days in jail. In an admirable burst of civic pride and private generosity, $25,000 was raised quickly, and the replacement was installed in October 2008. I was struck by the odd coincidence of the evil spirit that moved Lewis to steal a canoe continuing to live in the vicinity of Fort Clatsop. Of course, this evil spirit is anything but a local force.[9]

The replica of the tiny fort that the Corps built here is the most attractive feature of the site. As Fanselow recounts, the original fort, built entirely of logs from the abundant supply at hand, had deteriorated within ten to fifteen years of the expedition's stay. In 1901, the Oregon historical society began searching for the site, but it was not till 1955, the expedition's 150th anniversary, that a replica was built. The replica's design was based on drawings and descriptions found in the Corps' journals; it was lovingly maintained for more than 50 years to prevent the wet climate from wreaking the same fate as that of the original fort.

Then in October 2005, as the bicentennial of the Corps' arrival approached, the replica was accidentally burned. The same civic pride that just a few years later resulted in the prompt replacement of the Sacagawea statue was evident in the hundreds of volunteers who stepped up to rebuild the replica. Years of archaeological research contributed to a new replica even more faithful to the original. It was dedicated in December 2006, 201 years after the expedition had begun working on the original.[10]

Walking through the fort on a sunny day made it a little difficult to imagine the smells and feels that must have been the daily experience of the Corps through that wet winter. It measures only 50 feet square with two rows of huts separated by a "parade ground" down the center. One row had three small rooms, each providing compact quarters to eight of the enlisted men with two pairs of narrow bunk beds on either wall. On the other side of the parade ground were four rooms. The largest housed the two captains. Charbonneau, Sacagawea, and her baby, Pomp, shared another room. An orderly room housed the sergeant of the guard and his three men, a rotating assignment that was scrupulously observed. As Fanselow notes, it is not known where Clark's slave, York, slept; she guesses it might have been in the orderly room. The fourth room was used for smoking and storing meat, a constant need and challenge in the wet conditions.[11]

Monotony was the dominant theme of the winter as was recurring illness. Fleas were a constant annoyance. Although game was available, principally elk, it was of uneven quality and unreliable quantity. Dog meat obtained from the natives was a staple of their diet. Although strict military discipline was enforced, one of the few diversions allowed the men was regular sexual relations with the willing Clatsop women. Lewis treated the frequent cases of syphilis and all the other maladies the men suffered with his stock of medicines. There is no record of either captain having availed themselves of these carnal pleasures despite there having been offered.[12]

After about two hours at Fort Clatsop, I reluctantly departed to visit other sites in the limited time left in this last day of my solitary explorations. I drove down into the historic little port city of Astoria and crossed the magnificent Astoria-Megler Bridge, a 4.1- mile steel cantilever through truss bridge that spans the Columbia River connecting Northwest Oregon with Southwest Washington. The longest continuous truss bridge in North America, it was opened in 1966 replacing the ferry that had previously been the only means of crossing the turbulent river near its terminus in the Pacific. It is an impressive engineering accomplishment that is high enough on the

Oregon side to allow large container ships to pass beneath into the deep-water port at Astoria.[13]

I had hoped to reach the Lewis and Clark Interpretive Center at Cape Disappointment State Park on the north shore of the Columbia near Ilwaco, Washington, but the 25 miles took a little longer than I expected so I was too late to visit the Center, which closed at 5 p.m. From Fanselow's account, it's well worth a visit although being much smaller in scale and scope, not in preference to Fort Clatsop.

The most attractive feature of the peninsula is the wild and verdant topography of steep cliffs and hills, evergreen woodlands, and rocky outcrops. Narrow blacktop roads wind through the area, and I enjoyed wandering through the woods before making my way to the quaint seaside village of Ilwaco. This little town has shops and restaurants along its port and a Saturday Market that attracts tourists. According to Fanselow, the Ilwaco Heritage Museum is worth a visit. There are two functioning lighthouses on the peninsula. The Cape Disappointment Lighthouse, built in 1856, is the oldest operating one on the West Coast.

Just beyond Ilwaco, the Interpretive Center is located on rocky cliffs about 200 feet above the Pacific at the extreme southwestern tip of the Long Beach Peninsula, which stretches some 28 miles north by northwest along the state of Washington's southwest border. It is a popular vacation spot that claims its beach of 28 uninterrupted miles is the longest in the U. S. I can't help but believe there would be challenges to that claim, but I am again reminded of my historian friend's disdain for such "sterile claims to primacy." I decided not to spend time finding other claims to longer beaches.

The Interpretive Center includes a series of mural-sized timeline panels that guide visitors through the Corps of Discovery's journey west. It makes good use of sketches, paintings, photographs, and the words from the Corps' journals. It also features a short film, a gift shop, and a glass-enclosed observation deck that offers a panoramic view of the river, headlands, and ocean that Lewis and Clark saw upon their arrival at this western-most point of their journey in November 1805.[14]

After reaching the final miles of the Columbia River's path to the Pacific on November 7, the Corps of Discovery spent more than two weeks in punishing wet miserable conditions looking for a suitable place to spend the winter on the north shore of the river. On November

11, Clark wrote, "We are all wet as usual and our situation is truly a disagreeable one." Four days later he noted eleven straight days of rain and complained, "I can neither get out to hunt, return to a better situation, or proceed on."[15] Although they were ultimately able to do a good deal of exploring, passing on beyond Cape Disappointment and up what was later named the Long Beach Peninsula, they ultimately gave up on finding a suitable place for a winter camp on the north side of the river.

It is merely a coincidence that their frustrations and disappointment along the north shore of the river terminated at Cape Disappointment. John Meares (1756-1809), a British sea captain, fur trader, and adventurer of dubious integrity had sailed from China in 1788 and while trading for furs had attempted to confirm the existence of a rumored large river in the vicinity. Impeded by wind and tides, he came very close but failed to find the mouth of the Columbia and thus dubbed the prominent point Cape Disappointment.[16] Four years later, an American explorer named Robert Gray found the Columbia and sailed almost 100 miles up the river.[17]

In one of the more unusual incidents of the great expedition, the captains called their small company together in wet misery on November 24 to determine their next move. They had three options: 1. Stay on the north shore and continue to search for a suitable winter camp. 2. Retreat upriver to more agreeable grounds they had already found on the outward passage. 3. Cross over to the south shore of the river where they had been told by local Native Americans that the game was more abundant and the land heavily timbered with sources of fresh water flowing into the Columbia. Although the Captains were partial to the third option, they decided to take a vote. It was a first for the Corps, which had operated on a military command model. As Ambrose wrote, it was also "the first vote ever held in the Pacific Northwest. It was the first time in American history that a black slave had voted, the first time a woman had voted."[18]

Only Private John Shields voted against the third option. "York's vote was counted and recorded," Ambrose wrote. In his journal, Clark, using Sacagawea's nickname, wrote "Janey in favour of a place where there is plenty of Potas" [roots], Ambrose noted.[19] On November 26, after working its way slowly upriver to calmer water, the company crossed to the south shore; they were further delayed by foul weather until November 29 when they reached the present-day site of Astoria where they camped. A few days later they located what would become Fort Clatsop alongside a stream they dubbed the Lewis and Clark River. They had no way of knowing that the site, which Clark declared a "most eligible Situation," would prove to be a place of such protracted soggy misery.

Having driven 309 miles since leaving Bend that morning, I returned to Astoria around 5:30 that evening to my overnight room at the Astoria Riverwalk Inn. It was a high contrast to the luxury that I had enjoyed at the Pronghorn Resort, but it was clean and neat with a fine view of the Columbia out my window and a small deck outside my room. The tariff of only $64.30, taxes included, was hard to beat, and given the quality was among the best bargains of my trip. Tourism is a major feature of Astoria's economy now, so there are at least fourteen hotels in a range of prices and many restaurants along the Riverwalk.

Hoping for a fresh seafood dinner, I took the suggestion of the Inn's desk clerk and made my way on foot to the nearby Bridgewater Bistro (https://bridgewaterbistro.com). It proved to be a good choice. I enjoyed a delicious dinner of fresh salmon, sat at the little bar overlooking the river, and enjoyed the cordial company of a couple from Central Oregon. They were butter makers in town for an association event. Over dinner I told them of my journey and my envisioned book project.

In response to the three questions, they agreed that freedom was what they most prized about being Americans, the opportunity to move freely—she was originally from Maine—and take risks, as they had done in launching their enterprise in butter. They were in a holiday mood and reluctant to voice what worried them about our country although the wife did say "Trump" with a slight chuckle when I first asked. I was surprised by their suggestion that eliminating the national debt was what they would immediately change with a "magic wand." I wish now I had asked them to elaborate on this wish as I'd like to know why they would choose this among so many other possibilities. How did the national debt affect them? It is, of course, a huge, complex, and controversial subject, but not pursuing it with this amiable couple was a missed opportunity. Our conversation wandered in other directions over our good dinner and more than one fine glass of wine. It was an agreeable end to another memorable day, the last stop on my following the Lewis and Clark Trail to the Pacific. I would happily return to Bridgewater Bistro.

Chapter Twenty-Seven
Astoria: "The Little Town That Could"

December 7, 1805: The Corps selects its site for winter quarters, "Fort Clatsop," just south of present-day Astoria, Oregon.

View of Astoria across Columbia River from Southwest Washington

"Astoria is that little town that could, a city of 10,000 people on the Columbia River, just a few miles from the Pacific Ocean. Founded 200 years ago at the beginning of Oregon's North Coast, Astoria has been through boom and bust times more than once, weathering the collapse of both the Columbia River fishery and Oregon timber industry. It has risen again as a cultural haven, often referred to as "little San Francisco." Astoria is an old place that is newly hip. Here, Victorian mansions and maritime relics live in harmony with chef-driven restaurants and tattoo parlors."[1]

My overnight in Astoria was too brief for me to appreciate the spirit of the place as reflected in the above effusions by Oregon's tourism promoters. That came later as I read about the little city's history and had time to reflect. Equally helpful was a Zoom interview that I had on February 9, 2021, with Mayor Bruce Jones, whose term began in January 2019. Jones is a retired U.S. Coast Guard officer whose last assignment was serving as commander of the Astoria Station. I was pleased to discover that Mayor Jones is, like me, a Washington and Lee University graduate, class of 1982, ten years after me.

After 30 years of Coast Guard service that took him all around the country, Jones and his wife retired in Astoria, which he describes with affection. "It is," he said, "a beautiful, historic place with a real sense of community that is reflected in a strong ethic of volunteerism." He noted that the five-member, nonpartisan City Council works very well in a spirit of collegial, civil professionalism. He felt at home in the community very quickly and notes that his being a newcomer elected to the City Council and later as mayor with more than 58 percent of the votes reflects the warmth and openness of Astoria. Although he has enjoyed the work, he was plunged into the rough waters of the coronavirus in the second year of his term. It appears that his Coast Guard experience prepared him well to provide steady leadership in the most challenging of storms.

Astoria is a distinctive example of how America's towns and cities, buffeted by sometimes dramatic economic and cultural change manage to reinvent themselves and creatively adapt to new circumstances. My appreciation for how Astoria reflects the enterprise and adaptability of the American spirit was deepened by having recently read *Our Towns: A 100,000-Mile Journey into the Heart of America* by James and Deborah Fallows.[2]

As the subtitle suggests, it is an account of the Fallowses flying in their tiny, single-engine Cirrus SR22 back and forth across the country for more than four years to discover reasons to be hopeful in the face of an increasingly toxic and divided nation. Their protracted journey had ended in 2017 shortly before I set out on my much-more-modest adventure, but it was a joy to discover their account as I began to work on this book. Their thoughtful and appreciative stories of smaller towns and cities across the country deepened my appreciation for what

I had seen, especially in two towns that my journey had included: Rapid City, South Dakota, and Bend, Oregon.

I enjoyed meeting the Fallowses in February 2019 when they visited the Midtown Scholar Bookstore on North Third Street in Harrisburg, Pennsylvania, for a talk about their new book. I treasure my signed copy of the hardcover edition. Located just a few blocks from the state capitol complex, this independent bookstore is a small wonder, well worth a visit by any book lover within striking distance. Not only does it have a wide selection of new and used books stacked in floor-to-ceiling shelves on its two floors, but also regularly hosts talks and book signings by prominent and emerging authors on a variety of subjects. Knowing of the challenges that independent bookstores face in ordinary times, I have watched with admiration as Midtown Scholar Bookstore creatively adapted to the restrictions of the coronavirus.[3] May it continue to thrive.

Although the Fallowses did not include Astoria in *Our Towns*, they told me that they had a much longer list of other candidates than the 28 they included in their book. At the time, they were mulling a second volume. Astoria would be a good candidate, but so would many other American towns, including the three with which I am most familiar in Pennsylvania: Gettysburg, Harrisburg, and Reading. Each of them has been buffeted by changes that have brought out the best in generous and civic-minded citizens who have labored tirelessly to address the challenges and build new foundations for a brighter future. These stories of civic pride and often-volunteer service reflect the enduring spirit that Alexis de Tocqueville admired early on in his famed *Democracy in America* (1835).

Astoria, a thriving port city and the seat of Clatsop County, traces its founding in 1811 to the enterprising German immigrant John Jacob Astor, who is reputed to have been America's first multi-millionaire. Just five years after the Corps of Discovery spent the winter of 1805-06 nearby, Astor's American Fur Company built Fort Astor on the northwestern tip of what is now Oregon at the confluence of the Columbia River and the Pacific Ocean. He went on to command a monopoly in the booming fur trade of the early nineteenth century. In 1876, the Oregon Legislative Assembly incorporated Astoria.[4]

Known as the Beaver State, Oregon became the nation's 33rd state on February 14, 1859, just three years after the boundary dispute with England was resolved with the 49th parallel being the border between

Canada and the U.S. Today Oregon has an area of 98,381 square miles and a population of 4.2 million. A state of spectacular beauty and topographic variety, it rewards exploration in every direction. Its highest point is Mount Hood at 11,249 ft. Its lowest point could be said to be beautiful Crater Lake, a caldera formed by the collapse of an ancient volcano some 7,700 years ago. The depth of the crystal blue lake exceeds 1,900 feet.[5] That's 124 feet more than the World Trade Center in New York, America's tallest building and the seventh tallest in the world.

In the decades following Lewis and Clark's expedition, waves of American settlers made their way across the famed Oregon Trail and settled throughout the territory. Astoria, which is the oldest city in the state and the first American settlement west of the Rocky Mountains, became a thriving port initially dependent on the fur trade and logging. Today, Oregon is still the largest producer of timber among the contiguous states, but neither the fur trade, long-since ended, nor timber are principal economic forces for Astoria.

Fishing and fish processing grew as the major industry for Astoria well into the middle of the 20th century. As recently as 1945, about 30 canneries were located along the Columbia in or near Astoria. But following World War II, the commercial fishing industry declined along with the diminished Pacific salmon population. Mayor Jones acknowledged the decline but said commercial fishing continues to be an important part of the local economy with two major seafood processors remaining, Bornstein Seafood and Da Yang. The same is true of the forest products industry despite Astoria Plywood Mill, once the city's largest employer, having closed in 1989. Reflecting the declining industry in the city, the Burlington Northern and Santa Fe Railway ended its service to Astoria in 1996. "Tourism has grown as these industries declined," the mayor said.

Today Astoria appears to be a city shaped by creative and imaginative collaboration in making the most of its assets. Sport fishing is a growing attraction, and the city boasts a thriving art scene as well as a burgeoning microbrewery and brewpub business. Since 1982, when the city invested $10 million in port improvements, Astoria has become an increasingly popular port of call for cruise ships. A weekly street market is an additional attraction.

A city of only ten square miles, including about four square miles of water, Astoria's population, never large, peaked at 14,000 in 1920 and declined steadily thereafter to a low of 9,477 in the 2010 census. Growing since then, the 2020 census recorded a population of more than 10,000, and Astoria is projected to continue modest but steady growth in the coming years. Indeed, one priority for the city's current leadership is managing growth and providing affordable housing while protecting its natural beauty and historic treasures.

Mayor Jones affirmed the ongoing challenge of balancing economic development and historic preservation. He mentioned with pride the recently completed Riverfront Vision Plan that established four geographic sectors to guide the city's efforts to strike the correct balance between its strong spirit of entrepreneurship and an equally firm commitment to preserving the natural beauty and historic assets of the old town. He was particularly pleased with the number and variety of restaurants that are locally owned and operated. Aside from the usual presence of national fast-food chains, there are none of the large chain restaurants that seem to occupy almost every city of any size across the country. For a city of its size, the range of restaurants is impressive, numbering around 40 and including a broad ethnic variety from Thai, Chinese, and Japanese to Bosnian, Italian, Mexican, and Indian, as well as more traditional American fare in pubs and bistros. Naturally, excellent fresh seafood is abundant.

The mayor also mentioned Columbia Memorial Hospital (CMH), with almost 700 employees, as the largest employer in the community and thus a key economic force. Serving Astoria since 1880, CMH claims to be the "fastest growing rural hospital in the state." It is a 25-bed, full-service, not-for-profit Level IV Trauma and Critical Access Hospital and only one of five remaining independent hospitals in Oregon.[6] Its independence is a growing exception in the U. S. healthcare system, which seems to thrive on growing numbers of consolidated systems such as WellSpan, which absorbed the Gettysburg Hospital well over a decade ago.

Mayor Jones also mentioned with pride the 2017 arrival of The Knight Cancer Institute, which is affiliated with the Oregon Health & Science University in Portland. This long-planned partnership has expanded the local hospital's cancer treatment capacity.[7]

Among the major challenges facing the city is a housing shortage and rising real estate values caused by recent growth and particularly by people moving from Portland and other larger cities seeking refuge from the coronavirus as well as the usual stresses of urban life. Most of these newcomers are relatively affluent and able to pursue their careers remotely. Although they bring welcome new energy and talents to the community, people of lower income face growing difficulty in finding affordable housing.[8]

Mayor Jones told me of one recent accomplishment that will provide housing for low-income residents. The old Merwyn Hotel, a four-story structure built in 1926 had fallen into disrepair in the 1980s and was closed in 1989. Sandwiched between City Hall and the Library, the old hotel sat derelict and decaying till a group called Innovative Housing, Inc. purchased it in 2018 and led a public/private partnership to acquire the funds for renovation as a 41-unit, low-income residence which opened in early 2021. Although the project will not solve Astoria's housing challenge, it is a promising step in that direction and an example of community vision and collaboration that combined historic preservation with entrepreneurship.

Another example is the city's grand old Venetian-style Liberty Theater, a 1920-vintage "motion-picture palace" and vaudeville venue that had fallen into disrepair and was a vacant eyesore till it was restored in 2006. Built soon after a devasting fire in 1922, the theater had been a symbol of the city's rebirth. Its second incarnation complete with the original decorative architecture and a 631-seat main auditorium is now a proud symbol of Astoria's commitment to the arts, historic preservation, and economic development.

Among the town's more unusual annual events is the Fisher Poets Gathering, held in late February since 1998, where artists with ties to the fishing industry congregate in growing numbers to share their poems, tales, and songs celebrating that legacy. Its popularity has been boosted by stories on NBC's Today Show, an article in *Smithsonian* magazine, and a documentary film called "Fisher Poets."

Of course, like me, thousands of Lewis and Clark tourists travel to Astoria each year to visit Fort Clatsop and the related historical sites that commemorate and interpret the arrival of the Corps of Discovery as well as the culture and history of the native peoples who have inhabited the area for more than 13,000 years.

Another point of pride for the community is the soaring Astoria Column built on Coxcomb Hill above the town. The 125-foot column of steel and concrete features an interior spiral staircase of 164 steps leading to an observation deck that affords a spectacular view of the entire area. Its exterior *sgraffito* frieze commemorates the history of the area from pristine wilderness to the arrival of the first explorers, the further development of the area following the arrival of Astor, and finally the arrival of the railroad. It was built in 1926 with funding from the Great Northern Railroad and Vincent Astor, a great-grandson of John Jacob Astor. The mayor noted that a nonprofit friends group supports the maintenance of the Astoria Column and raised $1 million for a complete restoration of the frieze in 2013-14. It was added to the National Register of Historic Places in 1974.[9]

As a bicycle enthusiast, I was delighted to learn that Astoria is the western terminus of the TransAmerica Bicycle Trail, which runs 4,250 miles to Yorktown, Virginia, along mostly rural two-lane roads through ten states. It was opened in conjunction with the U.S. Bicentennial, and in that year 2,000 riders completed the entire trip. Many others rode parts of it.[10]

In some circles, Astoria may be best known as the setting for the popular 1985 film *The Goonies*, which I distinctly recall enjoying with my children, admiring the lush and rugged landscape, charming Victorian homes, and shots of the river. At the time, I had no idea where the film was made, but Astoria has been quite a magnet for other films. Among them are *Short Circuit*, *The Black Stallion*, *Kindergarten Cop*, *Free Willy* and its sequel, *Teenage Mutant Ninja Turtles III*, *The Adventure Home*, *Benji the Hunted*, *Come See Paradise*, and others.[11]

With characteristic enterprise, Astoria seized on its success as a film location by creating the Oregon Film Museum in 2010, the 25th anniversary of *The Goonies*. The museum wisely celebrates not just films made in Astoria but the more than 400 that have been made throughout the state. Housed in the old county jail, which was featured in the opening chase sequence in *The Goonies*, the building itself is a stately two-story, neoclassical structure built in 1913 and now listed on the National Register of Historic Places. Yet another delightful Astoria attraction, it features hands-on exhibits related to films made in Oregon, props from *The Goonies* and other films, as well as an opportunity for visitors to make their own short films.[12]

The Columbia River Maritime Museum, where Mayor Jones serves as Deputy Director, is yet another attraction. As described on its excellent website, it "is a unique combination of experiences where an extensive collection of seafaring vessels, maritime artifacts, and fine art come to life through exciting and informative exhibits, demonstrations and hands-on activities."[13] Opened in 1963 in the Old Astoria City Hall and expanded in 1982 to its current location on the waterfront, it has gained a national reputation for the quality of its exhibits and the broad scope of its collections that focus on the Columbia River as well as the Pacific Northwest. Oregon's official maritime museum, it was the first in the state to be accredited by the American Alliance of Museums.

Among its prized exhibits is the retired U.S. Coast Guard lightship Columbia, which served as a floating lighthouse for almost 30 years guiding ships through the treacherous waters at the mouth of the Columbia. In 2013, the museum opened the Barbey Maritime Center for Research and Industry nearby in the old 6,000 square foot train station originally built in 1925 for the Spokane, Portland & Seattle Railway. The mayor noted that "the museum uses the renovated building for adult and youth education programs and community events."

The maritime museum's adaptive re-use of local facilities reflects, yet again, the entrepreneurial spirit of Astoria. Remodeled and expanded in 2001-02, the museum is now located in a handsome, modern facility of more than 44,000 square feet that offers visitors a panoramic view of the river and an appealing variety of exhibits as well as a 36-seat 3D theater. Its collection exceeds 30,000 objects, 20,000 photographs, and a 10,000-volume research library.[14]

From the Fallowses' *Our Towns,* I learned to look for "bellwether institutions" that most thriving communities seem to share. These include an engaged community college, a vibrant public library, and a local newspaper. Astoria checks all those boxes.

The Astoria Board of Education founded Clatsop Community College (CCC) in 1958; it was the state's first community college. Its first building was in the old high school. The original curriculum included two years of classes that could be transferred to a four-year college and two-year programs in electronics, business, automotive and building construction. Today, CCC serves 857 students (43% are full time) at its main campus on a hillside overlooking the Columbia River and two other sites offering specialized training including its maritime science program and small business and economic development services. The student-teacher ratio of 16:1 is lower than the state's community college average of 28:1. The broad curriculum of 35 areas of study ranges from Accounting and Art to Veterinary

Medicine and Welding. It's clear that CCC is an engaged partner in meeting the community's workforce development needs and providing opportunities for motivated students to move on to more advanced study. Mayor Jones mentioned the program that enables motivated high school students to complete an associate degree at the community college while completing their high school diploma.[15]

Although small in stature, Astoria's public library is actively engaged in the community and offers a variety of programs for all ages including early literacy programs for children up to five years old, activities especially for teens from grades six through twelve, monthly game days, book discussion groups, author visits and musical performances. It offers public access to the internet through its computers on a time-limited basis (one hour/day/user). It also provides a community meeting space in its Flag Room. With other community stakeholders, the library recently conducted a study exploring the feasibility of relocating to a new facility as part of the city's Heritage Square initiative. Although that project is currently on hold, the creative energies of this community lead me to believe the much-needed expansion will one day be realized like so many other projects that once seemed beyond achieving.[16]

The community's local newspaper, *The Astorian,* has been in continuous publication since its founding in 1873. Formerly *The Daily Astorian,* the paper began publishing three times per week in 2019, reflecting the challenges that small-town newspapers across the country are facing. I remain grateful to have a local newspaper that publishes six days per week here in Gettysburg. I enjoyed perusing *The Astorian's* on-line offering and appreciated the opportunity to purchase a one-day pass for only 99 cents.

A recent story that caught my eye further reflects Astoria's vitality. "Italian Market Coming to Astoria," Jan. 12, 2021, tells of a local family of teachers launching an Italian pasta and sausage shop to be known as Gaetano's Market & Deli. "The shop will offer homemade pastas, sauces, sausages, lasagnas, salads and sandwiches to-go, along with meats, cheeses and breads. The market portion will include beer, wine and a gourmet selection of groceries, including peppers, vinegars, oils, marinated vegetables, condiments and dried pastas." Having spent time in Italy, the founders aim to provide an added dimension to the food scene in their community. Starting a small business at any time is a high-risk proposition; doing so during a pandemic is something else. Learn more on their attractive Facebook page: https://www.facebook.com/gaetanosmarketanddeli/.

In the conclusion of *Our Towns*, the Fallowses list ten and a half "signs of civic success." I've touched on most of them in this profile of Astoria. The playful "half" sign, "perhaps the most reliable gauge," is "at least one craft brewery, maybe more, and probably some small distilleries, too."[17] Following the elimination of "musty Prohibition-era restrictions on home brewing" during Jimmy Carter's administration, the craft-brewing business exploded and continues to grow. There are now more than five thousand across the country, and here again, Astoria shines.

Mayor Jones mentioned several local breweries, but there appear to be at least eight in or near Astoria plus a couple of small distilleries. Fort George Brewery and Public House, which opened in 2007, occupies an old riverside warehouse that had been vacant since the 1980s. Praised by *Lonely Planet* as "one of the state's best and most reliable craft brewers," this popular destination is clearly booming. It boasts 40 varieties and ships to Oregon, Washington, and Idaho. In 2013, it was included "among the fastest growing breweries in the U.S." by *The New Yorker.*[18]

The mayor also encouraged me to check out Buoy Beer as another example of a thriving local brewery; it set up shop in a long-vacant waterfront cannery that dates to 1924. Not only are these creative beer-loving entrepreneurs, but they also have a touch of the poet in their souls:

Here, one of the West's most relentless rivers meets the wilderness of an entire ocean. The unstoppable meets the unyielding. And here, a community with grit and backbone make that meeting work.
The river that built a town is home for building this beer. *A place where hard work and hustle matter; where the local color has seen a little weather; where the newest generation wasn't born yesterday.*
This is beer with history to it; a story to unfold, a tale to be told. *Brewed from this confluence of pride and place. New beer, with a few centuries under its belt. Beer you can savor and share. Made of a few pure ingredients and a whole lot of local flavor.*
Just like the town it comes from.
BEERS UP![19]

It's worth noting that as of 2014, Oregon had 208 breweries, more than all but three other states in the U.S.: California (509), Washington

(251), and Colorado (217). With 58 breweries, Portland claims more than any other city in the world. If one is a craft beer fan, Oregon is clearly a destination, and Astoria deserves a visit.[20]

Although I became increasingly fond of Astoria in the months and years following my visit there in 2017, I would not want anyone to think it is a place without challenges and drawbacks. The weather, although generally mild, with cool winters and mild summers, would not be ideal for all. The soggy winter of 1805-06 was not an aberration. Indeed, Astoria has the distinction of being tied with Lake Charles, Louisiana, and Port Arthur, Texas, for having the highest average humidity in the U.S. Having grown up in Georgia, I know something about humidity. Average temperatures make a difference. If I had to choose between the Mediterranean climate zone of Astoria and the steamy summers of the Gulf Coast, it would not be a difficult decision. But for those who enjoy a good cleansing sweat as soon as they walk out the door every morning between April and October, the Gulf Coast would surely deliver.

When I asked Mayor Jones about crime in Astoria, he expressed relief that "serious crime" was not a major challenge. He noted that it had been years since there was a murder in the city, and various sources bear this out. It looks like the last murder in the city was recorded in 2010. As I consulted various on-line data bases, I learned that comparing crime statistics can be tricky. There appears to be no single, authoritative source for such data and a lack of consistency in who reports and how it's done.

After studying some of these data, I had a helpful email follow up with the mayor who then conferred with his police chief. The chief prepared a detailed four-page analysis of the city's crime data and some helpful cautions about comparing such data across states much less across the country. The bottom line is that these statistics can be misleading and confusing to the untrained. The chief's data show that Astoria's most frequent recorded crimes in 2019 and 2020 were criminal trespass and disorderly conduct. The chief also cautioned that many compilers of crime statistics will include all crimes in a given zip code and then label it with the principal municipality in that area. He pointed out that Astoria's zip code covers 149 square miles and several other municipalities.

When I initially shared my findings with the mayor, he said that a small number of individuals with "behavioral health problems" are the source of hundreds of police calls each year and thus drive their crime stats up in a way that distorts his own experience and that of most Astorians, who feel that there is very little crime in their community. He noted that a relatively small homeless population—perhaps 90 individuals—is an intractable problem that Astoria shares with many other cities across the country.[21]

Another challenge facing Astoria is its aging underground infrastructure. As Mayor Jones explained, the main business district of the city alongside the river looks relatively flat, bounded by steep hills to the south. This was not what Lewis and Clark saw when they arrived in the area that would become Astoria. Almost all the original buildings were built on posts and then the early residents filled in the watery shore over time. The result is a soft and wet soil that plays havoc with any utility that runs underground.

Mayor Jones mentioned landslides as another chronic challenge of Astoria's location. A recent article in *The Astorian* covered this topic well: "More than half of Astoria is prone to shallow landslides, and more than one-third to deep landslides. At least 120 slides have hit the city, including more than 80 in the past 150 years. The city's Community Development Department, supported by its engineering and public works staff and new state guidelines, is creating a geological hazard ordinance to help keep residents on stable footing."[22]

Having lived across the U.S., Mayor Jones readily acknowledges that every city and every region has different challenges. He didn't seem to think that Astoria had more than it could handle and was clearly pleased that he and his wife had finally settled in a community where civic engagement, pride, and volunteerism are deeply rooted values.

Near the end of *Our Towns*, the Fallowses recall the assessment of Philip Zelikow, a professor at the University of Virginia, who observed that Americans across the country "are figuring out how to take advantage of the opportunities of this era, often through bypassing or ignoring the dismal national conversation." These "positive narratives," however are "lonely and disconnected," he argues. "It would make a difference to join them together, as a chorus that has a melody." "That is the American song we have heard," the Fallowses concluded.[23]

During my visit to Astoria and in research following my return, I, too, heard that "American song," not just in Astoria, but across the country in communities large and small. Despite the grim and disheartening events of the intervening four years, I have hope that the spirit so evident in Astoria will endure and ultimately guide our country to a better and brighter future.

Chapter Twenty-Eight
A Long Way Home

March 28, 1806: The Corps departs Fort Clatsop for its return journey, arriving amidst great celebration in St. Louis on September 23, 1806.

Mount St. Helens, July 18, 2017

Sunday, July 16, began with 8:30 mass at the little frame St. Mary's Star of the Sea Church on the slopes overlooking Astoria. I then headed off to the Portland airport to meet my wife, who was flying in for an eight-day tour of Portland, Seattle, and Vancouver, British Columbia. It was our first time in the Pacific Northwest, and we enjoyed many of the tourist and historical attractions in and around these lovely cities. Although we enjoyed them all, Vancouver was our favorite.

We spent two nights at The Benson Hotel in downtown Portland. Highlights included a memorable visit to the famous Powell's

Bookstore where we had the pleasant surprise of running into a couple who are friends from Gettysburg. They were visiting family in the area. On the morning of the 17th, we toured Washington Park with its magnificent rose garden where we admired yet another statue of Sacagawea. In the afternoon, we drove up the Columbia to Cascade Locks and boarded the Columbia Gorge Sternwheeler for an hour's excursion through the magnificent vistas of the river. Before returning to Portland, we visited the Cathedral Ridge Winery in Hood River. Our return to the hotel was plagued by terrible afternoon traffic, but we were compensated by an outstanding seafood dinner that evening at Jake's, one of Portland's many fine restaurants. A disturbing feature of Portland was the large number of homeless people camping in the city's parks and wandering hopelessly through its streets. How can this disheartening sight be an ordinary feature of so many American cities? One would think the richest nation in human history could do better.

On the 18th, we left for Seattle, some 175 miles north, but detoured to visit Mount St. Helen's, the active stratovolcano that erupted with devastating impact in May 1980. The entire area offers visitors one breathtaking vista after another until one reaches the visitors center on a peak across from the crater formed by the eruption. The trip was well worth it. We arrived at The Warwick Hotel in Seattle that evening, very tired but grateful for a good meal in the hotel.

We stayed only two nights in Seattle, so the 19th was our only full day for touring. We packed as much as we could handle into this single day and enjoyed our visit to the city's iconic Space Needle, were swept away by the Chihuly Garden and Glass gallery, and to my surprise Dottie agreed to ride the Great Wheel off Pier 57, a peaceful contrast to the hectic street scene of the Pike Place Market. We dined that night at the cozy Petra Mediterranean Bistro on 4th Avenue. One day is inadequate for a visit to Seattle, but we greatly enjoyed our wee taste of its diverse sights, sounds, and pulsing energy.

On the 20th, we returned for another hearty breakfast at CJ's Eatery near our hotel, where we had breakfast the previous day. On the road by 9:45, we arrived mid-afternoon at Hotel Opus in the lively waterfront district of Yaletown in Vancouver. We were greeted warmly with a glass of Prosecco and guided to our elegant room where we spent the next three nights.

Our tour of Vancouver included a whale-watching tour through the Salish Sea aboard the "Salish Sea Dream" to Victoria, which we toured by bus before visiting the spectacular Butchart Gardens. And, yes, we did see whales but not till our return trip just beyond Victoria's harbor.

On Saturday, July 22, we visited the Capilano Suspension Bridge Park, a treetop experience through heavily wooded evergreens on seven lengthy suspension bridges and other winding paths that immerse visitors in a taste of Canadian forest wildness. Although understandably crowded on a Saturday, it was a memorable excursion. After returning to the city and enjoying a good lunch at the Cactus Club Café, we caught a little water taxi near our hotel and ferried over to Granville Island. Almost immediately upon arriving, we knew this would not be a place where we would tarry for long. It was a chaotic collection of every tacky, touristy shop one could imagine. The highlight was a large company of nude or nearly nude male and female bicyclists winding through the avenues proclaiming, "more ass, less gas," to the bemused onlookers. Knowing that Granville Island could not possibly top that spectacle, we hopped aboard the water taxi and headed back to our hotel.

The following Sunday morning, we wandered the streets of Vancouver on our way to the Cathedral of Our Lady of the Holy Rosary for mass. It's a lovely old Gothic structure with some fine stained glass. We made our way back to the hotel and were on the road by 11:30. We arrived at a Holiday Inn near the Portland airport around 6 p.m., had dinner at the airport, and had a short, final night together before her early flight out on the 24th.

After dropping Dottie at the airport, I headed east on I-84 along the Columbia Gorge as the sun rose in glory over the river's morning mist. I had a sudden stab of joy realizing that I was finally headed home. I couldn't help but think of the emotions that Lewis and Clark's wilderness-hardened troop must have felt as they at last were able to make their way back up the mighty river in the late spring of 1806. It would take them about six months to get back to St. Louis, where they arrived on September 23, 1806. My return trip took six days.

I did not plan to retrace the Corps of Discovery's return trip. Instead, I was eager to take in a few sights that were important to me and to make a much quicker return. My first goal was to reach Vernal, Utah, where I had lived with my older sister and parents when I was too young to remember. My principal goal in Vernal was to visit the nearby Dinosaur National Monument. On the way to Vernal, I would stop by the Great Salt Lake just so I could say that I had.

On July 24, I drove about 475 miles to Mountain Home, in southwest Idaho, east of Boise. I stayed at the Mountain Home Inn, a comfortable Best Western, and had a simple dinner at the adjacent AJ's restaurant, retired early and had a good night's sleep.

The following day I drove all the way to Vernal, some 538 miles with my detour to see the Great Salt Lake. Although a very long day of driving, a little more than 12 hours including stops along the way, it was filled with beautiful vistas. These included the rolling, brown hills south of I-84 out of Mountain Home through the Snake River Valley to the magnificent gorge outside of Twin Falls, Idaho, famous as the site where daredevil Evel Knievel attempted to fly across the Snake River Canyon in 1974, unsuccessfully as it turned out due to a mechanical failure that almost cost him his life.

The Great Salt Lake, located further west of Salt Lake City than I had realized in planning my travel that day, proved to be a substantial detour, but it was worth seeing this vast, salty remnant of the much larger, late Pleistocene Lake Bonneville that was ten times the size of the Great Salt Lake and covered much of present-day western Utah and extended into Idaho and Nevada until around 16,800 years ago.

The Great Salt Lake now has an average surface area of 1,700 square miles but fluctuates greatly depending on weather, ranging from the recorded low of 950 square miles in 1963 to the historic high of 3,300 square miles recorded in 1988. Only the Great Lakes in the U. S. are larger, and they are very much larger, indeed. Lake Superior, for example, measures almost 32,000 square miles, and the smallest of the Great Lakes, Ontario, is at least four times the size of the Great Salt Lake's average surface area. Still, it's a great sight to see on a sunny summer's day, and it certainly stirred my imagination to think of Lake Bonneville's vast pre-historic reach across this section of the country. It was about the size of today's Lake Michigan, which deepened my appreciation of our Great Lakes' scale and reminded me of my first climbing across the dunes along the shore of Lake Michigan north of Indiana. Gazing across this vast, inland sea, I wondered what the first explorers must have thought. Were they surprised to discover it was not salt water?

While I'm recalling my brief visit to the Great Salt Lake, it seems worthwhile to note that it's far from a "Dead Sea," as some call it. The lake is fertile habitat to millions of native birds, brine shrimp, various shorebirds and waterfowl including being the world's largest staging population for Wilson's phalarope, beautiful migratory waders with sharp, slender beaks for spearing their prey along salty shorelines. They winter in salty lakes found in the Andes of Argentina. Although I don't recall spotting this species on my visit, I did enjoy seeing plenty of people swimming, boating, and frolicking in the lake.[1]

After leaving the Great Salt Lake around 6 p.m., I made my way east around Salt Lake City and arrived at Park City in time to find a quick dinner. The home of the Sundance Film Festival, this ski resort drips with affluence. Indeed, with a population of about 8,000, it reaps more than $529 million per year from the hordes of tourists that drive the booming economy. I was not surprised to learn that in 2008, *Forbes Traveler Magazine* listed it among the 20 "prettiest towns" in the U.S. As I pulled into the neatly landscaped shopping mall where I found a Subway, I watched with dismay as a ragged and dirty family of five dug through a dumpster behind a fast-food restaurant. This, too, is a disheartening feature of our beautiful, wealthy country. Why?

Leaving Park City, I made my way through beautiful Heber Valley, known as Utah's Little Switzerland, up into the sparsely populated mountains of the lower Wasatch Range and then on to Vernal, 145 miles east of Park City. I arrived around 9:30 at the Ledgestone Hotel, my overnight lodging, where I was relieved to get a quiet night's sleep despite a gathering of Harley-Davidson enthusiasts who were staying there as well.

My destination on July 26 was Cheyenne, Wyoming, but in the morning, I headed first to the Dinosaur National Monument, a few miles east of Vernal and straddling the Colorado state line. Having long been fascinated by the ancient fossils of the Jurassic Period, 150 million years ago, I spent a delightful morning there. I first visited the enclosed exhibit that covers a huge cataract of fossils that were washed downstream by an ancient flood. I then drove through a small portion of the surrounding hills and river valleys within the preserve. First discovered in 1909 by paleontologist Earl Douglass of the Carnegie Museum in Pittsburgh, the area around his find was declared a national monument in 1915. It was initially comprised of only 80 acres, but in 1938 the U. S. Government expanded the preserve to more than 210,000 acres in Utah and Colorado. It contains more than 800 paleontological sites. One could spend many days—or even a lifetime—exploring this vast expanse.[2]

I reluctantly left Dinosaur National Monument around 12:30 p.m. and took a northwesterly route through the Flaming Gorge National Recreation Area in the Uinta Mountain Range of northeast Utah. This combined a passage through another magnificent wilderness area and the most direct way to I-80, which runs through southern Wyoming. Cheyenne was 365 miles away. I stopped for an excellent lunch at the rustic Flaming Gorge Resort and arrived at the stately old Plains Hotel in downtown Cheyenne around 7:30 p.m. I discovered that my arrival coincided with the annual week-long celebration of Pioneer Days, which resulted in my paying one of the highest room rates of my trip for a huge second-floor room with a tiny bath that appeared to have been added after the hotel was first built early in the 20th century. It was not my most elegant accommodations, nor the quietest with the exuberance of celebrating visitors in the street just below. In retrospect, Laramie, just 50 miles west of Cheyenne, might have been a better choice.

After a restless night, I got up early, took a walk around the handsome capitol with its golden dome, had a great breakfast at the hotel and hit the road. Home was still more than 1500 miles away. My consolation was a planned round of golf at River's Edge Golf Course in North Platte, Nebraska. I cannot now recall how this course came to my attention. It's certainly not among those that make lists on *Golf Digest* but having not swung a club since my memorable round at Tetherow on July 14, I was descending into golf withdrawal. In such a condition, as all golfers know, almost any course of any condition will be welcome. It was 220 miles east.

I arrived in North Platte a little after noon. Located at the confluence of the North Platte and South Platte Rivers, which simply become the Platte River east of town, North Platte describes itself as a "railroad town," and justly so. It was founded in 1866 when it became, briefly, the western terminus of the First Transcontinental Railroad, which ultimately stretched 1,912 miles from Council Bluffs, Iowa, to the San Francisco Bay in Oakland, California. The construction began in 1863 and ended in 1869. The Union Pacific Railroad is still a major presence in the town of some 24,000 which claims that its Bailey Yard is the largest railyard in the world. It also celebrates the North Platte Canteen, a volunteer enterprise that provided food and hospitality to millions of troops who passed through North Platte during World War II.[3]

I am pretty sure the citizens of North Platte would be offended if I failed to mention the Buffalo Bill Ranch State Historical Park just north and west of the city. Also known as Scout's Rest Ranch, it is a living history state park that dates to 1878 when William "Buffalo Bill" Cody (1846-1917) purchased 160 acres near the Union Pacific tracks as headquarters for his famed "Wild West" show and the beginning of a successful cattle ranch that grew to 4,000 acres when it was sold in 1911.[4]

River's Edge is one of four courses in North Platte, another 18-hole and a 9-hole public, as well as Iron Eagle, a municipal course, which appears to be a bit more highly regarded than River's Edge. After a quick lunch at its sports bar and grill, "Another Round," I made my way alone to the first tee, which overlooks the North Platte River running the length of the fairly straight par four. It was the only round I played entirely alone, and given my destination that day, I was glad I could get through in two and a half hours. Although it was a lovely summer's day, the course was not crowded. Another solo golfer was a few holes ahead of me, and I never caught up with him.

Of course, my erratic play slowed me down a bit looking for wayward balls in hedges. Losing my tee shot on the first hole was a sign of things to come. I'd like to think that not having played for almost two weeks and having spent too many hours driving contributed to my poor play on an otherwise not terribly challenging course. Relatively flat as it lies alongside the river, the course measures 6258 yards from the tips and is rated 69.7/122. I played the white tees (6053 yards, 68.7/120).[5] My score was so gosh-awful I am reluctant to record it here. Let's just say that net of my handicap, my score was 86 on the par 71 track! I did play a good deal better on the back nine than on the front. Still, it was great to be out again.

I departed the course around 3:45 and reached Lincoln about four hours later. I had driven 460 miles and played 18 holes. After late dinner at a nearby Ruby Tuesday's, I was rewarded with a long, restful sleep.

Friday, July 28, dawned bright and clear, a promising day for driving to my destination of Naperville, Illinois, to visit with old friends who had once lived in Gettysburg. The Wilcoxes had owned and operated the charming Doubleday Inn, a bed and breakfast that sits along the ridge north of the borough and was the site of horrific fighting on July 1, 1863, the first day of the historic battle. The Doubleday Inn is the only one of many in the area that is located on the battlefield itself. Being innkeepers for about ten years was a second career for the Wilcoxes after Charles retired early from banking. They are among the most outgoing and personable couples I have ever met and made many friends from far and wide throughout their career and in their time in Gettysburg.

Soon after taking up golf in my 50th year, I discovered that Charles shared my passion, and we became regular golfing buddies. In the mid-90s, he and I launched an annual spring trip to Myrtle Beach along with other friends from Gettysburg; it lasted for more than ten years. Lots of good memories as I learned the game and attempted to develop something like a reliable swing, still a work-in-progress.

On the way to Naperville, I passed through Omaha (again), enjoyed the lovely rolling hills and miles of cornfields across Iowa and paused for an hour to tour and admire the Des Moines Capitol, its gracefully designed and landscaped grounds, and numerous monuments. It is surely one of the most beautiful state capitols that I have seen. Particularly memorable was its Civil War monument with a huge symbolic granite statue of Iowa portrayed as an imposing nude woman seated with her lap draped holding up her large breasts as an offering of sustenance to her loyal sons. It is an image that has stuck with me.

I arrived around 6:45 at my friends' home in the almost too-perfect-to-be-real, affluent city of Naperville where I enjoyed a delicious home-cooked meal with the Udes, who are close friends and neighbors of the Wilcoxes. He had been one of our Myrtle Beach regulars for many of our memorable trips. It was a delightful reunion, great food, good talk, lots of laughter.

The next morning, Charles, Vern, and I headed out to the Prairie Bluff Golf Course in nearby Crest Hill for what would be the 16th and last round on my trip. The green fee of $70 was at the upper end of that expense but not the highest, a distinction held by the Coeur d'Alene course. My total for green fees was just over $930. I continue to be grateful for some very generous discounts along the way.

Designed by two-time U.S. Open Champion (1978 & 1985) Andy North and Roger Packard, Prairie Bluff is a beautifully maintained public course sprawling across 230 acres of rolling prairie with ponds in play on five of the holes and a lot of tall grass to catch wayward drives all around the course. It plays 7007 yards from the tips with a rating of 73.5/129. We played the white tees, at 6054 yards, 74.8/126, which proved more challenging than it initially appeared. My lackluster score showed that playing it sight unseen, even with helpful partners, adds to the difficulty. It has a ten-acre driving range, generous putting green, and a short-game practice area. The handsome stone and wood clubhouse includes a well-stocked pro shop, a comfortable casual restaurant and bar with patio, and space to host banquets of up to 200 guests.

Saturday evening, I took the Wilcoxes out for dinner. They made an excellent selection of Hugo's Frog Bar, one of many fine dining options in Naperville's elegant downtown. This highly rated restaurant, praised for its great seafood and steaks, originated in Chicago. In addition to its Naperville site, I was delighted to discover another in Philadelphia at the Rivers Casino on the Delaware River waterfront. Although it proved to be one of the more expensive meals on my journey, the quality of the food, the service, and the company made it well worth it. By the time I returned home, my food expenses totaled $2798.91. This included snacks and groceries that I stocked along the way so that I did not need to eat every meal in a restaurant. Most of my breakfasts were included in my hotel room rate.

On the morning of July 30, forty days since departing Gettysburg, I left Naperville and headed east unsure whether I had the energy to drive almost 700 miles in one final day. As it turned out, I got a second wind in the afternoon somewhere around Toledo and decided to go for it. I arrived home at 8:30 p.m., 12 hours after leaving the Wilcoxes' home, having logged 688.2 miles. My total round-trip mileage was 9,713.6. It was good to be home.

Afterword
The Enduring Struggle

October 11, 1809: Meriwether Lewis commits suicide at Grinder's Inn on the Natchez Trace, 70 miles southwest of Nashville, Tennessee. He was 35 years old.[1]

When I began work on this book in the fall of 2017, I had no idea that its completion would coincide with the tumultuous and disheartening end of the Trump presidency. As I worked on the book, the increasingly distressing and exhausting chronicle of Trump's tenure as President cast a shadow over my research and recollection of my journey. Like most Americans, I was shocked by Trump's improbable election and took small consolation that he lost the popular vote by some three million and that his success was the result of razor-thin margins in three states. Not for the first time did our arcane Electoral College show its need for a complete overhaul or perhaps simply being long overdue for the dustbin of history.

When Trump was elected, I told friends and family that he was the most mentally disordered, dishonest, and dangerous man ever to occupy the Oval Office. Nothing in the ensuing four years changed that assessment, and the heart-breaking catastrophe that he incited following the November 2020 election would seem to leave little room for debate. But this is America, after all, so the debate over Trump's legacy continues even in the face of his second impeachment and the unsurprising failure of his being convicted by the Senate. Never was the difference between "not guilty" and "innocent" so stark. How this will play out in the months and years to come will determine much about what kind of country we have become. The Midterm Elections in 2022 will be the most obvious measure of where we are headed, but much in the coming months could give us cause for hope. President Biden's success in carrying out his ambitious agenda will surely be a leading indicator, but the challenges he has faced thus far are not encouraging.

For now, however, I continue to hope that our better angels will prevail and that Trump's toxic influence on the battered and divided remnant of the Republican Party will recede. Senator McConnell's unstinted condemnation of Trump following the impeachment trial left little doubt about that Senator's perspective, and there appears to be substantial evidence, mostly unspoken in public, that a great many other Republicans share McConnell's dismay and disdain despite their failure to vote their consciences in supine fear of Trump's apparent death grip on the base of the party that has become a personality cult.

By contrast, Joe Biden's substantial victory with a margin of more than seven million votes and the diversity of his support suggests a Democratic Party that increasingly reflects the emerging future of our country. It has been said that demographics are destiny. If that be so, it appears that the Republican Party, as currently configured, has lashed its future to a shrinking base. Although the emergence and growth of white supremacists and domestic terrorists are real and profoundly disturbing, it does not appear to represent the heart of our nation.

As I traveled the Lewis and Clark Trail in 2017, I could not imagine how ugly and disheartening the Trump presidency would become, and few with whom I met brought it up. I naturally wonder how my conversations would have gone if I had taken the trip in the summer 0f 2020. I have little doubt that I would have found stalwart supporters who might not defend some of his more outrageous actions and words but would still express support for his policies. It is clear and disheartening that Trump's hold on the Republican Party remains strong.

Although I learned a great deal in my travels, I may have learned more about Lewis and Clark and about our country in the years following my return. I read several helpful books that informed my thinking as I wrote this account. One that stands out is Jon Meacham's *The Soul of America: The Battle for Our Better Angels* (2018). It is a bracing look at several darker times in our history and the ultimate triumph of those better angels beginning with the Civil War and ending with the incomplete civil rights legacy of Martin Luther King, Jr. Meacham's central argument is that American history has been defined by a constant tension between fear and hope. He was clearly

243

writing with the dark fears unleashed by Donald Trump hanging heavily over his shoulder, but he argues that despite our having been "frequently vulnerable to fear, bitterness, and strife, . . . we have come through such darkness before" and emerged stronger. Meacham is hopeful but not Pollyanna about our nation. He readily acknowledges that "imperfection is the rule, not the exception."[2]

Meacham also recalls FDR's conviction that "[t]he Presidency is not merely an administrative office. That's the least of it . . . . It is pre-eminently a place of moral leadership. All our great Presidents were leaders of thought at times when certain historic ideas in the life of the nation had to be clarified."[3] In this context, Meacham recalls Truman's guiding political insight: "You can't divide the country up into sections and have one rule for one section and one rule for another, and you can't encourage people's prejudices. You have to appeal to people's best instincts, not their worst ones."[4] As Michelle Obama more succinctly observed at the Democratic National Convention in 2012, "Being president doesn't change who you are, no, it reveals who you are."[5]

That Meacham fondly hoped to sway the toxic impulses of Donald Trump would be fatuous, but I would like to think he was writing more for future American Presidents rather than the one who so clearly had him worried. In the face of Trump's incessant appeals to fear, division, distrust, and the very worst instincts of the public, Meacham's writing this book was, in itself, a triumph of hope over fear. For me anyway, it was a cool salve of encouragement in the face of almost daily dismay.

Although the Trump presidency is now thankfully behind us, the toxic legacy that he unleashed and encouraged remains. The horrific assault on the nation's Capitol on January 6 leaves scars that will not be as easily repaired as the physical damage done to this venerable symbol of our democracy. The country remains deeply divided. Mistrust of our institutions is widespread. But I do believe, with Meacham and with President Biden, that what we have seen and experienced over the past four years is not the whole story of America. My travels across the country and back have bolstered this hope.

I was struck to see that Meacham quotes St. Augustine's familiar definition of a community's soul as "an assemblage of reasonable beings bound together by a common agreement as to the objects of their love."[6] This was familiar to me mainly because President Biden quoted the same definition in his inaugural address. The quotation from St. Augustine succinctly describes one of my enduring impressions from my trip. Yes, we are a divided country, divided along a wide variety of lines from regional differences to race, class, religion, ethnicity, and history. But we are bound together by a set of enduring ideas about what's most valuable about America. I continue to believe that there is a good deal more common agreement about what we love than what divides us.

Since developing the three questions that I posed during my travels, I have given them a great deal of thought:

1. What do I most value, most appreciate about America?
2. What worries me most about America today?
3. If I had a magic wand, what are one or two things in the American past or present that I would change to make our country a better place?

It seems only proper that I should conclude by offering my own answers.

First, I agree with what many offered—freedom, opportunity, possibility, which is to say hope. As Americans we hold certain truths to be, as Jefferson eloquently put it, self-evident: "that all men are created equal, that they are endowed, by their Creator, with certain unalienable Rights, that among these are Life, Liberty, and the pursuit of Happiness." That these rights are not guarantees and that our history demonstrates repeatedly our failure to make them so for every man, woman, and child who has ever resided in this nation is equally self-evident. Yet, despite the bloody struggles and manifest failures, we have not ceased to aspire, to hope. Indeed, we continue to be a beacon of hope for countless individuals all around the world.

Second, like so many others, I am deeply worried about the darker angels so starkly and disturbingly invoked and inflamed by Trump and manifested in armed militias, deep distrust, alienation, fear of the other, conspiracy theories, and most recently in the deadly insurrection of January 6. That so many seem to believe in building walls rather than bridges is a grim repudiation of our most noble and sacred vision to be a "shining city on a hill," a bastion of hope for all those huddled masses yearning to be free. We have been reminded and challenged recently to embrace that hopeful vision in Pope Francis's *Let Us Dream*. As Meacham demonstrated, the dark angels that undermine that vision have been present from the earliest days of our

245

settlement. Hope can be found in our never yet having completely surrendered to those dark angels.

Third, if I had a magic wand, I would erase our original sin of slavery and dream of a history where black Africans were never brought to our shores to suffer the unspeakable horrors that are so deeply woven into the fabric of our nation. These crimes against humanity continue to haunt and poison us and something like reparation seems necessary. Closely related is our genocidal treatment of the Native Americans who occupied this land for thousands of years before the first Europeans arrived. I dream of another history embodied in Jefferson's instructions to Lewis and Clark. In such a history, we would have seen the native peoples as neighbors to be honored and respected. They had so much to teach us about how to love the land and the creatures who occupied it. Only in recent years have we begun in halting steps to recognize the gifts that these original inhabitants have to offer.

Of course, as some of my more-thoughtful respondents recognized, my third question was the most fanciful. We don't have magic wands; we can't re-write history and undo what has been done. The darkest and ugliest episodes are part of who we are, and out of them have come stories of heroic struggle perhaps nowhere better illustrated than in the continuing aspirations of the Civil Rights Movement. Martin Luther King's dream of the beloved community is alive and continues to inspire. It will take no magic wand one day to make that stirring dream a reality.

Itinerary: June 20-July 30, 2017

June 20   Gettysburg to Clarksville, Indiana, through Western Maryland, West Virginia, & Louisville, Kentucky (583 miles)

June 21   Clarksville to French Lick via Jasper, Indiana (152 miles)

June 23   French Lick to St. Louis via Wood River, Illinois (283 miles)

June 26   St. Louis to Kansas City, Kansas, via Washington, New Haven, Hermann, and Jefferson City, Missouri (285 miles)

June 28   Kansas City, Kansas, to Omaha via Council Bluffs, Iowa (235 miles)

June 29   Omaha to Yankton, South Dakota, via Sioux City, Iowa, and Spirit Mound, Vermillion, South Dakota (219 miles)

June 30   Yankton, South Dakota, to Fort Pierre, South Dakota, via Chamberlain, South Dakota (240 miles)

July 1   Fort Pierre to Rapid City, South Dakota, via Deadwood Trail, The Badlands National Park, Custer State Park, and Mount Rushmore (332 miles)

July 2   Rapid City to Bismarck, North Dakota, via Mobridge, South Dakota (350 miles)

July 3   Bismarck to Williston, North Dakota, via Minot (230 miles)

July 4   Williston to Great Falls, Montana (459 miles)

July 6   Great Falls to Anaconda, Montana, via Helena (191 miles)

July 7   Anaconda to Coeur d'Alene via Beaverhead/Deer Lodge National Forest, across Skalkaho Pass to Travelers Rest to Lolo Pass and back (371 miles)

July 9   Coeur d'Alene to Lewiston, Idaho, via Circling Raven Golf
            Club and Saint Maries, Idaho (156 miles)

July 10   Lewiston to The Dalles, Oregon (257 miles)

July 11   Touring Columbia Gorge and Mount Hood (192 miles)

July 12   The Dalles to Pronghorn Resort, Bend, Oregon (137 miles)

July 15   Bend to Fort Clatsop, Astoria, Oregon (261 miles)

July 16   Astoria to Portland via Portland International Airport (107
            miles)

July 17-23 Touring Portland, Seattle, Vancouver, BC

July 24   Portland International Airport to Mountain Home, Idaho (474
            miles)

July 25   Mountain Home to Vernal, Utah, via Great Salt Lake (538
            miles)

July 26   Vernal to Cheyenne, Wyoming, via Dinosaur National
            Monument and Flaming Gorge (421 miles)

July 27   Cheyenne to Lincoln, Nebraska, via North Platte (460 miles)

July 28   Lincoln to Naperville, Illinois, via Des Moines, Iowa (500
            miles)

July 30   Naperville to Gettysburg via Toledo, Ohio, & Pittsburgh (688
            miles)

Total miles recorded, including detours and diversions: 9713.6

Courses Played

Wed., June 21	Sultan's Run, Jasper, IN	Ch. 3
Thurs., June 22	Donald Ross, French Lick, IN	Ch. 3
Sat., June 24	Tapawingo National, St. Louis, MO	Ch. 5
Sun., June 25	Missouri Bluffs, St. Charles, MO	Ch. 5
Tues., June 27	Shoal Creek, Kansas City, MO	Ch. 9
Wed., June 28	Tiburon, Omaha, NE	Ch. 10
Fri., June 30	Hillsview, Pierre, SD	Ch. 12
Mon., July 3	Hawktree, Bismarck, ND	Ch. 15
Thurs., July 6	The Old Works, Anaconda, MT	Ch. 18
Sat., July 8	Coeur d'Alene, Coeur d'Alene, ID	Ch. 20
Sun., July 9	Circling Raven, Worley, ID	Ch. 21
Wed., July 12	Jack Nicklaus Course, Bend, OR	Ch. 25
Thurs., July 13	Crosswater, Sunriver, OR	Ch. 25
Fri., July 14	Tetherow, Bend, OR	Ch. 25
Thurs., July 27	River's Edge, North Platte, NE	Ch. 28
Sat., July 29	Prairie Bluff, Crest Hill, IL	Ch. 28

About the Author

Lex McMillan is President Emeritus of Albright College in Reading, PA, where he served as president for 12 years. He retired in 2017 after serving for more than 37 years in administrative positions of increasingly broad scope and responsibilities at four liberal arts colleges in Virginia and Pennsylvania. He established a reputation as a skilled administrator and inspiring leader; a creative strategic thinker; and an effective teacher, writer, and public speaker. An avid (bogey) golfer and enthusiastic bicyclist, he serves on several local nonprofit boards in the Gettysburg area, where he now lives. He earned his B.A., *cum laude*, from Washington and Lee University, his M.A. in English Literature from Georgia State University, and his doctorate in English Literature from the University of Notre Dame. He and his wife, Dorothy, have five grown children and seven grandchildren.

Notes

Preface
[1] Alvin M. Josephy, Jr., ed., *Lewis and Clark Through Indian Eyes* (New York: Vintage, 2007), p. 192.
[2] (Chapel Hill: UNC Press, 1962).
[3] *Meriwether Lewis, Thomas Jefferson, and the Opening of the American West* (New York: Simon & Schuster, 1996).
[4] Fourth Edition, Falcon Guides, 2007.

Chapter One
[1] *Thomas Jefferson and the Stoney Mountains: Exploring the West from Monticello* (Urbana: Univ. of Illinois Press, 1981), p. 138.
[2] "The Seeing Eye," *Christian Reflections* (Grand Rapids: Eerdmans, 1967), p.168.
[3] "Indians of North America," *National Geographic* map, Dec. 1972).
[4] *Ibid.*

Chapter Two
[1] *Undaunted Courage,* p. 117.
[2] https://www.fallsoftheohio.org/discover/.
[3] http://lewisandclarktrail.com/legacy/louisclark/statue.html.
[4] http://www.campdubois.com/html/history.html.

Chapter Three
[1] Ambrose, p.117-118.
[2] *Dubois County Free Press*, April 30, 2015.
[3] Alvin Ruxler, quoted by Ross Millin, "Supreme Sultan," www.newlineza.com/supremesultanusa.html.
[4] "The Itinerant Golfer's Take on Sultan's Run Golf Club," http://www.golftripper.com/sultans-run-golf-club/.
[5] https://www.frenchlick.com/golf/donaldross.
[6] https://frenchlick.com/golf/petedye/mansion.
[7] http://theaposition.com/anitadraycott/golf-road-warriors/grw-frenchlick/899/pete-dye-throws-down-the-gauntlet-at-french-lick.
[8] https://frenchlick.com/golf/petedye.

Chapter Four
[1] (New York: Harper Collins, 2007), p. 146.
[2] Ibid.
[3] https://www.fhwa.dot.gov/interstate/history.cfm.

[4] https://www.usatoday.com/story/news/nation/2017/04/01/highway-rest-stops-disappearing/99868368/.
[5] https://en.wikipedia.org/wiki/Cahokia.

Chapter Five
[1] http://lacledeslanding.com.
[2] https://www.forbes.com/sites/johnmariani/2018/11/07/st-louis-missouri-is-rebounding-from-a-long-decline-by-focusing-on-its-historic-heritage/#5c27119a24a3.
[3] Ibid.
[4] https://en.wikipedia.org/wiki/Central_Park.
[5] https://www.stlouismo.gov/government/departments/parks/parks/Forest-Park.cfm.
[6] http://www.thedredscottfoundation.org/dshf/index.php?option=com_content&view=article&id=156&Itemid=53.
[7] NPS, "Jefferson National Expansion Memorial, 2013.
[8] William Sloan Coffin, *Credo* (Louisville: Westminster John Knox Press, 2004), p. 84.
[9] https://www.britannica.com/biography/Daniel-Boone.
[10] https://www.discoverstcharles.com/listing/lewis-%26-clark-statue/1230/.
[11] https://lewisandclarkboathouse.org.
[12] https://www.discoverstcharles.com.
[13] http://www.mobluffs.com/course/.
[14] https://news.stlpublicradio.org/health-science-environment/2020-04-24/construction-underway-on-missouri-bluffs-development.

Chapter Six
[1] http://bellefontainecemetery.org/destination/history/.
[2] https://www.theatlantic.com/national/archive/2011/03/our-first-public-parks-the-forgotten-history-of-cemeteries/71818/.
[3] http://westviewcemetery.com.
[4] http://bellefontainecemetery.org/destination/history/.
[5] https://www.senate.gov/artandhistory/history/common/generic/Featured_Bio_Benton.html.
[6] http://bellefontainecemetery.org/destination/art-architecture/.
[7] https://en.wikipedia.org/wiki/Wainwright_Building.
[8] https://wustl.edu/about/campuses/danforth-campus/william-p-eliza-mcmillan-hall/.
[9] www.laduenews.com/business/columns/persons-of-interest-michael-mcmillan.
[10] https://www.findagrave.com/memorial/202/william-clark.
[11] https://www.nps.gov/parkhistory/online_books/lewisandclark/site9.html.

Chapter Seven
[1] http://bellefontainecemetery.org/destination/history/.
[2] https://en.wikipedia.org/wiki/Maysville,_Kentucky.
[3] *Undaunted Courage*, p. 105.

[4] https://superbowlentertainmentguide.info/place/the-john-colter-museum-new-haven-mo.html. https://aboutstlouis.com/local/museums/john-colter-museum-63068.
[5] https://en.wikipedia.org/wiki/John_Colter.
[6] https://www.visitjeffersoncity.com/lewis-and-clark-monument-at-the-lewis-and-clark-trailhead-plaza; http://sabratullmeyer.com/artist.asp.
[7] https://en.m.wikipedia.org/wiki/Katy_Trail_State_Park.

Chapter Eight
[1] Fanselow, *Traveling the Lewis and Clark Trail*, p.45.
[2] https://kceconomy.org/2017/03/24/kcs-population-growth-suggests-strong-economy/.
[3] http://www.kansascity.com/news/local/article141841529.html#storylink=cpy. March 31, 2017.
[4] https://berkleyriverfront.com.
[5] https://en.wikipedia.org/wiki/Alcohol_laws_of_Kansas.
[6] http://americannutritionassociation.org/newsletter/usda-defines-food-deserts.
[7] https://www.flatlandkc.org/news-issues/awaiting-oasis-kcks-food-desert/.
[8] Elle Moxley, https://www.kcur.org/arts-life/2020-06-12/who-was-j-c-nichols-the-mixed-legacy-of-the-man-whose-name-could-be-taken-off-kansas-citys-most-famous-fountain.
[9] "Kansas City: Economic Competitiveness Has Slumped," *The Kansas City Star*, 6/12/2014.

Chapter Nine
[1] Ambrose, p. 149.
[2] https://www.shoalcreekgolf.com.
[3] JT, email, 12/23/17.
[4] WT, email, 1/16/18.

Chapter Ten
[1] Ambrose, p. 150.
[2] Fanselow, p. 44.
[3] Fanselow, p. 60.
[4] Fanselow, p. 60.
[5] http://speziarestaurant.com/spezia/omaha/.

Chapter Eleven
[1] http://www.siouxcityhistory.org/historic-sites/106-sgt-floyd-river-museum-a-welcome-center.
[2] Fanselow, p. 68.
[3] Fanselow, p. 71.
[4] Fanselow, p. 71.
[5] Ambrose, pp. 169-75.

Chapter Twelve

[1] Ambrose, Chapter Fourteen, "Encounter with the Sioux: September 1804," pp. 165-175.

[2] https://en.wikipedia.org/wiki/Dignity_(statue).

[3] Fanselow, p. 84.

[4] https://www.cityofpierre.org/136/Amenities.

[5] https://en.wikipedia.org/wiki/South_Dakota_State_Capitol.

Chapter Thirteen

[1] *Ambrose, p. 178.*

[2] *https://historicpierrefortpierre.com/historic-trails-deadwood-indian-etc/.*

[3] ("Badlands," official NPS visitor's brochure, National Park Service, U. S. Department of the Interior, undated.

[4] https://www.nps.gov/badl/index.htm.

[5] https://www.fs.usda.gov/blackhills.

[6] *The Essential Lewis and Clark*, Landon Y. Jones, ed., (New York: HarperCollins, 2000), p. 15.

[7] C. S. Lewis, *The Four Loves* (New York: Harcourt Brace Jovanovich, 1960), p. 143.

[8] *Tatanka*, https://gfp.sd.gov/parks/detail/custer-state park/.

[9] https://en.wikipedia.org/wiki/Mount_Rushmore.

Chapter Fourteen

[1] https://sdexcellence.org/Ben_Ash_1986.

[2] Ambrose, p. 187.

[3] Ambrose, p. 225.

[4] https://www.sdhspress.com/journal/south-dakota-history-6-2/fort-manuel-its-historical-significance/vol-06-no-2-fort-manuel.pdf.

[5] Peter Cozzens, *The Earth is Weeping: The Epic Story of the Indian Wars for the American West* (New York: Alfred A. Knopf, 2016), pp. 466-67.

[6] Cozzens, pp. 4-7.

[7] Cozzens, p. 466.

[8] https://mobridge.org/sitting-bull-monument; http://heritagerenewal.org/stone/sittingbull.htm; https://www.nps.gov/libi/learn/historyculture/sitting-bull.htm.

[9] Fanselow, p. 89.

[10] https://en.wikipedia.org/wiki/Kenel,_South_Dakota#cite_note-confidence_report_2015-5.

[11] https://history.sd.gov/preservation/docs/MarkersMasterAlphabetical.pdf.

[12] https://en.wikipedia.org/wiki/Sioux.

Chapter Fifteen

[1] https://hawktree.com/golf-course.

[2] https://www.aoc.gov/art/national-statuary-hall-collection/sakakawea.

[3] https://www.waymarking.com/waymarks/WMHKA8_Buffalo_sculpture_Bismarck_North_Dakota.

[4] https://bennettbriendesigns.com.
[5] Fanselow, p. 96.
[6] Fanselow, p. 101.
[7] *Essential Lewis and Clark*, p. 28.
[8] https://www.parkrec.nd.gov/lewis-clark-interpretive-center.
[9] Fanselow, p. 105.
[10] "She Survived Sex Trafficking. Now She Wants to Show Other Women a Way Out," By Aryn Baker, Photographs by Lynsey Addario, *TIME*, January 17, 2019.
[11] https://kaygolfcoursedesign.com; https://www.thelinksofnorthdakota.com.

Chapter Sixteen

[1] https://www.history.nd.gov/historicsites/mycic/mycichistory.html.
[2] Fanselow, p. 112.
[3] https://www.history.nd.gov/historicsites/buford/index.html; Cozzens, p. 466.
[4] https://townofbainville.com.
[5] https://ci.wolf-point.mt.us/community/page/history-wolf-point.
[6] https://en.wikipedia.org/wiki/Wolf_Point,_Montana.
[7] William Least Heat-Moon, *Blue Highways: A Journey into America* (New York: Little, Brown and Co., 1982), , p. 272.
[8] Heat-Moon, p. 271.
[9] https://en.wikipedia.org/wiki/Fort_Peck_Indian_Reservation.
[10] https://en.wikipedia.org/wiki/Fort_Peck_Indian_Reservation.
[11] https://www.uscanola.com/crop-production/.
[12] https://agr.mt.gov/AgFacts.
[13] https://www.nass.usda.gov/Statistics_by_State/Montana/Publications/Annual_Statistical_Bulletin/2018/Montana-Annual-Bulletin-2018.pdf.
[14] https://apnews.com/article/electoral-college-census-2020-government-and-politics-politics-86e1a31aeeea02004a3c71abd58097ee.
[15] https://www.farmflavor.com/montana/montanas-top-10-agricultural-products/10/.
[16] https://www.hmdb.org/m.asp?m=142526.
[17] Lewis, June 3, 1805, Jones, ed, p. 53.
[18] Fanselow, p. 145.
[19] Fanselow, p. 146.
[20] https://en.wikipedia.org/wiki/Fort_Benton,_Montana; http://www.fortbenton.com.

Chapter Seventeen

[1] Ambrose, p. 237.
[2] http://wmpaulyoung.com/the-shack/.
[3] Fanselow, p. 158; http://www.lewisandclarkfoundation.org/home.php.
[4] Ambrose, p. 250; from *Lewis and Clark: Pioneering Naturalists* (Urbana: University of Illinois Press, 1969), p. 332.
[5] Jones, ed., p. 69.

[6] https://www.amazon.com/Lewis-Clark-Confluence-Time-Courage/dp/B01GWC36KU.

[7] Fanselow, p. 159.

[8] https://en.wikipedia.org/wiki/Great_Falls_(Missouri_River).

[9] https://en.wikipedia.org/wiki/List_of_dams_in_the_Missouri_River_watershed.

[10] https://en.wikipedia.org/wiki/Black_Eagle_Dam.

[11] https://en.wikipedia.org/wiki/Great_Falls,_Montana.

[12] https://en.wikipedia.org/wiki/C._M._Russell_Museum_Complex.

Chapter Eighteen

[1] Jones, ed., p. 72.

[2] https://en.wikipedia.org/wiki/Helena,_Montana.

[3] https://mhs.mt.gov/education/Capitol/History.

[4] https://en.wikipedia.org/wiki/Montana_State_Capitol.

[5] https://www.visitmt.com/listings/general/state-historic-site/montana-state-capitol.html; https://mhs.mt.gov/education/Capitol/History.

[6] https://missoulian.com/news/state-and-regional/mystery-of-capitol-dome-statue-solved/article_44857203-4ae1-5bd7-a0e4-c869ce182430.html.

[7] https://helenair.com/news/local/ornament-honors-mysterious-capitol-sculptor/article_cce2e44f-f5e3-5369-8876-af75f77b06d1.html.

[8] https://mhs.mt.gov/education/capitol/art/exterior.

[9] https://en.wikipedia.org/wiki/Irish_Brigade_(Union_Army).

[10] https://www.waymarking.com/waymarks/WMWK98_Thomas_Francis_Meagher_Helena_MT; https://www.ricksteves.com/watch-read-listen/read/articles/the-amazing-life-of-waterfords-favorite-son; https://www.britannica.com/biography/Thomas-Francis-Meagher; https://dailyhistory.org/How_Did_Thomas_Francis_Meagher_Really_Die%3F; https://en.wikipedia.org/wiki/Thomas_Francis_Meagher.

[11] Jones, ed., p. 72.

[12] Jones, ed., p. 75.

[13] Jones, ed., p. 75.

[14] https://www.playoldworks.com/golf/history.

[15] https://www.msgagolf.org/wp-content/uploads/2016/11/MSGA-Newsletter-November-2016.pdf.

[16] https://www.playoldworks.com/golf/course-designer.

Chapter Nineteen

[1] https://en.wikipedia.org/wiki/Skalkaho_Pass.

[2] https://en.wikipedia.org/wiki/Skalkaho_Pass.id_plant=XETE; https://en.wikipedia.org/wiki/Xerophyllum_tenax.

[3] Lewis, Aug. 24, 1805, Jones, ed., p. 108.

[4] http://stateparks.mt.gov/travelers-rest/.

[5] https://en.wikipedia.org/wiki/Traveler%27s_Rest_(Lolo,_Montana).

[6] Quoted in Fanselow, p. 218.

[7] https://en.wikipedia.org/wiki/Lolo_Pass_(Idaho–Montana).

[8] https://www.fs.usda.gov/detail/r1/specialplaces/?cid=stelprdb5108516.

[9] https://en.wikipedia.org/wiki/Coeur_d%27Alene,_Idaho.

Chapter Twenty
[1] Ambrose, pp. 292-298.
[2] https://www.cdaresort.com/play/golf.
[3] https://www.golfdigest.com/story/selling-golf-as-an-experience-not-just-a-round-of-18.
[4] https://www.cdaresort.com/play/golf.
[5] Matt Saternus, Co-Founder, Editor-in-Chief, PluggedInGolf.com:
https://pluggedingolf.com/coeur-dalene-resort-golf-course-review/.

Chapter Twenty-one
[1] http://www.bronzewest.com/bronze-sculpture-article-2.html.
[2] https://www.cdacasino.com/golf/circling-raven-golf-course-tour/.
[3] https://thegolfwire.com/circling-raven-open-for-play/.
[4] http://americangolfer.blogspot.com/2009/08/golf-digest-ranks-circling-raven-no-17.html.
[5] https://thegolfwire.com/circling-raven-voted-the-best-idaho-course/.
[6] https://www.golfcoursearchitecture.net/content/gene-bates-develops-renovation-plan-for-circling-raven.
[7] https://www.cdatribe-nsn.gov.
[8] https://www.golfcoursegurus.com/reviews/circling-raven-golf-club/.
[9] https://en.wikipedia.org/wiki/St._Maries,_Idaho.
[10] https://stmarieschamber.org.
[11] *Indian Eyes*, p. 136.
[12] *Indian Eyes*, p. 192.
[13] *Indian Eyes,* p. 192.
[14] https://www.theguardian.com/world/2012/may/04/us-stolen-land-indian-tribes-un.
[15] https://en.wikipedia.org/wiki/Indian_reservation;
https://www.theguardian.com/world/2012/may/04/us-stolen-land-indian-tribes-un.

Chapter Twenty-two
[1] https://www.pbs.org/weta/thewest/people/s_z/whitman.htm;
https://en.wikipedia.org/wiki/Henry_H._Spalding.

Chapter Twenty-three
[1] Fanselow, p.222.
[2] http://lewisandclarktrail.com/section3/idahocities/nezpercelewiston.htm.
[3] https://lmtribune.com/obituaries/carol-grende-carmona-53-big-arm-mont/article_50a7a767-a2e1-5b29-ab52-ae03f22c8392.html.
[4]https://www.waymarking.com/waymarks/WMVY68_Tsceminicum_Lewiston_ID
[5] https://lmtribune.com/feature/sacajawea-fountain-once-more-graces-citys-pioneer-park/article_b8684ea8-530d-5c1e-98f7-2d9ce25f18e9.html.
[6] Ambrose, p. 304.

[7] https://en.wikipedia.org/wiki/Snake_River.

[8] Ambrose, p. 300.

[9] https://baldwinsaloon.com.

Chapter Twenty-four

[1] Ambrose, pp. 306-307.

[2] Fanselow, p. 247.

[3] https://traveloregon.com/places-to-go/regions/columbia-river-gorge/.

[4] http://www.ci.the-dalles.or.us/historygeo.htm.

[5] Ambrose, p.306.

[6] https://en.wikipedia.org/wiki/1984_Rajneeshee_bioterror_attack; https://en.wikipedia.org/wiki/Rajneesh.

[7] https://en.wikipedia.org/wiki/Historic_Columbia_River_Highway#Rowena_Crest

[8] https://en.wikipedia.org/wiki/Columbia_River_Gorge.

[9] https://thegorgeguide.com/rowena-crest-viewpoint/.

[10] https://stateparks.oregon.gov/index.cfm?do=park.profile&parkId=112.

[11] https://vistahouse.com.

[12] https://en.wikipedia.org/wiki/Edward_Goldsmith.

[13] https://en.wikipedia.org/wiki/Mount_Hood_Highway.

[14] https://en.wikipedia.org/wiki/1980_eruption_of_Mount_St._Helens.

[15] Winchester, p. 4.

[16] https://en.wikipedia.org/wiki/Mount_Hood.

[17] https://en.wikipedia.org/wiki/Timberline_Lodge.

[18] https://en.wikipedia.org/wiki/Works_Progress_Administration.

Chapter Twenty-five

[1] https://www.opendoorsuk.org/persecution/wwl20-trends/.

[2] http://www.crosswater.com/golf.

[3] https://www.golfspan.com/how-many-golf-courses-are-in-the-us.

[4] *Golf Digest*, Feb. 21, 2019.

[5] BB email, July 14, 2017.

[6] Email from Cody Johnson, July 25, 2017.

[7] https://www.fs.usda.gov/recmain/deschutes/recreation.

[8] http://dmkgolfdesign.com/about/philosophy/.

[9] https://www.findagrave.com/memorial/12776799/solomon-tetherow.

[10] http://archiveswest.orbiscascade.org/ark:/80444/xv52172.

[11] https://www.oregonencyclopedia.org/articles/lockley_fred_1871_1958_/#.X-DQzS1h1N0.

[12] https://breakingeighty.com/tetherow-golf-club.

[13] Zeb Weld email, 12/20/17.

Chapter Twenty-six

[1] Ambrose, p. 310.

[2] Ambrose, p. 310.

[3] Fanselow, p. 263.

[4] https://fortclatsopbookstore.com/product/arrival/.

[5] Ambrose, p. 335.
[6] Ambrose, p. 335.
[7] Ambrose, p. 336.
[8] http://www.banderasnews.com/1801/art-jim-demetro-gallery-vallarta.html.
[9] https://www.bendbulletin.com/localstate/new-sacagawea-statue-placed-at-fort-clatsop/article_2de6892c-3a0d-5e5d-9bbe-38e6cd36a90f.html.
[10] Fanselow, p. 263.
[11] Fanselow, p. 263.
[12] Ambrose, p. 325.
[13] https://en.wikipedia.org/wiki/Astoria–Megler_Bridge.
[14] https://parks.state.wa.us/187/Cape-Disappointment.
[15] Fanselow, p. 257.
[16] https://en.wikipedia.org/wiki/John_Meares.
[17] Fanselow, p. 259.
[18] Ambrose, p. 316.
[19] Ambrose, p. 316.

Chapter Twenty-seven

[1] https://visittheoregoncoast.com/cities/astoria/.
[2] (New York: Pantheon Books, 2018).
[3] https://www.midtownscholar.com.
[4] https://en.wikipedia.org/wiki/Astoria,_Oregon.
[5] https://en.wikipedia.org/wiki/Oregon.
[6] https://columbiamemorial.org.
[7] https://columbiamemorial.org/services/cancer-care-center/.
[8] Edward Stratton, "Housing options in the works for Astoria: Hundreds of apartment units on the drawing board," *The Astorian*, Jan. 11, 2021; https://www.dailyastorian.com/news/local/housing-options-in-the-works-for-astoria/article_9fa251b4-5129-11eb-9e96-9b9405829915.html.
[9] https://en.wikipedia.org/wiki/Astoria_Column.
[10] https://en.wikipedia.org/wiki/TransAmerica_Bicycle_Trail.
[11] https://en.wikipedia.org/wiki/Astoria,_Oregon.
[12] https://astoriamuseums.org/explore/oregon-film-museum/.
[13] https://www.crmm.org.
[14] https://en.wikipedia.org/wiki/Columbia_River_Maritime_Museum.
[15] https://www.clatsopcc.edu;https://www.communitycollegereview.com/clatsop-community-college-profile.
[16] (https://www.astorialibrary.org/dept/Library.
[17] Fallows, p. 407.
[18] https://projects.newyorker.com/story/beer/.
[19] https://www.buoybeer.com/?age-verified=1f1985717f.
[20] https://en.wikipedia.org/wiki/Brewing_in_Oregon.
[21] https://www.neighborhoodscout.com/or/astoria/crime; https://www.city-data.com/crime/crime-Astoria-Oregon.html.
[22] https://www.dailyastorian.com/news/local/astoria-tries-to-keep-development-on-solid-ground/article_263c34b4-46b9-11ea-80ff-d73ed8d40eb4.html.

[23] Fallows, p. 400.

Chapter Twenty-eight
[1] https://en.wikipedia.org/wiki/Great_Salt_Lake;
https://en.wikipedia.org/wiki/Lake_Bonneville.
[2] https://www.nps.gov/dino/index.htm;
https://en.wikipedia.org/wiki/Dinosaur_National_Monument.
[3] https://en.wikipedia.org/wiki/North_Platte,_Nebraska.
[4] https://en.wikipedia.org/wiki/Buffalo_Bill_Ranch.
[5] https://www.golfriversedgenp.com.

Afterword
[1] Ambrose, p. 475.
[2] Jon Meacham, *The Soul of America: The Battle for Our Better Angels* (New York: Random House, 2018), p. 6.
[3] Meacham, p. 12.
[4] Meacham, p. 12.
[5] https://www.washingtonpost.com/blogs/post-partisan/post/president-obama-is-an-introvert-so-what/2012/09/17/.
[6] Meacham, p. 7.